LII
IN T
BALA

LIFE
IN THE
BALANCE

COMPANION TO
THE AUDUBON TELEVISION SPECIALS

DAVID RAINS WALLACE

HARCOURT BRACE JOVANOVICH, PUBLISHERS

SAN DIEGO   NEW YORK   LONDON

FRONTISPIECE: *Spanish shawl, Sea of Cortez, West Mexico.*

*Requests for permission to make copies of any
part of the work should be mailed to:
Permissions, Harcourt Brace Jovanovich, Publishers,
Orlando, Florida 32887.*

*The Audubon Television Specials, to which this book is a companion,
are a co-production of the National Audubon Society, Turner Broadcasting,
and public television station WETA/Washington, D.C.*

*Library of Congress Cataloging-in-Publication Data
Wallace, David Rains, 1945–*
   Life in the balance.
   *Issued in conjunction with a series of television
programs produced by the National Audubon Society.*
   Includes index.
   *1. Nature conservation. 2. Nature conservation—
United States. I. National Audubon Society. II. Title.
QH75.W35   1987   333.95'16'0973   87-254
ISBN 0-15-151561-1*

*Designed by Dalia Hartman
Maps by Earth Surface Graphics
Printed in the United States of America   First edition   A B C D E*

CONTENTS

PREFACE

Peter A. A. Berle
President, National Audubon Society

> *One touch of nature makes the whole world kin.*
> —Shakespeare, *Troilus and Cressida*

From the time early man began using stone tools, nature was a force both to be conquered and a force that sustained life.

As the millenia passed, there were animals to be hunted, forests to be cleared, shelters to be built. Yet this activity—undertaken by a world population that seems incredibly small by today's numbers—had a miniscule effect on the environment, and man lived largely in harmony with nature.

When the Romans built aqueducts to meet increasing demands for water, there were only three hundred million people on the planet, compared to five billion by the mid-1980s. Astonishingly, about two-thirds of that increase has occurred during the twentieth century.

This explosive population growth, combined with the overlapping effects of the Industrial Revolution and worldwide agricultural development, has radically altered the face of planet Earth—a process chronicled compellingly in this book.

The losses of habitat and species have been staggering. One small anecdote from North America may be worth several thousand additional words: The first National Audubon Society television special,

"Condor," details the desperate plight of a magnificent species which once ranged over a large part of the continent. Boxed into a smaller and smaller area that finally shrank to just a portion of southern California, it now struggles to breed in zoos.

"Condor" is the story of what the inexorable pressures of development and population have done to just one species. The extinction of this bird would be a conservation tragedy, but the condor's difficulties pale in comparison to the global trends resulting from the growing stress mankind is placing on the world's resources, resulting in deforestation, desertification, ocean pollution, and the greenhouse effect.

Yet "Condor" is fundamentally a story of hope—as are all television programs in the Audubon series, on which this book is based. "Condor" is the story of biologists risking life and limb in rugged mountain terrain to study a severely endangered species, understand its habitat needs, and even capture its eggs for hatching in zoos—all so that the bird may someday be re-established in its native habitat.

This approach is what distinguishes the Audubon specials and this book from other treatments of nature subjects. Audubon's emphasis is on the positive impact people can have on our natural resources—and on the future itself.

This theme, both in book and broadcast form, is a logical outgrowth of the historic role the National Audubon Society has played in helping Americans understand what it means to live in harmony with nature and what it takes to resolve the issues that arise when people and natural resource protection come into conflict. Taking direct action at the local, national, and international levels is an Audubon imperative.

Audubon carries out its mission with the idea that the individual *can* make a difference—whether in saving condors, protecting wetlands, controlling the spread of toxic materials, or ensuring that land, air, and water will remain for our grandchildren.

The Audubon philosophy is fundamentally a message of hope. While the prospect of man-made environmental and nuclear disaster may seem overwhelming today, natural threats to local survival—wild beasts, hurricanes, floods, famine, and disease—must have seemed no less threatening to our primitive forefathers. And yet history has been punctuated by the efforts of individuals who have changed the course of events. So in that spirit, we of the National Audubon Society offer *Life in the Balance*.

LIFE
IN THE
BALANCE

WILDERNESS EARTH

A DRAGONFLY RESTS on a branch overhanging a small stream one July morning. It is newly emerged from the brown nymphal skin. As a nymph, it crept over the rocks of the stream bottom, feeding first on protozoans and mites; then, as it grew larger, on the young of other aquatic insects. Now an adult, it will feed on flying insects, and will eventually mate. The mature dragonfly is completely transformed from the drab, immature creature that once blended with underwater sticks and leaves. Its head, thorax, and abdomen glitter beryl and azure; its wings are iridescent in the sunlight.

Dragonflies and their relatives have been crawling out of streams since the Permian period some 270 million years ago, before the dinosaurs evolved. Today, they are among the most widespread life forms, with at least 4,500 species in their insect order, 412 species in North America alone. Few have more ecological importance: in their role as predator, they serve as a natural instrument of balance for the insect population and, in their role as survivor, as a kind of bellwether for the environment.

Yet the environment in which our dragonfly lives is very different from that in which its ancestors thrived for so many millions of years. The water in which it spent its nymphal stage contains traces of petrochemicals, sulphuric acid, chlorine, and other substances rare or unknown in streams 200 million years ago, or even 200 years ago. And the dragonfly's course may take it through urban environments its ancestors' many-faceted eyes never beheld.

Nevertheless, when its new wings have hardened in the sun, the dragonfly darts among the automobile windshields and plate-glass shopfronts as nimbly as it might through a Mesozoic swamp. It snatches a bluebottle fly in the basket-like trap of its six legs and lands on a car-radio antenna to devour its first adult meal. The metallic brilliance of its body and wings does not look out of place in that cityscape. Indeed, if we were to study its intricate miniaturization, we would marvel at a structure that would make cars seem primitive and clumsy in comparison. From an engineering standpoint, the dragonfly's ability to fuel, guide, repair, and above all reproduce itself is far superior to any machine humanity has produced.

A dragonfly soaring unnoticed through city streets suggests the wildlife that teems literally unseen in our midst. We tend to think of lions and elephants, or at least squirrels and songbirds, when we hear the term *wildlife*. Yet a great many more wild creatures live about us than we realize. Whether we are shoppers or commuters, skyscraper-bound executives or cowboys on the open range, we have enormous numbers of wild organisms on and within our bodies—organisms ranging in size from the *Demodex* mites that inhabit our eyelash hair follicles to the bacteria that cover every square centimeter of our skin.

One might say that these life forms are insignificant compared to the trees, wildflowers, birds, and mammals we most often associate with wildlife. But size is a superficial measure. From an overall biological standpoint, the *only* significant wildlife are bacteria, fungi, algae, and invertebrates. Life on Earth proceeded very well for most of its roughly three billion years with only these forms of life. Vertebrate animals and higher plants have only appeared in the past four hundred million years. If they disappeared tomorrow, their smaller relatives would survive very well without them.

If bacteria, algae, fungi, and invertebrates disappeared tomorrow, on the other hand, life on Earth would quickly end. Their great age has not reduced their importance to the biosphere—the thin layer of air, land, and water that supports life. The photosynthetic microbes that first introduced oxygen into the primeval atmosphere did not become obsolete once oxygen reached its present level; photosynthetic microbes still produce most atmospheric oxygen. Similarly, bacteria, fungi, and algae are still the basis of soil formation, decomposition of dead organic matter, and other biotic processes that make life possible for plants and animals.

The Earth will always be a wilderness precisely because life depends on a myriad of apparently insignificant wildlife. Civilization may have "tamed" some species of microbes to produce foods such as wine and cheese and drugs such as penicillin, but human control over

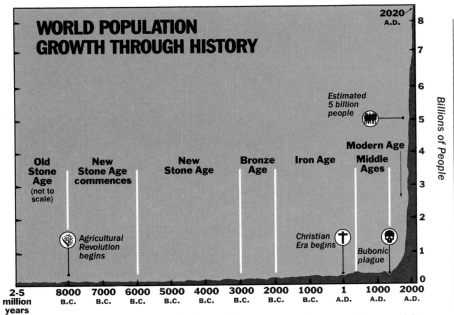

WORLD POPULATION GROWTH THROUGH HISTORY

2020 A.D.

Billions of People

Estimated 5 billion people

Modern Age

| Old Stone Age (not to scale) | New Stone Age commences | New Stone Age | Bronze Age | Iron Age | Middle Ages |

Agricultural Revolution begins

Christian Era begins

Bubonic plague

| 2-5 million years | 8000 B.C. | 7000 B.C. | 6000 B.C. | 5000 B.C. | 4000 B.C. | 3000 B.C. | 2000 B.C. | 1000 B.C. | 1 A.D. | 1000 A.D. | 2000 A.D. |

This population chart shows growth in human numbers through history. Today's world population projections indicate that if current growth rates continue, the number of people on Earth will double by the first quarter of the new century, from five billion to ten billion.

the microbial world will always be tenuous because that world is so complex and fast-evolving. To this day, civilization's control over the invertebrate world of insects remains quite marginal.

But even if the Earth retains a fundamental wildness, we should still be concerned for wildlife. The interrelationships within nature are such that if we do away with entire landscapes of plants and animals, we may not affect the planet's essential wildness, but we will surely affect the quality of its life. The quality of water in the dragonfly's stream affects not only the dragonfly, but the people who will drink that water when it eventually reaches a downstream reservoir. If dragonfly nymphs can no longer use a stream's water, its usefulness for humans is likely to be impaired as well.

Although we depend on wild microbes for life, our dependence hardly ends there. Humans evolved not on a planet of bare continents and algal oceans, or even on one of giant club mosses and ancient dragonflies, but on one of wildflowers, flowering trees, deer, and songbirds as well. City dwellers may no longer see those creatures in the wild, but they use much that originates from wild plants and animals. They would start their days less comfortably without sheets and clothes of cotton (African savanna shrubs) or wool (Asian bighorns), or beverages and foods (Arabian coffee, Asian oranges, Persian wheat, and Southeast Asian chickens).

Of course, these organisms have been domesticated so long that their wild origins seem beside the point, but, once again, this is a superficial outlook. The roughly ten thousand years of their domestication is very short in proportion to the roughly four million years of human evolution, during which wildlife was the only source of sustenance. Wildlife is still of major economic and cultural importance today, as anyone who eats seafood or uses lumber or firewood knows. Even most domesticated organisms need wildness at some point in their lives: feedlot steers would not produce beef if the wild microbes in soil had not allowed farmers to produce soybeans and corn to feed the steers.

Tame plants and animals have the same genes as wild ones, except that tame organisms tend to have less genetic diversity because humans have bred out traits considered undesirable. Diversity is one important reason for conserving wild ancestors: they may retain traits valuable in the long run. A recently discovered wild ancestor of corn, for example, is a perennial plant, whereas its tame descendant is an annual. If we could breed the perennial trait into domestic corn, then farmers could grow corn without having to replant every year, and agriculture would save billions of dollars. Genetically diverse organisms are also more resistant to disease and environmental stress than genetically uniform ones.

Every wild organism is a genetic library of intricately coded information, a vast compendium of proteins and other complex chemicals existing nowhere else. Our own "wild" ancestors understood the importance of wide ranges of organisms and survived because of that understanding. To sweep aside the wealth offered by millions of species of wild plants and animals because we only use a small range of tame organisms (most humans now depend for food on twenty plant species) would be foolishly shortsighted.

The intricate diversity of wild creatures exists in a state of dynamic balance. As naturalist John Muir said, everything is connected to everything else. Changes in one part of the biosphere ultimately affect the whole. When the atmospheric changes termed "El Niño" resulted in significant warming of Pacific Ocean waters in the early 1980s, cold water fish species disappeared temporarily from some temperate coastal areas. Seabirds and fishermen suffered.

Wildlife populations have usually evolved an ability to recover from natural disasters, because natural changes tend to be part of continuous cycles. El Niño has occurred periodically for centuries. But many of the changes we impose on our biosphere are unprecedented, and wildlife have not had time to adapt. If highly efficient commercial fishing fleets continue to pursue fish species already stressed by natural phenomena such as El Niño, for example, the reduced fish populations may lose their ability to recover. Seabirds and fishermen may not only suffer, but starve.

Yet there is no inherent reason why humans cannot adapt to ecological realities as other creatures have. In spite of all the changes that humans have imposed on the biosphere, each of its great wild elements—air, land, water—retains the ability to support life. There are birds in the skies, beasts in the forests, grasslands, mountains, and deserts, and fish in the wetlands, rivers, and oceans. There will probably be wildlife as long as air, land, and water continue to cycle oxygen, nitrogen, carbon, and life's other essential components from the clouds to the land to the oceans and then back to the clouds. Whether the wildlife of tomorrow will retain both the abundance and diversity that has made it so important to humanity's own survival, however, will depend very much on humanity.

A Melanesian boy in Tana, New Hebrides.

T H E
SKIES

A PERSON STANDING on a ridgetop east of the Los Padres National Forest in southern California's Ventura County might not suspect that one of the planet's biggest, noisiest cities is a few dozen miles to the south. Ridges covered with forest, chaparral, or grassland extend in every direction without visible sign or sound of human presence, except the occasional brown slash of a fire road or the roar of a high-flying jet. The dry mountains seem untouched.

The California condor soaring over the ridgetops one hot April noon sees more than any human below would have seen, however. Civilization's influence on the land is always more visible from the sky than from the surface. The condor sees broad dirt roads leading to mountaintop broadcasting installations, bulldozer tracks where brush has been cleared, power lines marching over ridgetops, and the remains of mining ventures or failed homesteads piled in gullies. Farther, toward the southern and eastern horizons, he sees smudges of brown petrochemical haze and the sparkle of sunlight on distant car windows as traffic moves endlessly up and down U.S. 5, California's main freeway.

We can assume that the condor sees these things, at least. As with other species of vultures, condors have excellent eyesight; they must to locate carrion from great distances. It's hard to say what these things mean to the condor, whether they disturb or confuse him, or simply seem ordinary parts of the landscape.

It is likely, anyway, that the condor is more interested in his own affairs than in human activities. Young condors are very curious, as are most young animals, but this particular bird is mature, over a decade old. He has watched the ridges and roads innumerable times, moving from his treetop roosts in the national forest mountains to foraging areas in the foothills and valleys to the east.

We know that condors feed on dead animals and that they spend most of their time flying, presumably in search of dead animals. Beyond that, we have trouble imagining what it's like to be a condor because it inhabits an environment that humans have begun to penetrate only in the latest instant of evolutionary time. As surface dwellers, we tend to think of the skies as being less substantial than land and sea, although we know that life on land and in the sea could not survive if the atmosphere did not protect it from cosmic and solar radiation and provide the gases required for photosynthesis and respiration.

Yet meteorologists point out that the air's complex mixture of gases is as much a fluid as water, albeit less dense. Like water, air has mass. Gravity gives it weight: it presses on the Earth's surface with an average of 14.7 pounds per square inch. Like water, air flows both vertically and horizontally. It rises when warmed, sinks when cooled, and slides around the planet in great currents and eddies. These currents rise and lose moisture—rain—over the warm equator, sink and blow as dry winds over subtropical deserts, rise again over green temperate zones, then ultimately sink again over the cold, dry poles.

In this transparent but ever-moving fluid, an ecosystem has evolved, connected to land and sea, but unique in its characteristics. The California condor is a supreme example of this. With hollow bones and feathers, he weighs about twenty-three pounds, a fraction of what a similarly sized land or sea creature would weigh. Yet the strength of those bones and feathers allows his nine-foot wingspan to bear enormous stresses as he soars in powerful updrafts or dives to Earth with a roar of air against feathers that can be heard half a mile away. Everything else about the condor—from his automatically locking toes, which allow him to sleep on branches, to his toothless (teeth are heavy) but barbed mouth, which allows him to pull apart large carcasses—is finely adapted to a life spent largely airborne.

Condors are so well adapted to the sky that they may have trouble getting off the ground. Like their smaller relatives, turkey vultures, they can take off from a standstill under favorable circumstances, but if they are heavy from eating and the air is still they may have to run as much as forty feet. Once they are airborne, their vast wingspread and relatively large weight (as compared to other soaring birds) makes them so stable that they can soar for an hour without moving a wing.

California condor.

This majestic stability has led some observers to mistake soaring condors for airplanes. Because they expend so little energy in flying, condors can easily travel a hundred miles in a day and can go for several days without feeding.

The condor is part of a complex pattern of aerial life that crisscrosses the sky just as surely as the roads and power lines crisscross below. Whether or not the roads mean anything to him, it is certain that he perceives much in that aerial pattern. He knows the meaning of a pair of ravens flying over the forested peaks to the west. They are potential nest robbers, looking for food in the maze of rocky canyons where condors have their traditional breeding grounds. Yet he does not have a nest in the canyons this year—his mate disappeared the previous summer—so perhaps he doesn't notice the ravens. A group of dark shapes circling to the east captures his attention, though: he flies in that direction.

When the condor reaches the grassland hills where the shapes were circling, he sees them—birds—surrounding a dead sheep that is partly eaten, probably by coyotes. Two of the birds, both golden eagles, have already begun tearing at the carcass. The third, another condor, stands aside. The eagles don't pause when the new condor lands, and he doesn't attempt to feed either; he merely stands patiently aside like the first. If he were very hungry, he might try to drive the eagles away, but he is content to wait. He has all day.

As the condors wait, the pattern of the sky ecosystem flows above and around them, thinly but steadily. Monarch butterflies flutter by, occasionally heading from coastal wintering grounds toward milkweed patches in mountain meadows. Hummingbirds speed over like bullets, also bound for mountain flowers. White-throated swifts, already nesting in cliffs to the west, swoop after high-flying insects, along with cliff swallows from nesting colonies on freeway underpasses to the east. Western kingbirds that have wintered in Central America flutter and

BIRDS: AN "EARLY WARNING SYSTEM"

Many bird species are particularly vulnerable to environmental disruptions such as pollution and habitat destruction. Their metabolism makes them more susceptible to poisoning and starvation than some other animals, and wide-ranging species usually require large areas of relatively undisturbed habitat. Meat-, fish-, and carrion-eating birds such as falcons, condors, and eagles live at the tops of food webs, where environmental contaminants tend to become concentrated.

Birds are thus among the first groups of animals to be affected by various environmental threats. The case of DDT, which threatened many species, is a classic example,

Peregrine falcon.

and there are many more recent ones. Declining temperate-forest songbird populations are indicative of the problem of tropical-forest destruction; drought and wetland destruction have reduced populations of North American waterfowl to their lowest levels ever recorded; contamination of surface and ground water by agricultural runoff is causing birth defects in nesting water birds; over-exploitation of water supplies has reduced wading bird populations in southern swamps. Estimates show that the current rate of bird species extinction is fifteen times the natural rate.

Birds have been particularly important in the development of wildlife conservation because they are so visible and so sensitive to environmental changes. Other squawk around barbed-wire fences, and the air is full of the cries of meadowlarks nesting in the grass.

The eagles stay until late afternoon, feeding or simply dozing by the carcass. When the condor has finally fed, the sun is setting. He dozes a moment, then stretches and makes the awkward lunge by which condors take off. The awkwardness vanishes when he leaves the ground and spreads his wings. He seems to float upward toward the brightness above the western peaks. Even as darkness gathers in the hill folds below him, the pattern of aerial life does not dissipate; it merely changes. Although condors, swifts, swallows, ravens, eagles, and kingbirds are heading for roosts, some migrant songbirds such as warblers and vireos are preparing for a night of northward flight under the full moon. Owls begin to call in the live oaks, and hundreds of small bats move into the twilight to feed on the tiny beetles and bugs that the swifts and swallows leave behind.

Bats and birds such as swifts and swallows, which catch insects in the air, are even more specialized for winged life than condors. They have lost the ability to walk upright, and do everything but sleep and nest in the air. Swifts even copulate in flight, and some species

organisms may disappear almost unnoticed (most rare species are plants or insects), but it is impossible to ignore the demise of condors and eagles, particularly in today's America, in which from 22 to 30 million people are birdwatchers and an estimated 62.5 million people (a third of the population) feed wild birds. Thousands of birders fan out across the countryside in annual bird counts, and ornithologists use their results to monitor trends of bird survival. Ornithologists also are using bird-count data to *predict* bird survival trends. Counts indicate areas critical for breeding, feeding, or other use by birds. If such areas are under pressure from human activities, then the bird populations in question are likely to dwindle.

Southern bald eagle in nest with young on Marco Island, Florida.

build their nests with their own saliva, dispensing with the need to come down to get mud or straw, as swallows do. Swifts, in fact, never touch level ground, landing only on the walls of cliffs, caves, chimneys, or hollow trees.

Even if no bats, birds, or butterflies are visible, the skies are seldom completely without life, even in extreme conditions. Tiny spiders and insects have been found floating above Mount Everest and high in the stratosphere. Although they lack wings, spiders often spend much of their lives flying by a process called "ballooning." The spider secretes a long strand of silk which catches on the breeze and eventually floats the spider away, like a balloon. Eggs or cysts of many small animals such as crustaceans and protozoans may travel long distances after being picked up by the wind, which is one way isolated mountain lakes come to be so full of life.

The skies contain plants as well as animals. Air is loaded with pollen in spring and summer, as hay fever sufferers know. Spores of algae, ferns, and mosses, not to mention fungi, flow freely across the globe, as the worldwide distribution of many common species shows. Airborne animals don't seem to feed on this floating plant matter, as water animals feed on microscopic water plants, perhaps because it isn't concentrated enough. We know comparatively little about the lives of most insects and spiders, however. Aerial pollen and spores may yet prove to be food for at least some flying animals. Plants that grow on other plants instead of on the ground (called epiphytes) do get nutrients from airborne material.

Living things aren't the only components of aerial ecosystems. The sky is full of chemically complex minerals, often the same ones contained in soil or water—dust particles carried on the wind or salt grains evaporated from the ocean surface. Water vapor condenses around such particles to form raindrops, snowflakes, and fog droplets, and so recycles them to the surface, often far from their points of origin. The volume of particles that air can carry is enormous, as anyone who has been in a dust storm knows. Much of China is covered with soil blown from glaciated areas far to the north, and much of the American Northwest is covered with ash from volcanic eruptions like that of Mount St. Helens in 1980.

Life in the air is the product of long evolution, although we know less about it than we do about sea and land evolution. Fossils of light-bodied flying creatures are rarer than those of swimming or walking ones. Insects were probably the first fliers: mayfly fossils show that they appeared over three hundred million years ago. We aren't sure how the insect wing evolved, but one theory suggests it may have begun as a heat-gathering organ, and only later has it been used for gliding and active flying. Insects still use their wings to warm (and cool) themselves, as does the bumblebee when it prepares for morning takeoff by buzzing. Some vertebrate wings may have had a similar origin. Take, for instance, the flying reptiles of the dinosaur age. These included the largest fliers that ever lived, with wingspreads much wider than any bird's. Such creatures, able to spend entire days soaring effortlessly, perhaps led almost completely airborne lives. Their huge wings might have made them helpless on land.

Since birds and mammals maintain a constant body temperature internally, bird and bat wings may have originated less for heat regulation than for movement through a forest environment. The first known fossil bird, the *Archaeopteryx* of the Jurassic period, might not have flown very well because it had teeth, a tail, and bones like the small, walking dinosaurs from which it apparently evolved. It may have been too heavy for anything other than gliding, and it may have used its wings as much for batting down insects as for moving through the air. We know even less about how bats evolved because transitional bat fossils comparable to *Archaeopteryx* haven't been found. Ancient mammals that glide from tree to tree on skin flaps between hind and fore legs still live in Indonesian and Malaysian forests, suggesting that bats also evolved from gliding ancestors.

Whatever its past, aerial life has been as successful as other kinds, perhaps even more so. Insects are arguably the most diverse and abundant single animal group, and the vast majority fly at some time in their lives. Even burrowing ants and termites depend on flying drones and queens for reproduction. Birds are the most diverse class of vertebrates, with some 8,500 species known, and if the numbers of individual birds and bats were counted together, they might rival those of surface-dwelling vertebrates.

At least, they might have ten thousand years ago, when civilization was beginning. Migratory and resident birds were a major food source for early cultures. Hunters caught birds in nets and traps, and dried or salted them for storage. An elaborate technology of wild-bird exploitation developed as civilization grew, and almost every kind of bird was included: peasants caught sparrows and thrushes on limed twigs, and kings pursued herons and cranes with gyrfalcons and eagles. Yet birds remained abundant, while elephants, lions, aurochs, bears, and many other land animals disappeared from populated areas. In regions where large-scale urban societies arrived late, history records truly staggering bird populations. The best known of these was North America's passenger pigeon, which had an estimated population of from four to nine *billion* when European colonists arrived. Migrating pigeon flocks darkened the skies above towns for days, the birds flying so close together that hunters knocked down hundreds simply by flailing at them with long poles.

For our ancestors, the sky's abundance was like the ocean's. People weren't sure where migrating birds went until the nineteenth century: they thought the birds might hibernate in mud or on the sea bottom, or fly to the moon. People didn't worry if some kind of bird became scarce. There seemed to be so much space. When passenger pigeons disappeared in the 1880s, many simply assumed they'd moved west, or to South America, or even to Australia to escape the relentless hunting to which they'd been subjected.

Of course, the pigeons hadn't moved. Their communal nesting colonies had been exploited so ruthlessly by commercial hunters that the species could no longer reproduce successfully. Passenger pigeon pairs produced only a single young at each nesting. Mass-nesting was the only way they could maintain their population. The last known wild passenger pigeon was shot in Ohio in 1900, although a captive, "Martha," survived in the Cincinnati Zoo until 1914.

The effects of an "out of sight, out of mind" attitude began to become apparent with many other bird species as civilization entered into its highly expansive industrial phase. As passenger pigeon numbers fell from at least one hundred thousand remaining birds to zero in the last two decades of the ninteenth century, Carolina parakeets, Eskimo curlews, heath hens, and labrador ducks also reached the vanishing point.

Belated laws protecting pigeons (such as one passed by Pennsylvania in 1878, the year of the last mass nesting of the species at Petoskey, Michigan) proved useless because there was no way of enforcing them against the vested interests of market hunters and game merchants. Every town market had its game section, selling not only pigeons and quails but strings of robins and meadowlarks for roasting, and cardinals, warblers, tanagers, and finches as cage birds.

Yet attitudes toward these traditional uses were changing. An increasingly urban population began seeing wild birds not as supplemental food sources, but as objects of entertainment and recreation. In some cases, this was not good for the birds, as when they wound up stuffed on women's hats or in the display cases of amateur collectors. On the whole, though, the effect was beneficial because it created a constituency for protecting at least some kinds of birds.

Early conservation took two major forms. First, people tried to save birds by passing laws that regulated hunting and much commercial use. This kind of conservation has come to work well in countries with well-established judicial systems, where the wild bird market is mainly a thing of the past, and commercial hunting is no longer the main reason for species depletion. Game laws have worked less well where the laws are hard to enforce, as in much of the Third World. In places where war or other disaster brings massive social dislocation, it may not work at all. In recent years, birds have been machine-gunned by the thousands in Lebanon.

Conservationists soon realized that no amount of legal protection for birds would save them if they had no place to eat or nest. Even if passenger pigeon killing had stopped, the species might have disappeared anyway as farmers cleared the large forest tracts needed for feeding and nesting. The second form of conservation began around the turn of the century as private and public groups set aside sanctuaries for birds threatened by plume hunters of the millinery trade. The National Association of Audubon Societies hired wardens to protect egret and spoonbill colonies in Florida. President Theodore Roosevelt established the first national wildlife refuge, Pelican Island, at another Florida bird colony in 1903.

Protection gradually increased over ensuing decades. Large refuges were established for migratory waterfowl and shorebirds in the 1920s and '30s. By the 1940s, even hawks and eagles began to receive significant legal protection. Many states had paid bounties on birds of prey because of supposed depredations on game birds, but these were discontinued with no ill effects. The bald eagle received federal protection in 1940, although Alaska continued to offer a bounty on eagles until it became a state in the 1950s.

After centuries of decline, the skies were beginning to look more promising for wildlife in the 1940s. Although feeding and breeding habitat dwindled, the elimination of commercial hunting, enforcement of seasons and bag limits on sport hunters, and establishment of refuges had stemmed the nineteenth century's frightening tide of extinctions. An industrialized society had shown that it could change traditional attitudes and practices toward wildlife. It could maintain, if not the brimming abundance of pristine wilderness, at least healthy remnants of it, enough for the average citizen to enjoy in parks and refuges.

It wasn't as simple as that, however. At the same time that civilization was developing new ways of protecting threatened birds, it was developing new agricultural technology that, quite unintentionally, would threaten the life of the skies with pollution. The sky had been polluted long before the 1940s, of course. People had been complaining about the smoky, smelly air of cities since biblical times, and industrial smokestacks had darkened the air above nineteenth-century cities much more effectively than the largest passenger pigeon flock could have. Automobile smog had become a problem in a few areas such as Los Angeles by the 1930s, and Oklahoma dust settling on the U.S. Capitol in Washington during the 1930s drought had demonstrated that air quality problems could spread. Still, pollution was perceived as a domestic problem which might have serious effects on human health, but was unlikely to affect wildlife far from cities.

After the Second World War, however, a new wave of birds began disappearing rapidly and mysteriously. Prominent among them were raptors such as peregrine falcons, bald eagles, and ospreys. There were about two hundred peregrine nest sites in the United States east of the Mississippi River in 1940; in 1965, there was none. Peregrines remained in the west and north, but their populations were shrinking also, as were those in Europe, the Soviet Union, and Japan. Bald eagle and osprey populations dwindled almost as dramatically, and people noticed declines in almost all birds of prey as well as a bewildering variety of other creatures—brown pelicans, bats, even fireflies.

Biologists had noted high levels of the new chlorinated hydrocarbon pesticides such as DDT and Dieldrin in wild bird tissues since the 1940s. Adult birds had died of pesticide poisoning in some cases, but exposure wasn't invariably fatal. Then British biologist Derek Ratcliffe noticed in 1967 that peregrine eggs laid in the 1950s and '60s had markedly thinner shells than eggs laid before 1940. The shells were so thin that the parents broke them while sitting on the nest. Peregrines were declining because they were unable to fledge enough new birds to replace old ones.

Professor Thomas J. Cade of Cornell University found a definite correlation between this eggshell thinning and the high pesticide residues in peregrine tissues. Further studies proved that DDT broke down in the falcons' bodies into a substance called DDE, which interfered with the normal formation of eggshells. The DDT absorbed from duck, shorebird, or songbird prey (which had ingested it from feeding on sprayed marshes and crop fields) was destroying the peregrine falcon's reproductive capacity. Eagles, ospreys, and pelicans also suffered heavily from eggshell thinning. Brown pelicans disappeared from Louisiana, where the mouth of the Mississippi River disgorged vast quantities of pesticide residues from runoff of upstream farms and factories. Eagles disappeared from agricultural regions. Osprey nests stood empty over DDT-sprayed marshes.

The idea that the environment can be polluted not only with smoke and smells but with invisible traces of supposedly beneficial chemicals took years to sink in, but Rachel Carson's bestseller, *Silent Spring*, began to convince the public in 1962. DDT had seemed a panacea against crop pests and disease carriers, but it accumulated and persisted in the environment long after its use. Less persistent pesticides were available, as well as nonchemical techniques for controlling pests. After the Environmental Defense Fund and National Audubon Society forced national hearings on the issue, the federal government finally banned DDT in 1972, despite the protests of manufacturers, farmers, and public health officials who predicted mass starvation and epidemics.

Unfortunately, falcons kept disappearing although DDT was banned. Even after the pesticide was removed from general use, residues persisted in the environment, and persist to this day. One San Francisco Bay location near a former DDT factory showed its highest DDT concentration ever in bay sediments in 1986. Until 1979, American companies still exported DDT for use in other countries, and DDT residues traveled back to the United States on fruits and vegetables. The routine conservation methods of protecting birds and their habitats weren't enough in the peregrine falcon's case. Their reproductive capacity had to be protected, too.

Faced with these unexpectedly dire results of their tinkering with the biosphere, humans were forced to reverse one of civilization's oldest and most basic processes, the taming process. For millenia, people have been capturing and breeding wildlife with the intention of making it part of human culture. Now it became necessary to capture and breed wildlife not to tame it, but to maintain it in the wild. If peregrine falcons were to breed again in the eastern United States within the foreseeable future, there was no choice but to reintroduce birds.

This wasn't simply a matter of capturing peregrines in, say, the Arctic and releasing them in the east. The birds would have simply flown back to the Arctic (peregrine falcons get their name for their ability to migrate long distances). Somehow, a native race of falcons, hatched and fledged in the area, had to be reconstructed.

It was a complicated problem, requiring complicated solutions and much dedication and hard work from biologists and other workers. First, a stock of captive falcons had to be accumulated, a tenuous proposition because falcons seldom had been bred in captivity. (Falconers took their birds from the wild.) Even when this was accomplished, in the early 1970s, there was uneasiness because the captive falcons were mainly from Canadian and Alaskan races, and it was feared their fledglings might be genetically suited only for life in the far north.

Because of the uncertainties, biologists didn't depend entirely on eggs laid in captivity, but also took eggs from wild nests in the western United States, thin-shelled eggs that not might have survived in the wild. They patched cracked eggs with wax and glue to keep the embryos from drying out. Eggs had to be kept at precise levels of humidity and temperature, and when they hatched, the falcon chicks had to be fed every two or three hours. Once their eyes opened, they had to be fed by remote control so they wouldn't "imprint" on their keepers and identify with humans instead of other falcons. Human-imprinted falcons are unwilling to mate with other falcons but will attempt to mate with their human keepers, unlikely as it seems.

The complications of breeding captive falcons paled before those of releasing the fledglings into the wild. Simply turned loose, the young falcons would have starved to death or been killed by predators. They had to learn to protect and feed themselves before they could survive in the wild. Fortunately, birds have strong innate capacities for survival. Much of their hunting behavior is instinctive; with practice, they can learn to capture prey without being taught. It proved possible to prepare the birds for survival by adapting an old falconry technique called "hacking," whereby fledglings are allowed to learn to hunt but then conditioned to return to their masters.

Before their plumage was fully developed, the fledglings were kept and fed for a week in a "hack box." After that, the birds could fly out, but because they couldn't fly far, they would return to the box, where food was provided. This would go on for six weeks, about the time it takes a normal fledgling to mature. In falconry, the falcons were caught and tethered at the end of this period. In restoration, the box was closed, feeding was stopped, and the birds flew away, it was hoped, to find mates, raise young, and make falcon restoration obsolete.

Conservationists in the western United States also started breeding peregrines for release in the wild. Their job was a little easier because there were still some wild falcons nesting. In addition to hacking fledglings, it proved possible to remove thin-shelled eggs from wild nests (at considerable hazard to the removers, since falcons nest high on cliffs) and replace them with healthy nestlings. The falcon parents, apparently not too upset by the intrusion, would raise these foster chicks. The thin-shelled eggs could be hatched artificially, and those chicks also placed in foster nests.

Falcon restoration projects have succeeded in returning well over a thousand peregrines to the wild throughout the United States. A percentage of released birds succumb fairly soon to the dangers of life in the wild (as is normally the case with wild birds), but the others are able to establish themselves. People who had never seen peregrines have been seeing them in recent years, and peregrines have been showing up in places from which they've been absent for decades. New York bridges, Baltimore skyscrapers, and other eastern aeries are again home to peregrines.

The real test of restoration will be whether the peregrines can maintain their population. Some have produced young, but their number is still small in proportion to the numbers released. Conservationists expect it to grow as more and more birds mature and find nest sites. Eggshell thinning will continue to be a danger to peregrine nesting as long as DDT and other chlorinated hydro-carbons persist in the environment, however. Falcon restoration may have to go on a long time, and it is expensive and laborious. Yet for many people the likely alternative, skies without peregrine falcons, is simply unacceptable.

Banning of DDT *has* had a beneficial effect on wildlife in this country. Other species that suffered from eggshell thinning have shown definite signs of recovery. Brown pelicans have maintained their populations without much help from humans, although the vanished flock at the Mississippi's mouth had to be replaced with birds transported from Florida. The pelicans were simply trapped in the wild and moved to the Louisiana coast, but they accepted their new home, although a number died suddenly when a high concentration of DDT from an unknown source came down the river and poisoned them. For the present, Louisiana's state bird still lives there.

America's national bird has taken longer than the pelican to begin recovering from its post-1946 breeding decline, but its situation seems hopeful, too. The number of breeding bald eagle pairs recorded by the U.S. Fish and Wildlife Service in 1982 was almost three times that of 1962. This increase may be partly a factor of people looking harder for eagle nests, and eagles are still declining in some states, usually in connection with continuing water-pollution problems. Yet there is definite evidence that eagles are returning to many areas and breeding more successfully. In the Chesapeake Bay area, where average breeding success declined from 1.6 young per nest in 1936 to 0.2 young per nest in 1962, eagles were raising an average of 1.27 young per nest in 1985. Conservationists have used techniques similar to those of peregrine restoration to supplement the wild eagle population with hundreds of captive-bred birds. Our other large, fish-eating raptor, the osprey, also seems to have recovered from 1960s population lows. Osprey reintroduction efforts have been successful in some eastern states.

Yet DDT is only one kind of contamination that affects life in the skies. Industrial civilization produces thousands of toxic chemicals, and many may have DDT's potential for being toxic in unexpectedly far-reaching ways. For example, air pollution is threatening the survival of fish and other aquatic life over vast stretches of North America and Europe. Successfully hatching eggs won't do eagles and ospreys much good if they can't feed their young from the lakes and rivers they nest beside.

People used to think that smog produced by automobile exhaust

Smokestacks in North America release more than fifty million tons of sulfur and nitrogen oxides every year. The "acid rain" caused by these dirty emissions is deadly to fish and other animals.

and factory and power-plant emissions in industrial areas of the United States, Germany, France, and Great Britain was the problem only of the places that produced it—an unpleasant side effect of industrial development, but one that could be tolerated in exchange for economic growth. Then people in Scandinavia, Canada, and the American Northeast began to notice that fish and other animals in their lakes were disappearing. This situation has gotten steadily worse over the past two decades: many lakes are now actually lifeless except for certain bacteria. Scientific study showed that the lake waters were becoming so acidic that they either killed aquatic life outright or reacted with chemicals such as aluminum in lake bottoms to form toxic compounds.

Other studies have shown that rain falling from polluted skies can be highly acidic because oxides of nitrogen and sulphur in the air react with raindrops to form nitric or sulphuric acid, rendering the water as sour as vinegar. Every year, more than fifty million tons of sulfur and nitrogen oxides are released over North America. One does not always require scientific instruments to identify acid rain: merely standing out in a summer thunderstorm may be enough. The eyes burn and redden; the throat becomes raw. Even on "clear" days, acid particles in haze or mist can cause such symptoms.

A link between eye-reddening Midwestern rains and souring Canadian lakes was not hard to make, because normal weather patterns regularly carry masses of air from the Midwest to Canada, and from Germany and Britain to Scandinavia. Northern lakes tend to be rather acidic naturally. Glaciers have scraped lime-rich sedimentary deposits off much of the north, exposing acidic granite bedrock, and northern coniferous forests form humus rich in acidic tannin. Such lake waters have only a limited capacity for neutralizing acid precipitation, so their acidity exceeds the tolerance of the loons, trout, otters, and frogs. Acidification threatens more than nine thousand lakes and sixty thousand miles of streams in the eastern United States alone.

As with DDT, we will not avert the threat of massive contamination unless industry stops introducing such vast quantities of toxic chemicals into the environment. Automobiles and power plants can't be banned, but technologies exist for the substantial reduction of sulfur and nitrogen emissions at reasonable costs—costs far lower than those resulting from the economic damage acid rain causes every year. Washing can remove sulfur from coal before it is burned, and stack scrubbers can eliminate sulfur from power plant emissions. New ways of burning coal can reduce both sulfur and nitrogen emissions. Using a variety of such techniques where appropriate, industry can cut sulfur dioxide emissions by more than half within the next decade. Unfortunately, utility companies have resisted taking action on the grounds that not enough is known about the problem, although the National Academy of Sciences and the Reagan administration have both acknowledged the link between acid rain and massive environmental and economic damage. Only national legislation will ensure concerted action and bring the United States in line with other industrial democracies, which are developing policies to deal with the problem.

Deadly as DDT and acid rain are, society at least has been able to identify their dangers and begin to try to avert them. Even more frightening are the dangers we don't identify, the ones with causes so complicated they confuse us. Whether falcons, eagles, and pelicans ever fully recover from DDT, or loons and trout return to northern lakes, we at least know what went wrong. This is not the case with other dwindling wildlife.

The swift decline of the California condor in recent years has dramatically demonstrated the limitations of our present ability to identify and remedy a threat to wildlife. While it is clear to all concerned that the condor has declined because of human encroachments on its living space, conservationists have not been able to agree as to the exact causes of the decline, as they have agreed about falcon eggshell-thinning or lake acidification. Since the condor's living space encompasses about thirty-six million acres of southern California, halting the fatal encroachments has so far proved impossible.

In prehistoric times, several species of condor roamed the continent east to Florida, feeding on the remains of mastodons, camels, bison, and other big game that inhabited the vast grasslands of the past two million years. Condor bones found in Grand Canyon caves show that the species we know today nested there as recently as nine thousand years ago. When Spanish explorers first encountered condors in 1602, however, the species had retreated to the Pacific Coast. They then ranged from British Columbia to Baja California, although it is possible that they nested only in California, where mild climate and rich grasslands resembled prehistoric conditions. The spread of desert during the past ten thousand years may have driven condors from most of the Southwest by greatly reducing herds of large animals, and thus of suitable carrion. Condors may have survived on the Pacific Coast largely by eating dead sea mammals on beaches: whales, seals, sea lions, and sea otters were abundant.

We don't know how many California condors were alive when Lewis and Clark shot one on the Columbia River in 1805, but they were never common; the population may have been no larger than five hundred. It dropped quickly thereafter. Condors were extinct outside California and Baja California by 1900, and gone from the northern half of the state by 1940. A scientific study conducted by Carl Koford from 1939 to 1946 estimated the remaining population at sixty condors. Human activities obviously caused the decline: condors had been shot, poisoned by predator baits or lead bullets in carcasses they had eaten, and disturbed by egg collectors. The wildlife whose carrion they formerly had eaten had been decimated, while modern ranching methods limited the amount of livestock carrion available to them.

At that time, it seemed possible that condors would survive these pressures in their remote mountain strongholds. State laws had protected the species since 1905, and conservationists established sanctuaries in Los Padres National Forest in 1939, 1947, and 1975. The U.S. Fish and Wildlife Service classified the species as endangered in 1967. Yet the condor population continued to gradually decline as roads, dams, mineral exploration, residential development, power lines,

THE CONDOR COUNTRY

The historical range of the California condor, the bird with the longest wingspan in North America, encompasses a relatively small region of southern California's coastal and interior mountains and valleys.

Condor feeding range is largely in the grasslands and oak savannas that border the San Joaquin Valley. Most of this area consists of private ranchlands: carcasses of ranch livestock have been the main food source for condors for many years. Because so much of southern California has been urbanized, these ranchlands have exceptional ecological significance. Many other endangered species, including the San Joaquin kit fox, live on them, but the lands are increasingly attractive to developers.

Condor nesting range is in remote mountain canyons, some of the last wilderness in southern California. Nest sites are located in places inaccessible to most natural predators, usually in caves or crevices in cliff faces. Several potential sites usually are located within a condor pair's nesting territory. After the pair has visited the potential sites, the female lays a single egg on the bare floor of the chosen cave or crevice.

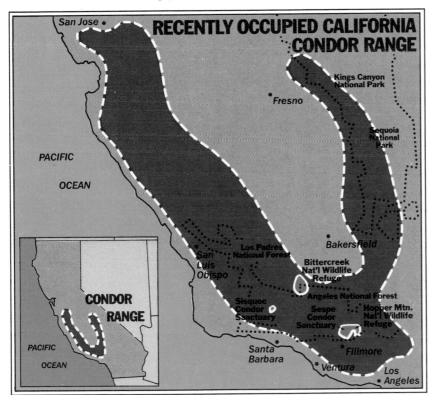

In April 1987, the last known wild California condor was captured at Bitter Creek National Wildlife Refuge. There are now twenty-seven condors in captivity in the San Diego and Los Angeles zoos, where biologists hope to breed them and eventually release a new population to the wild.

irrigated farming, and other man-made encroachments continued to spread into condor habitat. There was also a strong possibility of eggshell-thinning from DDT contamination, since southern California farmers used DDT heavily. The DDT ban didn't seem to help condors as it did eagles and ospreys.

Because of their small range and population, condors were already in much deeper trouble than eagles. Condors breed very slowly, each pair producing only a single chick every two to three years. By the 1970s, the population had dropped to around thirty, and extinction within decades seemed probable if the trend continued.

The situation was obviously very grave, but conservationists found it difficult to agree upon a course of action. Some said, reasonably, that the way to protect a bird threatened by human disturbance of its habitat was to minimize that disturbance. Others said that the danger to the species' very existence was too great, and advocated removing the survivors from the wild so their genetic diversity could be maintained. (Small, inbred populations may be susceptible to disease, birth defects, and other biological hazards.) Yet many conservationists feared that, if all condors were removed from the wild, there would be no incentive even to try to protect the habitat, making it impossible to eventually reintroduce captive-bred birds. Without wild condors, it also would be impossible to learn what exactly was threatening the species.

Authorities eventually decided to remove some of the condors for captive breeding, but to leave most in the wild, the rationale being that this would help to ensure the species' genetic survival while permitting study of wild birds and maintenance of habitat. A Condor Recovery Program began in 1980 under the auspices of the U.S. Fish and Wildlife Service, the Forest Service, the Bureau of Land Management, the California Department of Fish and Game, and the National Audubon Society. From 1982 to 1984, project biologists trapped nine condors, fitted them with small radio transmitters, and tracked the birds' movements after releasing them. Data collected suggested that condors used all parts of their range at various times of year, and that they weren't threatened by a food shortage within that range.

Biologists began a captive flock by removing five, mostly nonbreeding individuals from the wild, and by removing eggs from condor nests to be hatched in a special facility created at the San Diego Wild Animal Park. Biologists had seen one of the wild condor pairs lay a second egg in their nest after ravens broke a first. This suggested that the captive flock could be increased fairly rapidly by "double clutching," a technique that has been used with other endangered birds, including the Andean condor of South America. After a pair had produced one egg, biologists could remove it with the expectation that the pair would produce a second or third.

In 1984, the Condor Recovery Project looked promising. The wild condor flock seemed stable at five breeding pairs, and there were ten hatchlings from eggs laid by wild pairs in the San Diego and Los Angeles zoos. Biologists planned to release some of these hatchlings into the wild in 1985 to begin building up the wild breeding population.

Unfortunately, only one of the wild breeding pairs returned to its nest in 1985. The fate of the others was unknown. Then, in January 1986, the female of the last known breeding pair was found helpless, poisoned by a lead bullet she probably had swallowed while feeding on a deer carcass. She died despite the efforts of zoo veterinarians. In little more than a year, the known wild condor population had dropped to five birds. Plans to reintroduce young condors to the wild were shelved.

The rapid decline of wild condors led the U.S. Fish and Wildlife Service to the decision that all condors should be removed from the wild. Many conservationists objected to this expedient, however, on the grounds that removing the last wild birds would threaten the chances

THE CAPTIVE CONDORS

As part of the Condor Recovery Program, the San Diego Wild Animal Park established a facility for the captive propagation of the birds; its captive flock comprises some eggs and birds taken from the wild. The Los Angeles Zoo is also accumulating a captive flock of condors. Thus, if disease or other disaster wipes out either facility's flock, there will still be condors.

The recovery plan calls for the reestablishment of a wild population of sixty to eighty birds by early in the next century. The San Diego Wild Animal Park plays a key role in this plan. On a remote hillside at the edge of the park, away from the public areas, is the Condor Recovery Facility, nicknamed "the condorminium." In the first two years of the program here, ten chicks hatched from a dozen eggs that had been "double-clutched" from the nests of wild birds.

Captive California condors in the San Diego Wild Animal Park.

CONDOR MATING

Even to the trained human observer, male and female condors are indistinguishable. Biologists have had to devise a blood test to accurately determine the sex of individual birds.

Several mature condors have been caged together in the hope that they will eventually pair and mate. Studies of the related Andean condor made at San Diego and at the U.S. Fish and Wildlife Service's Patuxent Research Center suggest that no insurmountable obstacles exist to captive breeding of California condors. Successful

captive breeding of Andean condors is no guarantee of success with California condors, however.

Condors mate for life. Sexually mature at six, they may live to be thirty. No one knows precisely what attracts one bird to another. Male condors perform a flying courtship display prior to mating. Researchers at the Los Angeles Zoo are watching captive adult California condors closely so that we may learn more about the pair formation process.

Two condors flying in Los Padres National Forest, California.

of successfully reintroducing condors. In January 1986, the National Audubon Society obtained a temporary injunction against removal of the wild condors.

An appellate court dissolved the Audubon injunction in May 1986, however. The recovery team promptly took two of the five wild survivors into captivity, an eleven- to twelve-year-old male who was never known to have mated, and a twelve-year-old female whose first mate had disappeared in 1985, but who had formed a new pair and laid two eggs earlier in 1986. The remaining three birds, all males, were left in the wild during the summer of 1986, because hot weather increases danger of stress-related death or injury of birds while they are being trapped. The Fish and Wildlife Service gave the order for their capture in September 1986. The last wild condor was captured in April 1987

It is hoped that some of the twenty-seven condors presently in captivity can be released into the wild within a few years. In August 1986, a reconstituted Condor Recovery Program set forth three basic recommendations for future management: capture of remaining wild condors; major efforts to protect condor habitat; and high priority for reintroduction of condors into the wild. Habitat protection would include federal purchase of the sixteen-thousand-acre Hudson Ranch, a major foraging area for the remaining three condors before their capture, as well as designation of an endangered species macropreserve on the adjoining Carrizo Plains, an extensive grassland area where a

REARING CONDORS

Ornithologists at the San Diego Wild Animal Park raise condor hatchlings in virtual isolation, to minimize chances of the birds' "imprinting" on their human helpers. (*Imprinting* is a biological term for the phenomenon whereby a young bird gets its species orientation from older ones, usually its parents. A bird raised by humans, instead of by members of its own species, will identify with humans and will often try to mate with humans.) Young condors imprinted on people not only would fail to mate with condors, they probably would not survive in the wild, since they would lack the appropriate behavioral patterns. Young condors in the Los Angeles Zoo, which have not been kept isolated, may have to live out their lives in captivity.

The condor nestlings at San Diego Wild Animal Park were reared with the help of hand puppets shaped like the heads of adult condors. With ornithologists acting as puppeteers, the condor-puppet "parents" provided nurture and nourishment throughout the young birds' early lives. The efficacy of such techniques won't be tested until young birds are reintroduced into the wild. No one really knows if captive-bred condors will have the behavioral information necessary to sustain them in the wild, since we don't know how important contact with parents and other condors is to young condors. Young Andean condors have been successfully reintroduced into the wild. There is still a viable wild population of Andean condors, however. Some biologists wonder if California condors introduced into a world without other, wild California condors will survive and reproduce.

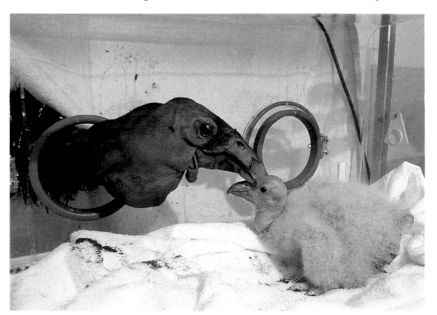

A condor hatchling feeds in the San Diego Wild Animal Park. The puppet prevents the hatchling from imprinting on humans.

number of organizations are cooperating to protect endangered species such as the San Joaquin kit fox and the giant Kangaroo rat as well as the condor. Biologists hope that if such a refuge can be secured, some of the original, experienced population of wild condors can be reintroduced there so that their ancestral traditions of foraging, roosting, nesting, and otherwise carrying on their lives will not be lost. The reintroduced zoo-reared birds could then learn how to survive from the experienced wild flock.

Some biologists disagree with the idea of perpetuating ancestral condor habits on the grounds that those habits have not allowed condors to survive in the wild under the pressures of the modern world. They would prefer to reintroduce into the wild only inexperienced condors whose behavior would not be influenced by the "bad habits" of the ancestral population. It also has been suggested that condors be reintroduced into a different area than southern California, such as the Grand Canyon, where pressure from civilization would be less.

Most conservationists feel, however, that removing condors to the Grand Canyon would only be postponing the basic problem of protecting the condor's habitat. Although condors once lived in the Grand Canyon, they did not survive there as long as in southern California, indicating that southern California is their optimal habitat. If it cannot be protected, then prospects for condors elsewhere are not promising. Northern Arizona may be under less pressure from civilization than southern California now, but that situation could change. In the end, society will have to face the hard choice between restraining some of its activities in order to give condors some room, and leaving them in zoos. Most people would probably agree, at least, that a condor in a cage is not much of a condor.

Society faces a similar choice in regard to the skies as a whole, between conservation and a continuing deterioration of air quality. The galloping expansion of automobile-dependent megapolises like Los Angeles could eventually affect the atmosphere enough to change the climate of the planet. The burning of fossil fuels such as gasoline and coal is measurably increasing the percentage of carbon dioxide in the atmosphere. Many scientists think an atmosphere significantly richer in carbon dioxide will raise global temperatures by causing a "greenhouse effect." Like the glass walls of a greenhouse, an atmosphere with more carbon dioxide could trap solar heat. The resultant rise in the temperatures of the Earth's surface could turn today's farm belts into desert and even melt the polar icecaps, drowning heavily populated coastal areas. A two-degree rise in global temperatures may occur within the next twenty years.

Such projections smack of science fiction, and people have grown weary of ecological doomsday scenarios. Yet our global climate has shown disturbing trends lately: we have seen a terrible drought in Africa, abrupt fluctuations of ocean temperatures, and unusually severe storms in many places. These phenomena may be a normal part of the atmosphere's complex and highly variable nature, but we don't know enough about the atmosphere to assume that we can go on polluting it without bringing major changes upon ourselves. If the condor's swift decline teaches us anything, it is that such changes can be as rapid as they are dire.

THE
FORESTS

CROWDED AS THE EARTH has become, there are still wild animals that people almost never see. One of these, a Florida panther, rests in the fork of a large live oak one spring evening and watches a pair of game wardens cross a sawgrass prairie in a swamp buggy. His ears twitch as the buggy roars past, but the panther does not seem to be disturbed by the noise. Although few people have seen him during the three years of his life, he has seen a number of them and hears even more, as swamp buggies, airplanes, helicopters, cars, and motorcycles cross parts of his territory.

Like other members of the cat family, the panther is a peculiar mixture of caution and curiosity. Although taught by his mother to avoid direct contact with humans, he is fascinated by the novelty of unfamiliar sights, sounds, and smells. This fascination almost cost him his life two years before, when he crossed the southern Florida highway called Alligator Alley for the first time while wandering in search of a home range. The sudden warmth of the smooth asphalt was arresting. Even more intriguing were the two bright lights that hovered on the eastern horizon like new stars and gradually grew even brighter. Fortunately for the young panther, the driver of the approaching pickup truck—who thought the eyes glowing above the road belonged to a deer—had quick reflexes. He slammed on the brakes and leaned into his horn in time to startle the panther into the roadside ditch. The cat has since been more careful about crossing Alligator Alley.

When the swamp buggy fades into the distance and the fireflies start to flash above the saw palmetto and waxmyrtle, the panther leaves his resting place and moves away through the trees. He is on one of the low ridges of hardwood forest that interrupt the bald cypress swamps and sawgrass wet prairies of the Fakahatchee Strand in southwestern Florida's Big Cypress Swamp. Although most of the many square miles of his home range are swamp and marsh, he spends much of his time on the forested ridges (which are also called hammocks after an Indian word for them). They offer what he needs most: concealment while he rests or ambushes deer and raccoons, and dry places on which he leaves the scent markings that establish his territory. The markings warn other male panthers of his presence and reserve the local prey populations and female panthers for him.

The panther pauses to sniff deer scat, then moves on, placing his feet so carefully that he makes almost no sound despite the heavy underbrush. Few creatures are better at moving through forest than Florida panthers. With small heads, low bodies, and long tails, they are perfectly balanced for the precarious world of windthrown trunks and undergrowth. Sensitive ears and noses allow them to perceive far through the screen of trunks and branches, while binocular, night-adapted eyes help make them extraordinary climbers and jumpers. Heart and lungs also are adapted to powerful, nimble movement in

Florida panther.

confined forest spaces. Panthers can jump as far as forty feet and reach speeds of thirty-five miles an hour in short sprints after prey, but they tire quickly after that. Their circulatory system is not adapted for maintaining high oxygen levels in the blood for long periods, as is the circulatory system of the grassland-dwelling cheetah.

The panther's adaptation to forest predatory life is reflected in its extraordinary natural range. The Florida panther is a subspecies of *Felis concolor*, the second-largest cat species in the Americas, also known as the mountain lion, cougar, and puma. Before Columbus, various subspecies of *Felis concolor* lived in almost every forest of the Western Hemisphere, from the southern beech forests of Tierra del Fuego to the spruce and fir forests of British Columbia and New Brunswick. Only the subarctic taiga of Alaska and northern Canada seems to have been without panthers. The species lived in grasslands and deserts as well, but never too far from places where it could stalk deer, javelina, or guanaco from cover. The three-year-old male in the Fakahatchee Strand is typical of panther adaptability, because he prowls a forest with both temperate and tropical affinities. Southern Florida hammocks support not only the live oaks, red maples, and slash pines common to the American Southeast, but also strangler figs, royal palms, and gumbo limbos that grow throughout the West Indies and Central America.

No other mammal (except man) was as widely distributed in the wilderness Americas as the panther. This shows something of the importance of forests and woodlands in the scheme of life. Before civilization, most of the continents were covered with woody vegetation, if not with two-hundred-foot-tall, closed-canopy tropical forest, then with hundreds of other variations on the theme of roots, trunk, branches, and leaves—deciduous forest, gallery forest, oak woodland, swamp forest, short-tree forest, cloud forest, brushland. The woody plant dominates all of these habitats with its ability to control the sources of terrestrial life: sunlight, water, and soil.

By the simple but efficient biological strategy of raising its leaves skyward on a stem stiffened with lignin and cellulose, the tree greatly increases its photosynthetic potential over that of ground-hugging, soft plants. A one-hundred-foot-tall tree exposes much more leaf surface to solar radiation than a one-foot-tall shrub because it has many more leaves. By invading the sky, the tree monopolizes sunlight with its dense screen of leaves, and soil moisture and nutrients with its extensive root network.

If the soil is poor in moisture or nutrients, the tree may extend its environmental control a step further and draw them from the sky itself. In tropical forests, where soils tend to be poor, trees get most of their mineral nutrients from rain, no meager supply since raindrops form around dust particles. Much of the rain in such forests never touches the ground: aerial roots and epiphytic plants absorb it first. So efficient are tropical forests at using precipitation that stream runoff in them is almost sterile, indicating that the trees have filtered out everything except water.

The tree's biological strategy is not only effective, but very old, evidence of perennial viability. Trees appeared very soon after plant life first emerged from the oceans some four hundred million years ago in the Silurian period. In a sense, they had to. Soft-bodied ocean plants such as kelp couldn't support themselves on dry land, and once plants evolved hard stems and branches, there would have been immediate evolutionary pressure, through natural selection, for them to grow taller. Taller plants would get more solar radiation for photosynthesis than the shorter ones they shaded. The first forests must have almost exploded across the continents.

By the Pennsylvanian period of three hundred million years ago, trees thickly covered the great lowland basins of the continents. The trees were quite different from today's, belonging to primitive plant groups represented now by the small horsetails and club mosses that still grow in moist woodlands. Some of them looked like giant versions of their descendants, some like nothing that grows now. Although probably not as diverse and efficient as today's, these forests were so extensive, and lasted so long, that they left fossil deposits many miles deep—deposits we dig up and burn as coal.

As the more efficiently reproducing seed plants evolved in the Mesozoic era, they too formed vast forests that dominated not only moist lowlands, but mountains and higher latitudes. These were the gymnosperms, whose descendants still comprise a large percentage of the Earth's forest cover, from the redwoods and bald cypresses of moist lowlands to the pines, spruces, and firs of the mountains and the far north. Ancient gymnosperm forests included many kinds of trees besides conifers: palm-like cycads and broadleaved joint firs which survive today, as well as extinct forms such as seed ferns. Gymnosperms were the dominant vegetation throughout most of the dinosaur age.

About one hundred million years ago, flowering plants evolved, probably from woody gymnosperms, although scientists aren't sure. Another forest explosion began. Capable of being polluted by insects, birds, and bats as well as by wind and water, and of spreading their seeds in equally ingenious ways, flowering trees (which include those with inconspicuous flowers such as willow and oak as well as those with showy ones such as magnolia and dogwood) quickly pushed gymnosperms to marginal habitats like mountains. Flowering trees occupied the world's great lowland basins with hardwood forests of an unprecedented diversity. In the more benign global climate of the late dinosaur age, they covered every continent, leaving abundant subtropical fossils such as magnolia and palm in Greenland and Antarctica. When the dinosaurs abruptly disappeared, flowering plants thrived, and have continued to do so through the ensuing sixty-five million years in forms very similar to the ones they have today.

These successive forest empires have had a formative effect on other land life. One might say that terrestrial animals evolved not so much to walk upon the ground as to move among the trees. Claws evolved in part for climbing tree trunks, and bat and bird wings probably evolved for gliding between them. With their tall canopies, forests have provided a kind of third dimension to land life, allowing it to retain and elaborate on the diversity it brought from the ocean depths. The most diverse habitats are coral reefs and forests. The most diverse forest, tropical forest, may contain as many as half the species on earth.

Forest diversity is a byproduct of the tree's basic biological strategy of raising its leaves to the sun. As leaf surface increases, opportunities for leaf-eating animals increase, along with opportunities for animals that feed on leaf-eaters. Trees respond to attacks on their leaves by evolving biological defenses that force leaf-eating animals to evolve new ways of feeding, which force predators to adapt, and so on, until forest life becomes an extraordinary tangle, with every organism depending on dozens of others for existence.

A single tree, for example, may depend on several species of symbiotic fungi to transfer water and nutrients into its roots, on several species of butterflies and bees to transfer its pollen, on a species of ant to defend its leaves from bugs and beetles, on several species of woodpeckers to defend its wood from grubs, and on several species of fruit-eating birds and mammals to spread its seeds in their droppings. Of course, the tree wouldn't die immediately if most of these organisms disappeared. Yet it would not grow and reproduce as well without them.

Forest diversity holds both opportunities and limitations for life. As the numbers of species multiply, adaptations become more ingenious and sophisticated. At the same time, however, individual organisms and species face increased competition from all the other ingeniously adapted organisms. The more diverse a forest is, the rarer the species in it tend to be. One can walk for a day through tropical forest and see hundreds of species but only a few individuals of each: a few spider monkeys, ocellated turkeys, chachalacas, agoutis, silk cotton trees. In temperate-zone forests, where cold winters and other factors limit diversity, a day's walk will reveal fewer species but more individuals of each: dozens of gray squirrels, ruffed grouse, oak trees.

The forest's interplay of opportunity and limitation has shaped humanity's relationship to it. Humans would never have evolved without forest diversity, because the large apes from which we descended evolved there. Our closest living relatives—gorillas, orangutans, and chimpanzees—are forest animals. On the other hand, humanity would probably never have evolved if our hominid ancestors had remained in the forest. Human characteristics such as erect posture, opposable thumbs, and enlarged brains probably developed after Pliocene drought forced early hominids into African grassland and savanna, where they eventually developed tools, fire, big-game hunting, and other cultural attributes.

Yet humans have always returned to the forest for its diversity. There may not be large game herds, but there are fruits, and birds, and honey, and a vast variety of plants with food and medicinal properties our early ancestors may have known already. Wild apes have a wide knowledge of plant uses, for medicine as well as food. The more human cultures diversified, the more forest diversity offered: bright feathers for decoration, hard or soft woods for building or tools, lianas and bark for weaving. Some peoples, such as Africa's Mbuti, or pygmies, developed hunting-and-gathering forest cultures and became as rare and scattered as other forest creatures. Other cultures developed along the forest edge, where they could maximize opportunities and avoid limitations: they learned to control the forest, girdling and burning trees, letting sunlight in to foster early crop plants such as bananas and cassava.

Early human cultures probably cut and burned most of the wild forests in the world repeatedly. The forests survived because the cultures were small and scattered. After one tribe entered a region, carved out a village site and gardens, hunted the local game into scarcity, and moved on, hundreds or even thousands of years might pass before another did.

This began to change as cereal crops and livestock allowed larger populations and more permanent settlements. Cultures continued to diversify, always finding more uses for trees: charcoal for metal-smelting, masts and timbers for ships, bark and seeds for spices, bark for tanning. Yet the trees did not grow back where goats and sheep pastured. Forests began to disappear, first from drier areas—the Mediterranean, the Near East, the Indus Valley—then from the humid river basins of Europe and China. When Columbus sailed for America, wood had become so scarce over much of the Old World that people were burning dung, peat, and straw to cook food and keep warm.

In the Americas, however, European explorers found forests even richer than their own vanished wilderness had been. Glaciers had not covered North America as completely as in Europe, and many species extinct there had survived in the New World. Although Native American populations were substantial, a lack of grazing livestock (except in the Andean highlands) and the consequent dependence on wild game led to less destructive treatment of forest. Even in the Aztec and Mayan city-states, where large tracts were cleared for agriculture, Spanish explorers found thriving forests and regarded them with pleasure and awe, remembering the sheep-bitten hills of their native land.

Pleasure and awe did not stop Europeans from abusing the New World forests. They accomplished in four hundred years what had taken ten thousand in the Old World, substantially deforesting first the highlands of South and Central America, then the river basins further north. The greatest of these, the Mississippi River basin forest, shrank away in little more than a century after United States civilization crossed the Appalachian Mountains. Settlers wrote home about the giant trees (forty-foot-circumference sycamores were the largest), built cabins and fences with them, fed hogs with the nuts, and burned the rest, planting crops in the ashes. They ate bear, deer, and squirrel meat for a few years, then switched to pork and chicken when the game supply ended. Forest predators—such as wolves and panthers—

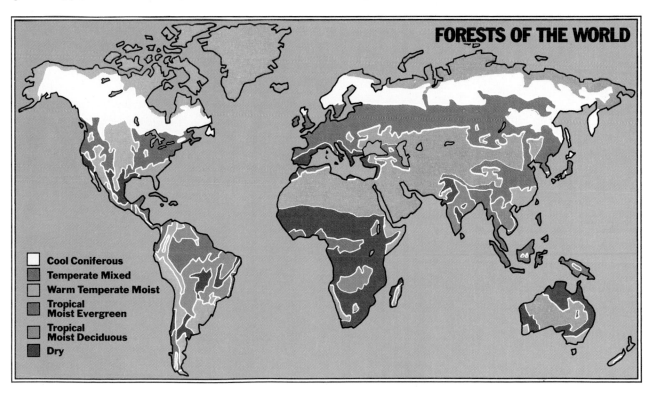

FORESTS OF THE WORLD

- Cool Coniferous
- Temperate Mixed
- Warm Temperate Moist
- Tropical Moist Evergreen
- Tropical Moist Deciduous
- Dry

lasted a little longer by preying on livestock, but settlers organized mass hunts to exterminate them.

In mountainous or northern areas, forests marginal to farming might have escaped cutting in earlier times, but industry followed agriculture quickly in America. Iron foundries and dozens of other enterprises used enormous amounts of timber before coal came into general use. As industrial cities grew, the demand for building lumber soared. Maine and Minnesota pine forests lasted only a few decades longer than Ohio and Kentucky oak forests, and the bald cypress and pine forests of the southeast were destroyed in the late nineteenth and early twentieth centuries. Acorn-eating passenger pigeons and bald-cypress-seed-eating Carolina parakeets went with them.

Forest liquidation had consequences other than the extinction of a few bird species. People in the growing cities began to wonder where their water supplies would come from, as cut-over upstream lands, without vegetation to absorb rain or protect soil from erosion, generated increasing cycles of floods and drought. They wondered where wood for future building would come from once the trees were all cut and the soil washed away. In response to such concerns, the federal government began taking control of much forest land under the Forest Reserve and Organic Administration Acts of 1891 and 1897, which authorized the president to set aside forest reserves to secure "favorable conditions of water flows, and furnish a continuous supply of timber." Under Theodore Roosevelt's administration, the government designated over a hundred million acres of national forests and created a Forest Service to manage them.

With such protective measures, and with regulations on private forestry practices, many industrial countries were able to check the trend toward deforestation. Timber barons could no longer simply cut all the marketable trees, burn the rest, and turn the land over to livestock after shooting all the wildlife. Rangers regulated livestock numbers so they would not preclude regeneration of young trees. Foresters allowed logged areas to regenerate naturally or replanted them. Forestry became a scientific enterprise which aimed to produce as much wood, water, pasture, wildlife, and recreational opportunity as possible without degrading the forest.

American forest conservation looked good in 1940. Many deforested areas were regenerating, and wildlife that had seemed about to follow pigeons and parakeets into oblivion was returning under protection. White-tailed deer, extirpated from many eastern states, returned once game laws were enforced. Colorful wood ducks nested in boxes that wildlife managers provided to replace the old-growth trees they had once used. In the West and Alaska, where substantial old-growth forest remained, the Forest Service established large tracts of wilderness and primitive areas where logging was excluded and the public could experience primeval forest.

Yet forests proved vulnerable to the same industrial developments that threatened the skies after World War II. Agricultural inventions such as DDT seemed to promise a limitless future food supply. Human population, already growing quickly because of improvements in health care, took an even sharper rise. The population of the United States doubled in roughly fifty years. In response to postwar baby-boom demands for increased housing, national forest policy changed markedly. Allowing the use of bulldozer technology developed during the war, the Forest Service opened millions of acres of western old-growth to intensive logging. Loggers clear-cut entire mountainsides, removed every living tree and scraped the residue bare to prepare for replanting with a few commercial species such as Douglas fir. Foresters treated plantations with pesticides and herbicides to remove competition from wild plants and animals. This caused the drastic reduction of some former administratively designated wilderness areas.

The Forest Service maintained that such developments were in keeping with scientific forestry. Yet many conservationists questioned whether the wholesale application of industrial technology would benefit forests in the long run. They doubted that the even-aged stands of one or two commercial tree species that the Forest Service and timber companies were creating were really forests at all. They feared that making trees into uniform crops would increase their vulnerability to pests, disease, and other destructive factors, and that many of the other plants and animals that had evolved in the old, diverse forests would be unable to survive in the tree farms.

Old-growth forest is quite different ecologically from second-growth. The large, old trees that predominate an old-growth forest produce much more of some kinds of wildlife foods such as fruits and nuts than do young trees. They also provide more nesting and shelter space for many kinds of animals in the form of treehole cavities, standing snags, and downed logs. A few species of wildlife may thrive when old-growth forest is cut, including deer, which feed on tree seedlings, and some species of songbird adapted to nesting in brushy habitat. Many other species—woodpeckers, squirrels, bears, wood ducks, martens, turkeys, spruce grouse—find that opportunities for food and shelter are greatly decreased in second-growth. Even deer may suffer in the long run from clear-cutting because it reduces environmental stability, leading to population explosions and crashes, winter die-offs, and disruption of migration patterns.

Many of conservationists' fears have been realized in the past forty years. The United States has probably lost one of its most spectacular birds—the ivory-billed woodpecker—to conversion of southeastern old-growth pine forest to commercial stands. A black, white, and red crested bird with a tin-horn call and a massive bill with which it could hammer its way through walls, the ivory-bill was common in early America. It was specialized, however, depending mainly on beetle grubs that it found under the bark of large, dead pines for food. Industrial foresters do not tolerate such trees because the beetles infesting them may spread to healthy stands. The last well-documented ivory-bill population, in the Singer Tract of the Tensas River bottomlands of Louisiana, disappeared by the 1940s, although there have been unsubstantiated sightings in southeastern swamps. The species still survives in Cuba.

In the West, another forest bird appears unable to survive logging of old growth. The spotted owl is a round-headed, black-eyed species with a call that sounds oddly like a small dog barking. Spotted owls depend on the coniferous old-growth forests of the West: they usually nest in large trees that have lost their tops to lightning or winds. They feed mainly on rodents that live in mature forests, such as flying squirrels and tree voles. They apparently have trouble sighting and catching prey in dense second growth. They also depend on the forest canopy for shelter from winter cold and wind. Clear-cutting not only destroys their breeding, feeding, and sheltering habitat, it makes spotted owls vulnerable to predation from the larger great horned owls.

Economically, the most important wildlife victims of industrial forestry are not land animals, but fish. Much of the forest that has been clear-cut since 1945 in the West has been on very unstable, steep slopes. Denuded by road building and log hauling, and liquified by winter rains, large amounts of soil from these slopes have eroded into creeks and rivers. The effects on the Pacific Northwest's several species of salmon have been disastrous. Salmon spawn in cold streams with clear gravel beds. By removing tree shade, logging causes streams to warm, and it smothers gravel beds with silt and sand from eroding slopes. Fish have difficulty spawning under such conditions and may not even be able to reach spawning streams because of logjams, also a result of clear-cutting.

Most Western rivers supported commercial canneries in the nineteenth century. Today there are barely enough salmon to go around among commercial and sport fishermen and traditional Indian subsistence users in the Pacific Northwest. Conditions are somewhat better in Alaska, where logging has been less extensive until recently. Overexploitation by canneries contributed to the salmon's decline, as did hydroelectric dams and pollution from cities and farmland. Yet the

Forest Service's contribution to salmon decimation is particularly unfortunate, since the congressionally mandated "multiple uses" of national forests include conservation of watersheds, water quality, wildlife, and fisheries. Regulations requiring uncut corridors along spawning streams and projects for rehabilitating damaged streams have restored some habitat for salmon in recent years, but Forest Service plans to expand logging into more ecologically fragile areas of the Northwest and Alaska will not be good for fish.

Industrial foresters seem to think that a commercial forest of a single tree species will meet wildlife needs as well as a natural forest of many species. Yet forests have thrived for over three hundred million years as diverse habitats. Simplifying them to suit industrial procedures could threaten the evolutionary viability not only of wildlife, but of the forests themselves. Trees have evolved into many species in response to a variety of environmental stresses. Different species have different tolerances, and if some species in a natural forest succumb to a certain stress, others will survive, and the forest will survive. The relatively diverse American deciduous forest had no trouble surviving the loss of chestnut and elm trees to disease epidemics. Planted forests may not have the same resilience.

Forests in Europe and America are under great stress from acid rain today, for example. As with lakes, acid rain raises the acidity of forest soils to a level at which toxic aluminum, usually bound chemically in them, is released and absorbed by tree roots. This gradually poisons the trees. Conifers seem especially vulnerable to acid rain, although hardwoods also suffer.

Thousands of acres of forest in central Europe are dead or dying from a combination of acid rain and other forms of toxic pollution such as ozone from automobile exhaust and heavy metals from automobiles and industrial emissions. Much of this central European forest comprises commercial conifers planted to replace logged-off native hardwood forests. On the other hand, in the American northeastern and midwestern areas most threatened by acid rain and other pollution, forests comprise native hardwoods. These are not dying yet, although their growth is slowing in some areas. American forests that are suffering the most from acid rain are the less diverse conifer stands at higher elevations in the northeast.

Forest diversity advocates have been making their case with increasing vigor in the courts and legislatures. Two of their major tools are federal laws: the Wilderness Act of 1964 and the National Forest Management Act of 1976. The Wilderness Act was largely promoted by the Wilderness Society, a group founded by professional foresters such as Aldo Leopold and Bob Marshall. The act provides for congressional designation of old-growth forests and other relatively undisturbed areas on federal lands as wilderness areas exempt from logging, road construction, mining, and other commercial activities that would degrade natural quality. Since 1964, Congress has designated about 32.6 million acres of national forest, national park, national wildlife refuge, and Bureau of Land Management property as wilderness in the lower forty-eight states, with another fifty-six million acres in Alaska. This is somewhat less than two percent of the coterminous United States, about the same amount of land that is now paved.

Because it involves only a small percentage of total federal forest land—the national forests encompass over two hundred million acres—wilderness designation will not assure forest diversity on a large enough scale to protect against catastrophes such as the death of central European forests. Conservationists must rely on the National Forest Management Act to do this. The act provides for equal consideration of, and protection for, all national forest resources. It prohibits logging that would cause irreversible environmental damage, limits clear-cutting, and mandates species diversity as a valid management goal. It directs the Forest Service to prepare plans for managing the forests over the next fifty years in ways that will perpetuate diversity.

Conservationists are deeply dissatisfied with the national-forest fifty-year plans that have been prepared so far. They find that most plans emphasize logging (with a doubling or tripling of logging roads) at the expense of natural diversity, and point out that logging may not even have economic benefits to the general public, since the government often spends more to make timber available to the logging industry (by building roads, replanting, suppressing fires, and providing other support) than it earns from selling the timber. The Wilderness Society has estimated that for every dollar the government spends in each of two Colorado national forests, it gets back three cents from one and four cents from the other.

Wilderness areas and management legislation undoubtedly have benefited forest diversity, particularly in the West. Yet presently designated wilderness may not be enough to save some low-elevation old-growth species, because most wilderness is in spectacular mountain-peak terrain, where there is more rock and ice than forest. Only about 725,000 of 3.2 million remaining acres of spotted owl habitat in western Washington and Oregon are designated as wilderness, and only 28 of the known 1,248 pairs of spotted owls live in designated areas. Biologists fear that if the remainder of this habitat is logged, as it apparently will be under present national-forest fifty-year plans, the remaining owls will be too isolated and inbred for the species to survive.

At least considerable areas of old-growth forest remain in the West, although that area is shrinking by forty thousand to fifty thousand acres a year in the Northwest alone. In the Southeast, where much less remains, another old-growth species may be in more trouble than the spotted owl. Like the ivory-billed woodpecker, the red-cockaded woodpecker depends on old-growth pine forest for survival. The medium sized, black-and-white species nests in holes that it excavates in pines eighty to one hundred years old, or old enough for the establishment of red-heart fungus, which weakens the tree's heartwood. It is a colonial nester, living in groups of from two to nine birds, and its colonies encompass a number of trees in which it makes holes. Colonies use some of these holes especially as nesting sites, sometimes for as long as fifty years.

Red-cockaded woodpecker colonies don't fit in with industrial forestry practices in the Southeast. Pines grow fastest during the first twenty to forty years of life, and loggers prefer to cut them in that period. Habitat suitable for colonies has dwindled steadily in this century: the species was placed on the endangered list in 1970, and a 1976 study suggested that the species was declining by as much as thirteen percent a year.

The Endangered Species Act of 1973 requires managers of federal lands to prepare recovery plans for listed species such as the red-cockaded woodpecker. Since there is little old-growth forest left in the Southeast, habitat will have to be re-created. By destroying underbrush and hardwood seedlings, lightning fires helped create the park-like stands of old pines to which the red-cockaded woodpecker was adapted. But such fires aren't allowed to burn unchecked today.

Red-cockaded woodpecker recovery will require considerably more than leaving a few nest trees. Guidelines prepared for national forests and wildlife refuges set specific goals for increasing populations of the woodpeckers and describe the amount and composition of habitat which should surround nesting colonies. They call for limiting the frequency of logging within one mile of existing nesting colonies and in some cases, in areas that might be colonized if habitat is suitable. Pines in the vicinity of colonies should be eighty to one hundred years old, depending on the species, unless additional habitat is set aside to allow the colony to expand or re-establish itself, in which case pines should be seventy to eighty years old. Pines in woodpecker foraging areas should be at least thirty years old, with forty percent aged sixty years or older. These are large tasks for land managers, but the species may not survive unless they are promptly and effectively implemented.

Unfortunately, not all southeastern forest species are capable of surviving in such relatively small and scattered habitat areas. A panther in the Everglades may require over a hundred square miles of habitat to support itself. Since a breeding population must include a number of males and females to be viable, a suitable panther habitat should encompass thousands of square miles, though it need not be completely undisturbed wilderness. Florida panthers evidently find more deer on the margins of commercial ranchlands than in the deepest swamps, because the ranchlands contain more deer forage. In the West, healthy mountain lion populations live quite near large cities. Yet habitat must be undisturbed enough to allow free movement after game and mates.

Hunting and habitat destruction had forced the eastern panther out of all but a few southern swamps by the early twentieth century. The subspecies has continued to dwindle, and now the Everglades contains the last known population. Panther reports from other areas such as northern New England occur, but few are verified. Not even the Everglades population is out of danger, since there are probably no more than thirty individuals. Biologists fear its food supply may be insufficient, because many individuals are in poor condition. Even worse, the population may be inbred, and consequently lack resistance to disease and infection.

Now, thousands of people move into Florida every day. On the

THE PANTHER AND THE DEER

For the Florida panther, the problem of survival comes down to the availability of deer. Southern Florida supported large populations of white-tailed deer before civilization modified the area.

During the winter and spring dry season, lightning fires often swept the swamps and forests of the region, where decomposing, desiccated peat made excellent fuel. The fires opened grassy prairies in the forests. Herds of deer thrived in these glades, sometimes moving into the swamps to feed on nutritious water plants. At the edges of the forest, Florida panthers waited in the early morning for deer, especially the young, sick, or old individuals.

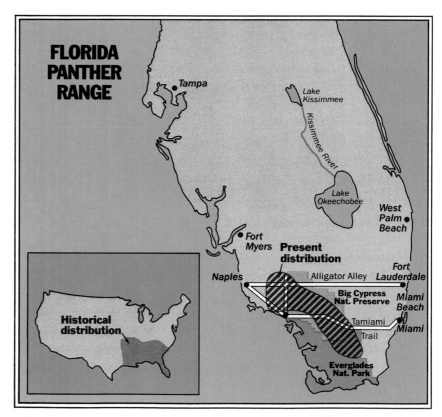

edge of panther country, developers are draining swamps and converting high ground to housing developments. Massive losses in northern Florida's citrus crop several years ago have resulted in conversion of southern Florida grazing lands to tomato fields and orange groves. As deer lose their feeding grounds and dwindle, panthers do too. Biologists suspect that the thirty panthers now estimated to live in southern Florida are all the area will support. Two male panthers captured in 1986 during radiotelemetry studies in the Everglades did show signs of inbreeding. Both lacked one testicle, probably a genetic defect, and a large percentage of their sperm cells were not viable.

Panthers are known to be breeding in the Everglades, but they may not be keeping ahead of losses caused by human activities. Automobiles have killed at least nine panthers on Everglades highways since 1979, and have probably wounded more. People continue to shoot panthers, although the eastern subspecies has been on state and federal endangered lists since 1968. Commercial and residential development still encroaches on panther habitat outside Everglades National Park and Big Cypress National Preserve.

Concern for the panther is growing. Florida has named it the

Male deer feeding on grass.

TRACKING A PANTHER

What does the Florida panther need to survive? In the last few years, a group of biologists has managed to put radio collars on several panthers and track their movements from the air. The information supplied by the collars is so complete, the biologists can not only tell where the animals are but are able to monitor vital clues to their health as well. The signals indicate pulse rate changes and even head movement.

The biologists use dogs to track and tree the panthers, then bring them to ground with tranquilizer darts after deciding that doing so will be safe for the men and for the animals. The big cats receive medical examinations, and sometimes treatment, before the biologists collar and release them. Examinations have revealed that panthers suffer from hookworm (a bloodsucking parasite) and a virus called feline panleukopenia, or feline distemper, which may be responsible for high mortality among panther juveniles. There also is evidence of anemia and malnutrition, suggesting that panthers are not getting enough of the right kind of food.

A Florida panther is tagged and collared.

state mammal and has proposed rebuilding Alligator Alley with wildlife underpasses at known panther crossing sites ("Panther X-ing" signs already exist) to minimize road kills. Yet the population may have fallen so low that further measures will be required to restore the panther.

The panther's situation is not as grave as the condor's, because sizable populations of the species exist elsewhere. Simply transplanting panthers from other areas to the Southeast, however, would not be a good idea. Florida panthers have evolved in environments like the Fakahatchee Strand and Big Cypress for millenia; individuals from outside the region belong to different subspecies, and whether they would be as well-adapted to the area is uncertain. If they were interbred with the remaining natives, unique genetic traits might disappear.

The better solution is to increase native panther numbers in southern Florida. Once the population recovers, surplus animals might be transplanted to other suitable areas in the Southeast, assuring that the loss of the southern Florida population—say, through hurricane— would not wipe out the entire native subspecies. Hardwood forests along the Gulf of Mexico coast—such as the Atchafalaya Basin—or Atlantic seaboard swamps such as the Okefenokee or Dismal are possible areas.

Increasing the Florida panther's wild population might be harder than increasing the California condor's, however. Panthers have been bred in captivity, but it's unclear whether young panthers can succeed in the wild if wild parents have not raised them. Technology may provide solutions to such problems in the future, and zoos are experimenting with breeding endangered species by embryo transfers, artificial insemination, and in vitro (test-tube) fertilization. If wild panther males prove infertile, artificial insemination of wild females with sperm from captive Florida males might be an alternative. If wild females prove infertile because of inbreeding or nutritional deficiencies, the implantation in their uteruses of fertilized eggs from captive Florida

---

"BIG GUY"

One night in November 1984, a car hit a male Florida panther on Alligator Alley. A truck driver saw the injured panther on the side of the road and succeeded in contacting the right people in Naples. The panther had dragged himself off the road and into a canal, across which he tried in vain to swim. A veterinarian pulled him out and operated on his shattered back legs, repairing multiple compound fractures with metal plates.

The injured panther, whom the veterinarian named "Big Guy," eventually recovered from his ordeal. Biologists hope Big Guy can help as part of a captive breeding program for his species, but initial evidence suggests he's not very fertile. Tests show that an estimated ninety-four percent of his sperm cells (and those of four other male panthers studied) are abnormal.

Because panthers are known to have trouble breeding, collecting these sperm samples may be vital to saving whatever genetic diversity they have left. One day, an artificial breeding program may make use of these samples.

Big Guy.

panthers might become possible; implanted fetuses might then grow to be born and raised as wild panthers.

We can't rely on these techniques yet, and even they won't help if the panther's habitat continues to deteriorate. But if we protect and restore its habitat, the panther might be able to survive on its own.

Precarious as the condition of some American forest species is, our expanding network of wilderness areas, wildlife refuges, and parks assures continuing diversity. Tragically, this may not be the case with many peoples who need healthy forests even more than Americans do. In developing nations, wood is still a major fuel for cooking and heating. The world population doubled in the past thirty-five years, and some countries experienced even faster growth, so that wood-cutting began to overtake tree regeneration in some areas. Firewood gets expensive as it gets scarce, and people are being priced out of the market.

Firewood-gathering is literally the last straw for forests already stressed by grazing and agricultural clearing. Not only forest wildlife, but forests themselves are disappearing from large areas. The situation is worst in semiarid regions, where trees are subject to drought. Africa, which has the highest birthrate in the world, is particularly hard hit on its northern and southern margins. Ethiopia already has lost most of its forest, with only four percent of its land forested, and other African countries have rates of demand for firewood many times the sustainable yield of their forests.

Loss of tree cover can drastically reduce a land's capacity to support life. Firewood scarcity forces people to use animal dung and crop residues for fuel—substances which would ordinarily maintain soil

NATURAL DIVERSITY

If the Florida panther is lost, it will be just one species in a multitude of extinctions about to take place. In the 1990s, we will lose some ten thousand species each year as agriculture and human overpopulation ravage the Earth's forests and grasslands. At this rate, by the end of the century, more than a fifth of the world's species will no longer exist.

There is a near vacuum of information about the physiologies and natural history of most wild animals, and scientists are working desperately to catch up. At the major zoos, a new kind of lab for the study and even preservation of endangered animals is springing up. The labs are managing "genetic banks" filled with frozen sperm and eggs from endangered species. Researchers hope that if the habitats can one day be restored, they will be able to replenish the wild populations.

A small group of physiologists is pioneering a range of new weapons in the battle against extinction: artificial insemination, in vitro (or test-tube) babies, and transfer of fertilized eggs into mothers of an entirely different species. Such fertilized embryos can now be kept frozen almost indefinitely. A research team at the Cincinnati Zoo has implanted such an embryo from a rare species of African antelope, the bongo antelope, into a female eland antelope in hope of increasing the bongo's population.

When settled regions become deforested and unproductive, people abandon their homes and seek new land. Many are moving into the equatorial forests of Africa, Southeast Asia, and the Americas, a vast area originally covering 12 percent of the Earth's land surface. These lush, highly diverse forests have seemed to offer civilization opportunities rivaling those of the temperate deciduous forests, which contributed so much to China, Europe, and North America. Loggers, farmers, ranchers, miners, and dam builders have been clearing them rapidly in the past three decades, and currently clear about twenty-seven million acres of tropical forest each year. Biologists fear they will lose virtually all of it if this process continues at the present rate.

Tropical countries such as Brazil and Indonesia hope to reap economic bonanzas from forest development, and for temperate nations that have heavily exploited their own forests to begrudge them the possibilities would be hypocritical. Yet why have tropical forests remained unsettled so long if they contain such opportunities? Why didn't early tropical forest civilizations such as the Mayan sustain growth as China and Europe did?

Humanity again may be confronting the limitations of forest diversity. Most of the temperate-forest land that civilization cleared during the past ten thousand years has had a good potential for sustained fertility. Paradoxical as it may seem, cold winters are an advantage to farming because they slow the buildup of crop pests and the breakdown of organic material, allowing humus-rich topsoil to accumulate. Cold weather sustains the fertility of soil rather as a refrigerator sustains the freshness of foods. Much temperate forest also grew on glaciated soil, which is particularly fertile because continental ice sheets have recently ground and mixed it, releasing mineral nutrients. Cold winters and glaciers have limited the diversity of temperate forests, but enhanced their agricultural potential.

In tropical forest, many soils have lain undisturbed for millions of years, and equatorial rains have leached mineral nutrients deep into the subsoil where tree roots cannot reach them. Leaf litter and other organic debris decomposes so quickly that a deep humus layer never forms on the topsoil. Native plants and animals can thrive upon such soils because they are adapted to them. Trees filter nutrients from rainwater, and animals maintain low populations and use specialized food sources. In effect, tropical forest stores its organic fertility not in soil but in living plants and animals—in diversity.

When such forest is cleared, most of its fertility evaporates. Temporarily enriched by the ashes of the burned forest, soils yield good crops for a few years. Then yields drop as nutrients leach away and pests proliferate, uninhibited by frost. Of course, there are places i fertility when returned to cropland. This is a serious matter for societies unable to afford artificial fertililizers. Trees no longer pump nutrients out of the subsoil with their roots and return them to the topsoil with their fallen leaves, and even noncultivated land declines in fertility. Wind and water erosion scrape away at the denuded topsoil. In effect the land loses its third dimension when the protecting screen of treetop is destroyed: life becomes flattened, desiccated. Such a cycle is o curring in parts of Asia and Central and South America as well as Africa.

A RESCUED TROPICAL MONKEY

Captive animals can be released back into the wild if their natural habitat is restored and the public is educated about the need to protect them. In one effort that took over a decade, scientists released captive individuals of a very rare Brazilian monkey, the golden lion tamarin, back into a Brazilian forest.

The forest that golden lion tamarins once called home extended for a thousand miles along the coast of Brazil. But developers have cut down 99 percent of the forest to make way for 123 million Brazilians who now live along the coast.

In 1970, only seventy golden lion tamarins lived in zoos; the wild population had dwindled to about 150 and had become dangerously inbred. The Brazilian government began the recovery process by setting aside a preserve. In a cooperative project, Brazilian and American scientists set about restoring the forest and conducted a campaign to inform Brazilians about the situation.

The scientists bred captive golden lion tamarins at the National Zoo, then gradually released them into the forest. Many died before the releasing procedures were perfected, but now they are interbreeding with the native animals, and the wild population has doubled. Even though only about 1 percent of the original habitat remains, these monkeys can now continue to breed and multiply until they are out of danger. But twenty other kinds of monkeys live here, including the muriqui, the most endangered of New World monkeys, and over half the plants in this forest live nowhere else. As the pressures of isolation mount, it will be too expensive to protect each species one by one.

LEFT: *The golden lion tamarin, a native of southeastern Brazil, is now very rare in the wild.*

RIGHT: *Aerial view of the Amazon Forest in Brazil.*

the tropical forest belt where soils have been renewed and enriched by river silt or volcanic ash, but its overall agricultural potential is not what its primeval lushness seems to promise.

As long as only a few people inhabited the tropical forest, they could farm it by clearing new fields every few years and letting the old ones return to forest. This becomes impossible, however, as mass settlement occurs and clearing overtakes regeneration. Denuded soil may bake into brick-like laterite in the tropical sun, reducing the land's ability to support not only crops, but even forest. With forest gone, climate changes. About half the moisture in tropical forest skies comes from the trees themselves, by transpiration. Without trees, annual precipitation drops; climate gets hotter and drier. Rain that does fall runs off the bare soil instead of being trapped by vegetation. Soil moisture and fertility decline further, and the final result may be sparse grassland or actual desert.

Mining, ranching, and logging companies make fortunes in tropical forest, but with little benefit to the poverty-stricken people who migrate there in search of a better life. Many settlers who moved to the Amazon region in the 1970s, for example, eventually had to sell their land to large cattle ranches because it no longer supported them. They then moved on and cleared new patches of forest, which they hoped to sell once fertility declined. Beef production also has been a major cause of forest destruction in Central America, where forest cover declined by almost half between 1961 and 1978, while cattle numbers almost doubled. Much of this beef, which is of poor quality because it is produced on low-grade forage, becomes hamburgers in North American fast-food restaurants.

Tropical forest destruction for cattle ranching slowed in the mid-1980s, however, because the market for beef declined. North Americans began worrying about the effects of high-cholesterol diets. Annual per capita beef consumption in North America declined by fifteen pounds from 1977 to 1985, and Latin American cattle herds stopped growing so fast.

Of course, Latin American tropical forest continues to disappear for many other reasons, but the leveling off of growth in ranching is a hopeful sign for temperate-zone conservationists concerned about destruction of the world's greatest storehouse of diversity. People in the temperate zone have affected the tropical environment for centuries through their appetite for spices, tea, coffee, chocolate, vanilla, hardwoods, sugar, and many other tropical goods. This relationship hasn't benefited the tropical forest much in the past, but the situation may change for the better in the future.

For example, much of the money that finances the destruction of tropical forest with dams, roads, logging, and mass resettlement projects comes from temperate-zone countries in the form of loans from international development banks such as the World Bank. In the past, banks made these loans with little consideration for environmental consequences. A dam project might wipe out dozens of plant and animal species and displace hundreds of indigenous peoples, but builders would ignore these problems in favor of creating hydroelectric power that a country's cities might not even need.

Recently, conservationists have challenged such loans, pointing out that the banks employ few specialists to consider environmental consequences and make little effort to monitor the harmful effects of the projects they fund. Because the U.S. government is a major source of development-bank funds, conservationists have brought such problems to the attention of congressional committees, with the result that funds have been withheld at least temporarily from one potentially destructive project—the Brazilian Polonoroeste Plan to cut a nine-hundred-mile highway through an Amazonian forest area the size of Great Britain, to colonize it, and to displace native Indians. An international task force sponsored by the World Resources Institute, the World Bank, and the United Nations Development Programme recently launched an eight-billion-dollar campaign to reverse tropical deforestation by 1991. The U.S. Congress has passed legislation requiring federal agencies to protect tropical forest and species diversity in financial dealings with other countries.

Conservationists have also argued that development in tropical countries need not be in the form of huge dams, grandiose resettlement projects, and million-acre clear-cutting. Rather than sweep the forest aside, successful developers could use forest diversity, as indigenous cultures have been using it for thousands of years. Many of the most important foods and medicines already in use come from the tropical forest, and many more are being developed. A wildflower called the rosy periwinkle recently became the source of a promising cancer drug. Tropical rivers such as the Amazon contain an enormous abundance and diversity of fish, a more efficient source of protein than beef. Some Amazon fishes grow to considerable size by swimming into the forest during seasonal floods and feeding on fallen fruit. Forest fruits and spices have considerable potential for new beverage and ice cream flavors, since many of the flavors we use now originated in the tropical forest. Cola and citrus drinks both did.

Bank loans to develop such resources and take advantage of indigenous peoples' considerable knowledge of tropical forest natural history might give greater returns in the end than flooding or burning away the forest. There have been a few recent moves in this direction.

The Kuna Indians, who live along the Panamanian west coast, received assistance from the Agency for International Development in protecting their traditional land uses from the spreading cycle of forest destruction.

An important part of the Kuna's plan is the maintenance of forest adjacent to their fields and villages, which brings up an indispensable aspect of tropical-forest conservation. Even if economic development is beneficial, the vital diversity of tropical forest will not survive unless large areas are protected. The situation is the same in the tropics as it is in the United States: many species—particularly those most beautiful and exciting to man, such as panthers, monkeys, macaws, great apes, orchids, African violets, and carnivorous plants—depend on wild forest. Since there are so many more species in the tropics—ten times more in the Amazon Basin alone than in the United States—wilderness preservation there is that much more crucial.

Americans cannot expect struggling tropical nations to set aside ten times as much wilderness as *we* have. We don't know how much tropical forest we would have to preserve to avert a catastrophic loss of species, because we don't know what most tropical forest species are; they haven't been named yet, much less studied. We do know that species are being lost already. An estimated twenty-five thousand

Coniferous old-growth forest.

AN OLD-GROWTH-FOREST SONGBIRD

The hooded warbler is a small, bright-yellow bird that nests in mature deciduous forests with well-established undergrowth throughout eastern North America. The species gets its name from the black hood that covers the top and back of the heads, necks, and throats of mature males.

In winter, hooded warblers migrate south to areas of tropical forest, from southern Veracruz and the Yucatan Peninsula in Mexico to southern Costa Rica and (rarely) western Panama. As in the summer, they live in mature, broad-leaved forests with well established undergrowth. They feed largely on insects.

Approximately ninety-nine other species of North American breeding songbirds migrate south to spend their winters in Mexico, Central America, and the Caribbean. Twenty-nine species of warblers alone winter in southern Mexico. An additional fifty-three North American songbird migrants range as far south as South America. Wintering North American songbirds average 30 percent of the total avifauna at seven sites in Mexico, 12 percent at eight locations in Central America, and 1 to 30 percent at twenty-eight locations in the Antilles.

Although measuring populations of small forest birds is hard, researchers have recorded definite declines in hooded warblers in eastern forests. A study that compared migrant populations in 1947 and 1982 at a site in the Smoky Mountains found that hooded warblers were among ten to sixteen migrant birds whose numbers had declined. Sharp declines in hooded warblers were recorded at one northeastern site. A study of a tract of virgin forest in West Virginia showed significant declines in populations of most migratory songbirds in the past thirty-five years. These declines have coincided with deforestation in tropical Mexico and Central America. If this deforestation continues, the United States can expect drastic declines in almost half its forest birds.

Adapted from "The Hooded Warbler," by George V. N. Powell and John H. Rappole, *Audubon Wildlife Report*, 1986.

Hooded warbler.

species are in immediate danger of extinction, and as many as two million species could become extinct within decades, perhaps half of those living today.

Many tropical countries are making commitments to forest preservation and establishing sizable national park systems. The small Central American country of Costa Rica has designated twice as great a percentage of its land as national parks—8 percent—as has the United States, and it has done so largely since 1970. Benefits to Costa Rica's economy have been substantial: in 1984, tourism produced more income than coffee, the country's number-one export. Tourists come to the parks to see their 850 species of birds (more than those of the United States and Canada combined), 700 butterfly species, and 320 reptile and amphibian species. Costs of establishing the parks have been substantial, however: land had to be bought, personnel paid, boundaries guarded.

With the help of the United States and international private conservation organizations, Costa Rica has gone a long way toward meeting the initial costs of its parks. Yet Costa Rica has a growing population, and its neighbors are in the midst of guerilla warfare. Such political problems combine with economic pressures to threaten recently established parks throughout the developing world.

If tropical forests are destroyed, the temperate zone will feel the loss. The remaining forest contains vast quantities of carbon dioxide in its biomass. When the forest is burned, as it is today at a rate of at least twenty-five acres a minute, most of that carbon dioxide returns to the atmosphere. There it combines with carbon dioxide released by the burning of fossil fuels to enhance the greenhouse effect, which scientists fear will change global climates.

North Americans may already be feeling the loss of tropical forest in their own woods. There has been a noticeable decline in the abundance and diversity of forest songbirds such as warblers, thrushes, vireos, tanagers, and flycatchers in recent years; destruction of old-growth forest in the United States has contributed to this decline. Many songbird species are adapted to nesting in large areas of undisturbed forest, but when such areas are fragmented by logging and residential development, songbirds become vulnerable to predators and nest parasites such as cowbirds. Most of these songbirds are migratory, however, and many species spend at least half the year in tropical Mexico, Central America, South America, and the West Indies.

Such wintering birds are as dependent on forest habitat in the tropics as they are during summers in the temperate zone. The more such forests are disturbed, the more their populations decline. An area studied by ornithologists in tropical Mexico contained 42 percent fewer wintering songbirds after disturbance than it had ten years before. Since deforestation is proceeding very rapidly in tropical Mexico, and the largest percentage of migrant species from the United States winter there, the future may already be dim for many species which Americans presently consider common—hooded warblers, American redstarts, Kentucky warblers, wood thrushes, scarlet tanagers, and ruby-throated hummingbirds. Virtual disappearance of rare species such as Bachman's warblers may be related to complete loss of habitat on deforested Caribbean islands. If the forests that still remain on the Central American Caribbean coast and northern tip of South America are also cut, and if United States forest fragmentation continues, a North American spring as silent as Rachel Carson's vision may become a reality.

T H E
GRASSLANDS

WHEN THE SUN SETS behind the Absaroka Mountains, the air temperature is already near zero and a north wind increases the chill. The Wyoming prairie looks lifeless under a thin layer of snow: there is no movement but the waving of dead grass stems. Not even a raven calls from the darkening sky above the foothills, and the wind makes only faint scratching sounds in the sparse sagebrush. The treeless place seems not only devoid of life, but hostile to it.

Yet there are signs of animal presence. A line of small tracks, evidently punched into new-fallen snow, lead to a burrow entrance on a knoll. The snow around the burrow shows more tracks, and a curious, elongated pile of newly dug earth extends several feet from the entrance.

As the first stars appear overhead, something comes out of the burrow so quickly and quietly that it hardly seems an animal at first, rather a diminutive spirit from a Plains Indian legend. Pale and slender, it is hard to distinguish from the snow. It disappears and then reappears, bounds a few feet over the snow, then stands up on its back legs to look around, revealing a sinuous, mink-like body, dark-colored forefeet, and a black mask across the eyes. It is a black-footed ferret, one of the rarest mammals in North America.

Rarity might seem an inevitable condition in such an austere place, but the ferret is prospering at the moment. She has spent three days feeding on the large white-tailed prairie dog from whose burrow she has just emerged. Killing the hibernating rodent was easy after she

Black-footed ferret.

dug out the soil with which he had plugged the burrow. That was lucky for her, since the prairie dog was almost twice her size and she'd been slightly weakened from several days without food.

Now she is in excellent condition, having absorbed, in effect, the prairie dog's entire past summer of grazing on short grasses and wild-flowers. A replenished layer of fat over her muscles keeps the wind from chilling them, and she moves easily away, abandoning the burrow which now contains only her droppings and a few scraps of bone and fur. She is not really hungry yet, but the drowsiness of digestion has ended and she is eager to find another source of food and shelter. She moves quickly, pausing often to glance around. Like other small predators (she weighs less than two pounds) she is subject to predation herself, from eagles, owls, coyotes, bobcats, and badgers.

Black-footed ferrets have been rare since John James Audubon first scientifically described the species from a skin a trader had sent him. A second specimen didn't turn up for another quarter-century, and only a few hundred museum skins exist to this day. It isn't the prairie's winter bleakness that makes ferrets rare. They lived north into

Canada in Audubon's day, and south into Mexico. If anything, the reverse is true: the ferret's rarity reflects abundance rather than scarcity.

The black-footed ferret is a vulnerable species because it specializes in one kind of prey—the prairie dog. Yet it was able to survive in small numbers over a wide area because huge prairie dog colonies covered the Great Plains, so thickly at times that explorers rode for days without getting from one side of a "town" to another. Preying on prairie dogs that often were bigger than they were, ferrets did not lead easy lives. Yet there were simply so many prairie dogs that some ferrets always lived to produce a new generation.

The black-footed ferret's life of precarious plenty is typical of the great wild grasslands that once stretched across the world's continental interiors. From a low-lying, apparently simple, sometimes monotonous vegetation, grasslands produced not only the most abundant, but the most diverse mammal populations that had ever existed. They produced not only North American prairie dogs, black-footed ferrets, bison, and pronghorns, but South American vicuñas and guanacos, African lions and wildebeest, Asian yaks and camels, and Australian kangaroos and wombats.

Grasslands are so central to the world we know that life without them is hard to imagine. Yet compared to forests, they are very recent, having evolved only in the past 100 million years and reached their present importance only in the past thirty million. Grasses are flowering plants, like oaks and palms, but they probably evolved later than flowering trees. This may seem paradoxical, since trees are so much bigger, but evolution is as likely to shrink organisms as enlarge them if this helps them to survive.

Shrinking and losing woody parts probably helped the ancestors of grasses survive adverse conditions. We don't know what those conditions were, because soft grasses leave few fossils, but they may have been like the adverse conditions to which grasses are adapted today. Grasses cover the ground almost everywhere woody plants don't grow: where soil is too dry or too wet, where fires are common, where wind or browsing shave vegetation. They occupy these open spaces with a growth strategy that is almost the opposite of the woody plant's. Whereas a tree reaches upward, growing from its branch tips, a grass crouches or creeps on the ground and grows from its leaf bases. This is the great advantage of grass in adversity: if fire, wind, drought, frost, or an animal kills its leaf and stem tips, the plant continues to grow. If the growing tip of a seedling tree dies, the tree must form another one or die. It often does the latter.

Grasses reap the advantages of growing near the ground surface throughout the year. In spring, they begin growth early because the soil warms faster than the air. As long as moisture is available, they can grow throughout warm seasons. During dry times, and when winter cold stops growth, grass leaves can die back to the base without losing much energy or moisture. Many grasses circumvent the adversities of frost and drought entirely by being annuals—sprouting, flowering, seeding, and dying in a single year. Next to forest, grassland is the largest terrestrial biome on the Earth. It presently comprises almost a quarter of the continental surface, and much of the eleven percent of the planet that is cultivated now was originally wild grassland.

Adaptation to adversity has made grasses enormously productive, compensating in sustained growth for what they lack in overall leaf surface. Although they make up only about three percent of the Earth's total plant matter, grasslands produce about fourteen percent of the new growth of all ecosystems every year. Because all this growth goes into leaves and seeds, not into woody stems, grassland productivity offers particular potential for those animals able to digest the silica-toughened leaves and stems, and lignin-coated seeds. To a considerable degree, animal evolution since the dinosaurs' demise some sixty-five million years ago has been a process of exploiting that potential.

For the first half of this period, grasslands remained subordinate to the great forests that had survived from the late dinosaur age. Global climate was warm and moist. In North America, subtropical forest grew north into Canada. Then climate cooled and dried for various reasons, and grassland spread over continental interiors. Like the forest it replaced, this grassland was of diverse climatic types—tropical, temperate, or boreal. Some of the richest grasslands grew in places, such as the American Midwest, where forest would have grown if frequent lightning fires had not burned the land. The grass in such relatively humid areas grew thick and tall. Farther into continental interiors, where annual rainfall wouldn't support trees, grasses were shorter and sparser.

Wherever grasslands grew, rich faunas of grazing and seed-eating animals evolved. By the Pliocene epoch, which began about ten million years ago, most of the present grassland animals had evolved, along with many spectacular creatures that are extinct today. A kind of exaggerated combination of Yellowstone and Serengeti national parks extended from South Africa across Europe and Asia to the American Midwest: herds of wild cattle, horses, camels, rhinos, elephants, sheep, goats, antelope, and deer preyed upon by wild dogs, big cats, hyenas, and bears. Giant birds resembling today's ostriches and eagles were common; so were small creatures very similar to today's prairie dogs, badgers, rabbits, foxes, burrowing owls, and plovers. In the isolated continents of South America and Australia lived completely different but equally rich faunas: giant ground sloths and rhino-like toxodonts in South America, ten-foot-tall kangaroos and lion-like marsupials in Australia.

The richness of Pliocene grasslands permitted many rare species such as the black-footed ferret to live around the great migratory herds and burrowing colonies. Among the rarest of these were probably our ancestors, the early hominids. Evolved from forest apes by about five million years ago, these creatures stood fully erect and must have been fast runners, yet they lacked the high-crowned teeth and many-chambered stomachs that allowed horses and antelope to be so abundant and widespread, as well as the claws and fangs that allowed lions and dogs to prey on the herds. Various hominid species lived by feeding on fruits, seeds, and soft-leaved plants, catching small animals, and scavenging big-game kills. These methods provided adequate diets, but did not allow hominids to become a major grassland species. For millions of years, hominids were confined to the east-African savannas, while other African natives such as elephants spread around the world.

About two million years ago, according to current theory, one hominid species called *Homo erectus* evolved specializations that enabled it to use grassland wealth more directly than before. Hominids had been killing and cutting up small animals with sticks and stones for a long time, but *Homo erectus* took this one step further. It began

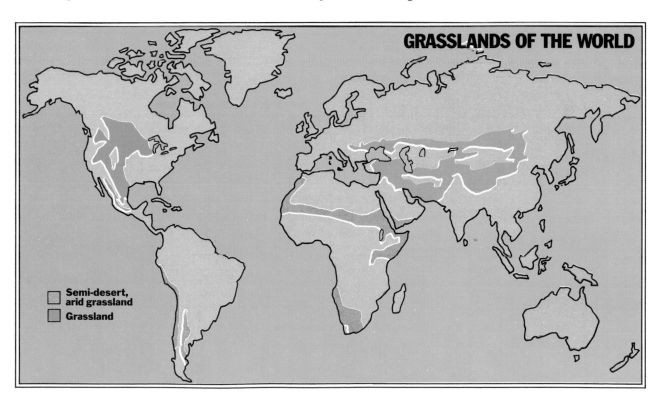

GRASSLANDS OF THE WORLD

☐ **Semi-desert, arid grassland**
☐ **Grassland**

to hunt in coordinated packs, which allowed it to kill big game, and it began to use fire, which allowed it to do many things: drive game, repel predators, cook food, control vegetation, and, eventually, extend its range outside its tropical homeland. *Homo erectus* spread gradually east to China and north to central Europe, finally becoming a major grassland predator in the process.

Despite increasing prowess with spears and hand axes, *Homo erectus* seems not to have had a particularly destructive effect on grassland ecosystems. Grassland wildlife remained highly diverse, although *Homo erectus*'s time coincided with the Pleistocene epoch, during which much of Eurasia and North America was covered repeatedly by vast glaciers. When the glaciers retreated, the grasslands spread again, often surprisingly far north. Lions once lived in Alaska. This began to change about two hundred thousand years ago, however, as a new hominid species evolved, probably from *Homo erectus*. *Homo sapiens* had a larger brain and may have been the first hominid to use true language, which would have allowed it to hunt more efficiently and thus to become more numerous.

Quite suddenly and quite recently, within the past fifty thousand years, much of the ancient grassland fauna vanished. Some of it—saber tooths, ground sloths—became extinct. Some of it vanished from large areas: rhinos, elephants, camels, and horses from North America; elephants, rhinos, and hippos from Europe. Changes of climate and vegetation such as the spread of deserts probably contributed to these extinctions, but it seems increasingly evident that human hunting cultures had become so efficient at killing certain species that they could wipe out entire populations. The disappearance of many species from the Americas coincides roughly with the first human migrations into the Western Hemisphere, and fossils clearly show that at least some of these species, such as mammoths, were major foods of ancient Native American cultures.

About ten thousand years ago, it seems, relatively high populations of skilled hunters suddenly ran out of their main food source, which also served as their major focus of cultural and religious significance (if cave paintings are any indication of paleolithic culture and religion). This first conservation crisis may have been traumatic. In any case, it was followed by radical changes in human behavior. With less big game to follow, people became more sedentary and depended more on small game, fish, and plant-gathering for livelihood. In a few places—the Middle East, Southeast Asia, Central America—hunting and gathering cultures became more sophisticated with the advent of agriculture. People had been using dogs for thousands of years for help in tracking and running down game; now they began to keep the young of many other animals around their increasingly permanent settlements. They had been using patches of edible wild plants for millions of years, now they began raising the plants around their villages. This may have been done for entertainment or mystical effect at first, but the plants eventually became major food sources.

Early domesticated organisms included many forest plants and animals, but the ones that would prove most important came from grassland: cereal grains and grazing ungulates. By domesticating these, people took control of grassland to a much greater extent than they could with more complex forest ecosystems. They were able to divert most grassland productivity to their own use because food energy created in grass leaves went directly into cows or grains without diversion through the forest's web of trunks and branches. With this unprecedented access to food, civilization began its explosive growth.

Great wild grasslands persisted throughout most of civilized history, however. Early agriculture developed mainly in river valleys, where climates were mild and soils were rich and easily cultivated with digging sticks and wooden plows. The high, dry grasslands of continental interiors had sod too tough and climates too severe for preindustrial civilizations. Some cultures learned to exploit high grasslands, but in doing so they had to abandon the settled life of mixed farming and become nomadic herders, completely dependent on their animals for food, and self-sufficient except when drought forced them off the plains. Then they became marauders on the settled peoples; often, they moved off the plains en masse to become warrior aristocracies dominating peasant tribes. Wild herds persisted in great empty spaces between these warlike nomads.

This uneasy state of affairs lasted until roughly two hundred years ago, as Mongol or Turkish nomads continued to periodically conquer the river-basin cities of China, Europe, and the Middle East. In the Americas, reintroduction of the horse by the Spaniards created an incipient nomadic herding culture among High Plains Native Americans; the American Indian culture was short-lived, however. River-basin commerce and industry reached a kind of critical mass around the time of the American Revolution and exploded into the world's interior grasslands for the first time. The expansion led to even more rapid growth as prairie grains poured back into river-basin cities.

American pioneers moving out of the eastern forest belt were unnerved at first by the tallgrass prairies they encountered in Ohio and Illinois. The summer prairie dazzled them with purple coneflowers, blazing star, butterflyweed, and wild strawberries that stained their horses' legs red, but they feared that treelessness meant lack of fertility. They feared the malaria of wet seasons and the prairie fires of dry ones.

They feared even more the completely treeless, Indian-haunted plains beyond Iowa and Missouri and called them "the Great American Desert." Many early wagon trains hurried past tallgrass and shortgrass en route to forested Oregon.

Such timidity was largely misguided, of course. With their eight-foot high bluestem, Indian, switch, and slough grasses, the tallgrass prairies soon would prove the finest croplands in history, and not surprisingly, since the corn and wheat settlers wanted to grow were grasses too. It was almost as though the Midwestern soils had been formed expressly to be farmed—first worked by glaciers to provide ample mineral nutrients, then mulched and fertilized by thousands of wild animal and plant generations, plowed by gophers, ground squirrels, and badgers, manured by bison and elk, until rich black humus topsoil lay two feet deep beneath the sod. Forest soil humus volume varies from 20 to 50 tons per acre of land; prairie soils contain up to 250 tons of humus per acre.

The only obstacle to cultivating tallgrass prairie was in breaking through the tough sod. Traditional plows broke or stuck on the masses of tough roots and sticky humus. The invention of special polished-steel moldboard plows that lifted and turned the sod without sticking solved this problem in the 1830s and '40s, and the Midwest became America's proverbial breadbasket by the time of the Civil War.

Tallgrass wildlife disappeared with the sod. The legendary Daniel Boone had followed well-worn bison trails across the Appalachians to Kentucky in the late eighteenth century, but trappers and traders had eradicated big game from much of the Midwest even before settlers arrived. Bison remained in great numbers only on the High Plains when Audubon traveled up the Missouri River in 1843. Small grassland creatures such as prairie chickens lasted longer in the Midwest, but eventually disappeared from most of their original range as cropland replaced tallgrass. Today, a few million acres of unplowed tallgrasses on rocky, sandy, or hilly sites are all that remain of an ecosystem that once covered all or most of a dozen states.

Great Plains wildlife went next as railroads crossed the continent after the Civil War. The United States government tacitly condoned bison slaughter as a way of opening the West (President Grant refused to sign protective legislation), and market hunters, settlers, tourists, cattlemen, soldiers, and Indians killed millions a year. After the Union Pacific Railroad divided the plains in 1869, it took only until 1879 to wipe out the southern bison, and only four more years to finish off the northern. Trains carried bison tongues and hides back to eastern markets, where the tongues were served as restaurant delicacies and the hides were used as rugs and industrial drive belts; later they carried bleached bones for crushing into fertilizer. A rancher on a thousand-mile trip in Montana reported that he was never out of sight of a dead bison and never in sight of a living one.

By 1900, wild bison survived only in the swamps of northern Alberta and the mountains of Yellowstone Park. Other big game fared almost as badly, shot on sight for food or sport. Pronghorn antelope dwindled from an original thirty to fifty million animals to fewer than fifteen thousand by 1915. Bighorn sheep had inhabited hilly and broken terrain throughout the Plains, but hunting restricted the species to inaccessible mountains; the same occurred with elk. Great Plains predators that had impressed early explorers with their size and abundance—"buffalo" wolves and grizzlies—succumbed to poison and trapping by the 1920s.

Pronghorn buck.

Yet the Plains remained wilder than the tallgrass prairies because they were harder to farm. West of the hundredth meridian, summer rain becomes unreliable; many attempts to found farming communities on the Midwestern model were unsuccessful. In 1862, the Homestead Act granted 160 acres of federal land (a normal-sized farm in the eastern United States) to anyone who farmed the Plains for at least five years. But a 160-acre plot wasn't enough to support a family where unirrigated crops were as likely to dry up and blow away as produce grain, and many homesteads failed. The act later was amended to grant larger acreage to farmers equipped to practice new dryland farming techniques—to use tractors to plant great expanses of winter wheat and to keep land fallow to conserve moisture. Some dryland farming prospered, particularly when grain prices were high, but the tractors bared and compacted the soil, making it vulnerable to wind erosion.

Ranchers had been on the plains before farmers and often stayed after them. They had their difficulties, too, not only with drought but with severe winters like that of 1886, which killed cattle from Texas to the Dakotas. Many ranchers grazed more stock than the grass could sustain and saw the grass replaced by mesquite, sagebrush, or tumbleweeds. Or by dust.

Exploitation of North American grasslands climaxed in the great drought of the 1930s, when overgrazing and plowing of marginal lands brought about the Dust Bowl. Wind-blown soil darkened skies from the Atlantic to the Pacific, and Congress passed the first grassland conservation legislation. The 1934 Taylor Grazing Act created a National Grazing Service (which exists today as the Bureau of Land Management), and the 1935 Soil Conservation Act created a Soil Conservation Service. Unlike the Forest Service, these agencies had little regulatory power, partly because much of the land they administered was private. Their function was mainly advisory, to help ranchers monitor their herds, and to urge farmers to adopt conservation practices—crop rotation to maintain fertility and discourage pests, terracing to prevent water erosion, and shelter-belt planting to limit wind erosion.

Conservation agencies and other government programs such as the Soil Bank, which paid farmers to remove lands from production for several years, did much to reduce soil erosion during and after the Depression. Prairie wildlife returned to some areas where homesteading had proved unfeasible. A National Bison Range had been set aside in Montana as early as 1908: bison herds were re-established on many other wildlife refuges and national parks. The wildness of such herds is a little debatable, since they live inside fences, but it's exciting to see them dotting areas such as the Dakota Badlands again. Pronghorns returned to much of their former range on their own, with help from game laws and sympathetic ranchers. Their numbers doubled from 1915 to 1924 and have doubled again many times, until they now number an estimated eight hundred thousand in Wyoming, Montana, and other states.

North American grasslands have not escaped the pressures of expanding human populations, however. Their very abundance has pressed them particularly hard in recent decades as they have become an internationally vital source of grain and legumes to countries forced to import food. As with forestry, technological innovation increasingly has industrialized farming and ranching. Both have become forms of clear-cutting in a sense, with vast stretches of cropland and range bulldozed, artificially fertilized, and treated with herbicides and pesticides that minimize competition from wild organisms. Large-scale irrigation, another technological innovation, is widely affecting grassland by permitting crop-growing deeper and deeper into the High Plains. Much of this irrigation is not sustainable because the water comes from "fossil" aquifers—deposits of groundwater accumulated during past, perhaps more humid climatic periods. Pollution of groundwater with artificial fertilizers and other chemicals is also a growing problem.

Like clear-cut forestry, such practices expose land to erosion and reduce its natural diversity. Before World War II, farmers left strips of grass and shrubs along crop-field fencelines, where wildlife and native plants survived. Modern machinery requires large fields, and farmers tend to crop as much land as possible to earn income so they can make payments on their large machines. Without vegetation to hold field borders, soil erosion increases. At present rates, about six and a half billion tons of soil a year are lost to wind and water erosion, which probably is a greater rate than that of the Dust-Bowl years. In parts of Iowa, the heart of the Midwest, a century and a half of farm erosion has reduced topsoil from fourteen inches deep to six or eight inches, topsoil that the tallgrass prairie took thousands of years to accumulate.

New technology sometimes works more efficiently than anybody wants it to, as with the pesticides that kill not only target pests but harmless and beneficial organisms. Predators such as wolves and coyotes can be destructive to livestock, and ranchers and government wildlife agents had used cyanide and strychnine to control them since the nineteenth century. Poison effectively exterminated wolves, but coyotes reproduce quickly, and the livestock industry couldn't get rid of them.

After the Second World War, however, a new poison called

Compound 1080 showed promise because it was cheaper and even more deadly than the older ones. Over the next two decades, Compound 1080 did indeed kill hundreds of thousands of coyotes, but it also killed countless numbers of every other kind of meat-eating animal on the Plains, animals unaware that the poisoned meat scattered about was meant for coyotes. (Compound 1080 is so acutely toxic that it proved to be a secondary poison, killing not only animals that feed on baits, but scavengers that feed on their carcasses.) Since coyotes breed faster than most of these animals, the result of the decades of Compound 1080 use was that most of the West still had plenty of coyotes, but increasingly fewer golden eagles, pine martens, bears, bobcats, mountain lions, ringtails, hawks, and owls. Under pressure from conservationists, the United States government withdrew Compound 1080 from predator use in the early 1970s, although in recent years it has allowed limited use again.

Black-footed ferrets probably died from Compound 1080 and other

SHEP FINDS THE BLACK-FOOTED FERRET

John Hogg is a Meeteetse, Wyoming area rancher and owner of Shep, the dog that rediscovered the black-footed ferret.

"Well, Lucille heard the dog having a big fight out here in the yard in the middle of the night. I don't know just what time, but anyway she thought maybe it was having a battle with a porcupine or something. So when we got up in the morning she said, 'You better go out there and see what happened,' she said. 'The dog might have some porcupine quills in it or something.'

"Anyway, I went out and checked, and found this animal laying out there in the yard. Gee, I didn't know what it was, I just thought it was a mink. So I just brought it back out and throwed it over the fence here and then we got to talking a bit after we'd eaten

breakfast and she said, 'What do you think about having that thing mounted, take it down to LaFrenchies?'

"So, we were going to Cody anyway, so I guess about nine o'clock we went down and took it in there and he took a look at it

and says, 'Wow, I think you got a black-footed ferret.' And I said, 'Well, what's that?' just not thinking, you know, and he said, 'That's an endangered species, I can't touch that.'

"I don't suppose anybody ever thought about a ferret being in this country. They had discovered them over in South Dakota and I suppose they'd keep looking in those areas where they knowed there had been some. They sure stirred 'em up for to start looking anyway. So we said, well, OK, we was going on to Cody so we just left it there. He called the game warden, and he sent it on to Billings, and that was the last we saw of the ferret. I guess they found some more here lately, one or two batches. I guess I heard they did anyway. I hope so."

Meeteetse, Wyoming rancher John Hogg and his dog Shep.

poisons during the years of heavy use, since they are known to eat some carrion along with their prairie-dog prey. The ferret doesn't owe its near extinction to the coyote-poisoning campaign, however, but to another poisoning campaign which has been much more successful. The huge prairie-dog towns on which the small populations of ferrets depended ate grass, which ranchers preferred to reserve for their livestock. Assisted by the United States government, ranchers poisoned prairie dogs so effectively with grain baits treated with Compound 1080 and other chemicals that the black-tailed prairie dog of the eastern Plains is now largely restricted to parks and refuges. The western white-tailed species has been also greatly reduced. Species that shared the prairie dogs' burrows or preyed on them also dwindled, including burrowing owls, badgers, and swift foxes, the Plains relative of the desert kit fox.

None dwindled as thoroughly as the black-footed ferret, however, which simply disappeared from most of its range as the prairie-dog population dropped by an estimated ninety percent. In fact, the ferret was thought to be extinct by 1980, attempts having failed to save the last known population, in South Dakota. Scientists had studied the South Dakota ferrets since 1964, and in the 1970s the U.S. Fish and Wildlife Service (which, ironically, had also been responsible for prairie-dog poisoning programs) captured some individuals and tried to breed them. One captive female delivered two litters, in 1976 and 1977, but the young did not live. Adult animals proved susceptible to a bewildering variety of diseases, and both captive and wild populations eventually died, leaving no other known population, although there were reports of ferrets, as there always seem to be reports where rare animals are concerned.

Then in September 1981, a rancher's dog near the small northwestern Wyoming town of Meeteetse killed a small animal apparently trying to eat from its food bowl. The animal was unknown to the dog's owners, so they took it to a taxidermist, who identified it as an endangered black-footed ferret and passed it on to the Fish and Wildlife Service. The Rocky Mountain foothills around Meeteetse are ideal ferret habitat—shortgrass rangeland supporting a complex of more than a hundred thousand white-tailed prairie-dog burrows. Fish and Wildlife biologists rushed to the scene, and within the month captured and radio-collared a ferret.

Studies conducted during the next few years revealed a thriving ferret population in the area. By driving around the eight thousand acres of prairie dog colonies at night and shining spotlights over the burrows, biologists counted hunting ferrets by locating their glowing eyes. In 1982, they counted sixty-one individuals, including twelve litters of young ferrets, which showed the population was breeding effectively. The count was even higher in 1983: eighty-eight individuals and eighteen litters. This number may have been partly a result of improved counting methods, but it was heartening for a species thought

GROWING UP UNDERGROUND

Although information about the black-footed ferret has multiplied since the species' rediscovery in 1981, much remains to be learned. Ferrets spend most of their lives underground, and what takes place there is open to speculation. Virtually nothing is known about juvenile ferrets' early development because they do not venture to the surface until they are almost six weeks old. When they do finally appear above ground, they are already approaching three-quarters of full adult size.

With their first exploratory ventures to the surface, the juvenile ferrets exhibit the same innocent curiosity found in the young of any species. Their mother is solely responsible for their care, since adult males are solitary and associate with females only during mating. When the juveniles start to increase their above-ground activity, the female will continually relocate her young. Only rarely will all of her litter be found in one burrow.

Juveniles generally come to the surface at dusk, play and wrestle until about midnight, then return to the burrow until an hour or two before sunrise. Meanwhile, their mother spends most of the night and even part of the daylight hours in search of food. There is little information about how ferrets kill prairie dogs because this usually

happens in tunnels, unobserved by man. One can only imagine how the ferret must take advantage of its small size and greater agility to outmaneuver the larger prairie dog.

BELOW: *Black-tailed prairie dogs in Wyoming.*

BOTTOM: *Young ferrets outside their den.*

two years earlier to be extinct. The 1984 total rose to 128 individual ferrets and twenty-five litters.

Biologists took advantage of the unexpected ferret bonanza at Meeteetse to study behavior and habitat needs with radiotelemetry, tracking, and direct observation. They found that individual ferrets have ranges of about a hundred acres—a large area for such a small animal—within which they move about nomadically, about a mile a day on the average. As with other members of the weasel family, they mark their territories with musk from scent glands that they rub against the ground or bushes. Males have larger ranges than females and live apart from them except when mating. Females raise litters of from three to five young alone, keeping them in a den burrow for the first six to eight weeks, dragging prey as much as a quarter-mile to the den.

When the young reach full growth at the end of their first summer, the mother apparently helps them to find home territories of their own. First she distributes the young ferrets in different burrows, then she leads individuals or pairs on increasingly long trips away from her territory. Such behavior is crucial to the species' survival, since not enough prey remains around the den burrow to support the young over the winter. Even so, most young ferrets don't survive their first year, and few individuals live more than several years.

Unfortunately, the ferret's prosperity in 1984 proved as short-lived as the California condor's. As with the condor, biologists and conservationists disagreed about how to save the Meeteetse ferrets. Some wanted to leave the entire population in the wild until a special captive-breeding facility could be developed in Wyoming. Others wanted to take advantage of the multiplying population to capture ferrets for transplantation to other prairie dog colonies or for breeding in zoos or other facilities outside Wyoming. As with the condor, bad luck hit the Meeteetse ferrets faster and harder than anyone had anticipated.

In June 1985, a University of Colorado graduate student doing a routine study of diseases in prairie-dog towns discovered sylvatic plague in fleas in Meeteetse prairie-dog burrows. This disease poses a serious threat to prairie dogs, who catch the fever bacteria from the fleas. (Also known as bubonic plague, the disease is serious to humans as well, but we are unlikely to catch it from prairie dogs unless we happen to spend time in prairie dog burrows.) That summer, spotlighting of ferret burrows showed a sudden drop in the ferret population. It was down to fifty-eight individuals, fewer than half the 1984 population.

Ferrets do not suffer from plague, but biologists feared the population could be decimated by lack of food if prairie-dog numbers fell significantly as a result of a plague epidemic. The Wyoming Game and Fish Department and the Fish and Wildlife Service began a program of treating prairie-dog burrows with an insecticide to kill fleas; they had treated most of the area by the end of the summer. The prairie-dog population fell by about 20 percent, however, and by October 1985, a count revealed only thirty-one ferrets remaining in the area.

Yet the situation did not seem too bad. A carefully selected population sample, captured during the summer, comprised six individuals whose lineages differed, and who therefore would presumably ensure against the possibility of inbreeding—a probable factor in the decline of the South Dakota ferrets in the 1970s (their unusual susceptibility to diseases may have been a result of inbreeding). Even if the wild population's decline continued, a nucleus existed for captive-breeding and eventual transplantation to the wild. There appeared to be no reason why the Meeteetse population should dwindle away completely, anyway, since thousands of prairie dogs survived.

But the bad luck was just beginning. In October, one of the captive ferrets developed a slight reddening on the top of its head and became listless. The veterinarian in charge thought it had scabies, a relatively minor disease, and treated it with antibiotics. It died after a few days, however, and autopsy revealed that it had canine distemper, a very serious viral disease for which there is no cure. The sick ferret had not been isolated from the others, furthermore, so they got sick and died too. Even worse, the distemper had been contracted in the wild, meaning that the dwindling Meeteetse population was threatened not only by food scarcity but by an incurable disease. How the distemper infected the ferret population is unknown. The disease can be carried by dogs, coyotes, raccoons, and even humans, who may transmit the virus by contact although they aren't susceptible to it. It may have gotten into the burrows during the dusting operations against plague, although the fact that the ferret population was already declining in June suggests otherwise.

The future of the Meeteetse ferrets suddenly seemed very grim. Biologists hastily captured six more individuals, vaccinated them against distemper, and placed them in isolation to protect them not only from distemper, but from other diseases such as influenza, which ferrets can catch from people and each other. Yet the basic problem of breeding the ferrets remained. Although related ferret species from Europe and Asia have been captive-bred (one species is a fairly common pet), the black-footed ferret has never succesfully raised a litter in captivity.

Intensive observation of the Meeteetse colony in the summer of 1986 found fourteen ferrets, including two females with litters, which allowed biologists to capture more individuals for breeding. Thus there is still hope for the Meeteetse ferrets, and even if they are lost, it will be early to call the species extinct. Ferrets are so small and secretive that they may survive in at least a few other places, as occasional sighting reports suggest. There was an unconfirmed report of another Wyoming population in the summer of 1986.

If we find another population, what shall we do about it? Some people have suggested that the Meeteetse ferret colony might not have met disaster if conservation agencies had not overrun it. Of course, the Endangered Species Act required the agencies to take action to protect and restore the species once they learned of the ferrets.

Ferrets are endangered because civilization has laid a heavy technological hand on the Plains; last-minute attempts to save ferrets by technological means such as captive breeding may not be enough to compensate for years of habitat loss and poisoning. Grassland abundance masks a considerable volatility, of which the Meeteetse ferrets' sudden population drop was an example. Because of the dry, exposed terrain, local conditions in grassland can change very quickly and

A PLAINS COMMUNITY

Nowhere is the geographic diversity of the North American landscape more apparent, or more majestic, than along the Rocky Mountain Front. Here, where the shortgrass plains of Wyoming's Bighorn Basin give way to the rugged volcanic buttresses of the Absaroka Mountains, the last known population of black-footed ferrets was discovered in 1981. The species had been presumed extinct until its rediscovery in Wyoming.

The ferrets live on a series of long, plateau-like terraces formed by the Greybull River and its tributaries as they flow eastward from the Absarokas into the Bighorn Basin. The grasses growing on the terraces support not only cattle, horses, and pronghorns, but also the prairie-dog colonies that provide the ferrets' main prey. In summer, the mounds that mark prairie-dog burrow entrances are alive with the large, squirrel-like rodents, which forage busily among the vegetation and communicate back and forth with noisy territorial calls and warning barks.

Prairie-dog colonies also support a variety of other burrow-dwelling animals and predators. Burrowing owls, snakes, lizards, and invertebrates find shelter in burrows, while coyotes, badgers, golden eagles and hawks prey on the prairie dogs and on the black-footed ferrets.

Burrowing owl.

extremely, with catastrophic effects on flora and fauna. Thousands of bison died in floods, droughts, and blizzards on the wild Plains. Grassland wildlife usually survived, however, because there was so much grassland. Prairie dogs and ferrets could die from disease or starvation over hundreds of square miles, but there always were other colonies to move back into the vacant territory. The wild grasses themselves could die over hundreds of square miles, but there always were thousands more square miles. This is not so today.

Ironically, the expansion of industrial technology into agriculture is threatening not only wildlife, but the farmers and ranchers who were expected to benefit most from the new techniques. The equipment required for highly mechanized, chemical-intensive farming is too expensive for most family farmers to buy outright, so they borrow. When farm-produce prices were high in the 1970s, most farmers could make enough money to make payments on their loans and still realize a profit. Some farmers also invested in rapidly inflating land markets in the '70s, confident that inflation would continue to increase the value of their property. When inflation and farm prices leveled off and dropped in the 1980s, many found themselves paying interest on their interest, and farm foreclosures became news in a way reminiscent of the Depression. Thousands of family farmers simply have left farming, often selling to corporate enterprises that practice even more industrialized methods.

Economics are forcing some farmers who want to stay in agriculture to experiment with less expensive methods. They don't have to look far to find them, since most traditional farming practices used

South Dakota prairie with wild sunflowers.

in the United States before World War II are cheaper than industrial-ized ones. Instead of growing enormous fields of one crop treated with commercial fertilizers, pesticides, and herbicides, traditional farmers grew a wide variety of plants and animals. This diversity allowed them to produce food without depleting soil fertility or letting large pest populations build up. Farmers rotated fields between grain, legume, and hay crops, fed some of the crops to livestock, and used the manure to fertilize the fields. Of course, traditional farmers used livestock instead of tractors to do the farm work, and a few modern alternative farmers (also called regenerative farmers) are trying even that. Most aren't going quite that far, but a National Academy of Sciences panel estimated that 5 percent of corn-belt farmers were using these alter-native methods in 1985. Making pesticide and herbicide applications only when needed led to significant savings for some farmers, and reduced pesticide use up to 75 percent.

Not all the methods under experimentation are traditional. Noth-ing is more traditional to farming than plowing, yet plowing alone is responsible for much soil erosion simply because it leaves soil unpro-tected from wind and rain. Completely exposed soil is abnormal in most natural grasslands, which tend to be dominated by perennial grasses. These live for many years and hold soil tightly with sod and roots even in droughts. Farming methods that reduce the need for plowing and tilling would save farmers an enormous amount of money and effort while saving the soil.

A method called "no-till farming," whereby seeds are planted in unplowed fields with special machines, has successfully reduced ero-sion. Unfortunately, it depends on heavy herbicide applications for weed control. Another method called ridge-tilling, successfully used since the 1950s, reduces plowing with less dependence on herbicides. The farmer grows crops along the tops of permanent soil ridges in the field: to plant, he scoops off only the top of the ridge, leaving the rest of the field covered by stubble. After the crop starts to grow, he uses cultivators to control weeds in the spaces between the ridges.

Some farmers are experimenting with crops that might grow more safely and profitably than the usual ones. Some plants which we regard as weeds such as amaranth, or pigweed—have been important food crops for other civilizations. Even ordinary crops such as corn or potatoes have many local and traditional varieties which modern ag-riculture has neglected, but which could have new uses. Native wild-prairie plants also have potential to become valuable crops; in fact, several already have, including the sunflower and the Jerusalem ar-tichoke, a sunflower relative which farmers grow not only for its edible tuber but as a source of alcohol fuel.

Wildlife benefits in many ways from regenerative farming. Small fields planted with diverse crops provide more habitat than unbroken expanses of monocultured crops. Reduced use of pesticides and herbicides results in larger populations of the songbirds and gamebirds that feed largely on weed seeds and insects. Reduced compaction and erosion of soil results in larger populations of the many invertebrates and microorganisms that contribute to natural soil fertility.

Of course, regenerative farming won't necessarily save wild grassland, although it can lessen the pressure to plow more prairie by sustaining the fertility of existing farmland. The problem with conserving wild grassland is that it has so much potential to produce wealth. As a result, the amount of grassland in national parks, wildlife refuges, and wilderness areas in the United States is small compared to the amount of forest, and almost all of it is in the shortgrass or mixed grass plains. The National Bison Range, for example, contains only eighteen thousand acres, enough to support 350 bison. Animals in excess of that number must be rounded up and sold. Exotic weeds such as goatsbeard and knapweed are invading the range and could reduce its

---

THE PRAIRIE FARM

The tallgrass prairies of the Midwest are the heart of American agriculture. As they go, our nation must choose a way to go as well: either toward soil erosion, wildlife decimation, and environmental contamination, or toward sound conservation practices and a sustainable future.

Dick Thompson, an organic farmer near Boone, Iowa, holds annual "field days" at his farm to demonstrate his techniques, machinery, and ideas to other farmers. He shows visitors how he feeds his hogs with organic grain (which reduces his veterinary bills) and how he experiments with crop rotation patterns, weed control measures, and fertilizer applications. Thompson also points out the hard cold facts about farm debt, the cost of farm chemicals

and heavy equipment, and the threats to wildlife and human health from chemical pesticides and excessive fertilizer. The Iowa Geological Survey determined recently that aquifers throughout the state contain high levels of nitrates (from fertilizer residues) and pesticides, and agencies have recorded similar findings across the corn belt.

Thompson's diversified, well-managed, profitable farm is a model for the large number of farmers who are trying to cut their costs and are converting to more environmentally sound farming. He believes that a well-managed farm is compatible with a healthy environment, and that the specialized, massive-scale farming encouraged by the agricultural establishment, with its reliance on heavy equipment and chemicals, has literally reached a dead end.

Thompson's ecologically balanced farming offers an economical alternative.

Dick Thompson on his organic farm near Boone, Iowa.

carrying capacity for bison even more by reducing the shortgrasses upon which they depend. Native shortgrasses cure on the stem, making a natural hay that remains nutritious through the winter.

Attempts to establish a tallgrass-prairie national park on virgin prairie remnants in Kansas or Oklahoma have foundered for years on resistance from ranchers, oil companies, and other economic interests; they fear that government acquisition of the land would restrict their activities. Nevertheless, such a park or a less restrictive national preserve may come into being soon, possibly in Oklahoma's Osage Hills. And many local and private conservation organizations have preserved tall-grass prairie remnants.

Restoring prairies to areas where they once grew is an increasingly popular conservation activity, from backyard prairies created with purchased or hand-gathered grass and wildflower seeds to a 650-acre prairie that conservationists are developing in the center of the Fermi National Accelerator Laboratory in Illinois, a project which has been underway for more than a decade, and which will include restoration of prairie birds and insects to the area, along with grasses and wildflowers.

The Bureau of Land Management and the Forest Service administer hundreds of millions of wild grassland acres, most of them in drier areas of the West such as the Great Basin. This land supports significant numbers of pronghorns, elk, bighorn sheep, and other big game as well as dozens of federally listed endangered species. It also supports millions of cattle, sheep, and goats, which compete with wildlife in various ways. Two million cattle and 2.3 million sheep and goats graze BLM lands every year, a number that many conservationists think excessive in light of BLM estimates that 60 percent of its land is in unsatisfactory condition because of overgrazing. The percentage may be even higher: a 1986 study by the National Wildlife Federation and the National Resources Defense Council found 71 percent of BLM lands to be overgrazed.

The 1976 Federal Land Policy and Management Act directed the Bureau of Land Management to protect wildlife and habitat on its land, but the livestock industry is as influential in management of public grasslands as the timber industry is in public-forest management. Livestock numbers remain high on BLM lands because the price per head that the government charges ranchers for grazing on BLM land remains much lower than the price private landowners charge. In 1985, the fee on public lands was $1.35 per animal; private landowners charged an average of $6.75 per animal for grazing on comparable land. Ranchers maintain that the quality of public forage is lower than that of private land, but that quality might improve if overgrazing were curtailed.

Wild grassland accounts for an increasingly small proportion of commercial livestock production as stock-raising has become more industrialized. Only 2 percent of all beef cattle feed on public grazing lands. BLM land supports only 4 percent of United States grazing overall, and rangelands worldwide produce only 16 percent of livestock feed. In countries such as India, where grain is too valuable to be fed to animals, livestock get much of their food from crop residues. They are turned out into the fields after harvest, which also helps to manure the fields.

Grazing pressure continues to increase on wild grasslands, however, as growing human populations require increased livestock populations. World cattle numbers grew from 777 million to 1.3 billion from 1950 to the present, which approaches the doubling of the human population that occurred during the period. Sheep and goat populations grew more slowly—from 1 billion to 1.6 billion—but sheep and goats can overgraze land even more severely than cattle.

The fate of wild grasslands throughout the world parallels that of North America's. Expanding human populations plow the most fertile and well-watered prairies and overgraze the drier ones, with consequent reductions of wildlife. The Eurasian species of bison comes even closer to extinction than the American, surviving only in a single Polish reserve. The saiga antelope, an ecological counterpart of the pronghorn, nearly reached extermination from the central-Asian plains before Soviet conservation measures restored it to a population of about two million. The Asian wild horse, called Przewalski's horse after a European explorer, is extinct in the wild, although it survives in zoos. The last wild herd was seen in Mongolia in 1969.

Until the late 1970s, it was thought that large wildlife herds might survive in the high Tibetan grasslands, closed to Western eyes after the Chinese takeover in the 1950s. Explorers in the 1920s had seen herds of wild yaks, wild asses, antelope, and ibex as well as brown bears and wolves. Recent expeditions found no large herds, however, and very little wildlife in general. Native pastoral peoples armed with Chinese submachine guns apparently had decimated them.

As with forest, the people who need wild grasslands most suffer most from their deterioration. All over the world, traditional herding peoples are caught between expansion of cropland farming into the best grazing land, and overgrazing of the drier areas into which they are being pushed. Modern governments view traditional nomadic movements with suspicion because they may cross national borders. Seeking to establish cash economies, governments try to convert subsistence-oriented land uses to commercial ones, destroying traditional, ecologically viable practices in the process.

TROPICAL GRASSLANDS

The cheetah of African grasslands suffers a plight similar to the panther of Florida forests. Drastic population reduction in the past has lowered its natural diversity, and human expansion has pushed it into shrinking islands of habitat.

The cheetah still has more room to survive than the Florida panther. In protected areas such as Tanzania's Serengeti, huge herds of wild ungulates still follow ancient migration patterns. After brief periods of rainfall, new vegetation sprouts. An estimated two million animals make circular annual movements in search of the new growth. The grasses have evolved to survive grazing by spreading out horizontally, by producing multiple shoots, and by regenerating quickly. Zebras lead, eating the upper layer of drying grasses. Next come the wildebeest, a species of large antelope, which reaches down for nutritious leaves and sheaths near the ground. The tiny Thompson's gazelle, with its slender mouth, favors cleared areas where it can find herbs and watch for cheetahs, lions, leopards, and hyenas.

Fast-growing human populations are closing in on the African grasslands, however. As villages and towns enter national and international economies, the market for tusks, skins, claws, horns, and other wildlife products becomes lucrative. Developing nations may lack the resources to defend wildlife against poachers armed with automatic weapons and high-performance vehicles. The poaching of some species, such as the leopard and the elephant, has become chronic. Poachers hunt others, like the black rhino, feverishly as the number of animals declines.

But one may not find the main threat to east African wildlife in the reserves themselves. The Masai, a nomadic people who rely on cattle grazing, have traditionally lived in the land surrounding much of the Serengeti; their numbers are low and they share the area with wildlife. But today, governments are converting these lands to large, fenced agricultural projects designed to feed rapidly growing urban populations and to bring foreign exchange. Disregarding the effects of poaching and intrusion, one study predicted that, as a result of geographic isolation alone, the reserves will lose 11 percent of their species in the next fifty years, and almost half in five hundred years.

Cheetah stalking prey.

The cycle of grassland deterioration parallels that of deforestation. As people exploit land, it becomes less productive, and so people exploit it even more to make up for failing productivity. Repeated cropping by livestock eventually eliminates the most nutritious, perennial grasses, and less desirable annual species replace them. Annuals may not grow at all in drought years. About a third of the world's grasslands have reached this stage of deterioration. The situation is worst presently in Africa's Sahel region, where years of drought have combined with overgrazing and loss of land to farming to drive many nomads to destitution and starvation. The final stage of grassland deterioration is desertification, when grassland becomes, in effect, desert. The Sahara Desert is spreading into former grasslands of the Sahel at a rapid rate.

Lions, elephants, giraffes, ostriches, cheetahs, and many other game species lived as recently as the last century in parts of northern Africa that are nearly devoid of big game today. Such species also lived in much of the Middle East and Asia within historical times. Very few areas now support grassland wildlife of such diversity. The savannas of eastern Africa are among the last, and they comprise a heritage of significance to all humans: humanity originated there, and there is proof of the abundance wild grassland can provide if conserved.

In Tanzania's Serengeti National Park, for example, millions of herbivores belonging to ninety-one species share the range without permanently overgrazing it. Each species has its own feeding preference—Thomson's gazelles and wildebeest graze short grasses, zebras graze longer grasses, giraffes browse tree leaves—so that vegetation remains diverse and healthy. Heavily grazed areas have time to regenerate as herds move on looking for new growth. Thus the amount of animal life sustained is much greater than in less diverse ecosystems. A study in the Sahel showed that savanna grassland there would support from three to seven times more wildlife than grazing livestock.

East-African grasslands are faced with the same demographic and economic pressures as others, unfortunately. Their wildlife might have been decimated already if not for the tsetse fly, which carries a kind of encephalitis (also called sleeping sickness) that is highly debilitating to livestock as well as people. Wildlife carry the disease, but are mostly immune to it. During the colonial period, authorities conducted mass slaughter campaigns against wild herds in attempts to remove the reservoir of infection and make the savannas safe for ranching. Since independence, African governments have shown increased sensitivity to the value of their wildlife heritage as sources of national pride as well as tourist revenue, yet high birthrates are forcing croplands to the edges of parks. Pastoralists such as the Masai, forced out of traditional grazing lands by farmers, come into increased conflict with wildlife.

Yet conflict between livestock and wildlife is not inevitable; they have coexisted for thousands of years. Livestock were wildlife themselves a very short while ago by evolutionary standards, and they retain natural grazing and browsing preferences which they will practice if ranges aren't overstocked. Even wildlife will overgraze range if they are confined and crowded: most conflict between wildlife and livestock occurs on deteriorated range.

In the United States, ranchers tolerate considerable numbers of pronghorns and deer on their cattle ranges because those animals eat largely different kinds of plants than do livestock. Sport hunters cull surplus wildlife here, where there is no shortage of protein in the average diet. In places like Africa, where diets tend to be low in protein, wildlife eventually could become a significant supplement to livestock as a commercial meat source. An experiment in commercial harvest of both cattle and native game from a ranch in Kenya has proved as much as ten times more productive than conventional ranching, even in a period of drought.

If the technique can work in Africa, it probably can work in many other places. Saiga antelope have been used commercially in the Soviet Union; so have bison in the United States. On public lands, wild herds perhaps should replace domestic ones. Of course, turning wild ungulates everywhere into commercial meat supply would not be desirable, since we want to leave room on the planet for other meat eaters, such as lions. Still, the more we increase productivity on commercial grassland, the more land we will have available to set aside as parks, wildlife refuges, and wilderness areas.

T H E
MOUNTAINS

TWO BULL MOOSE LOITER in a stand of lodgepole pines. The trees are old and many have fallen, making a labyrinth of trunks, but the huge deer move through it almost soundlessly. A creek mutters through a meadow nearby; otherwise the place has the particular hush of summer nights in the Montana mountains, where frost can occur anytime, and crickets seldom sing. Despite the stillness, the moose are restless. They have just heard something unfamiliar.

The sound comes again, a throaty wail from a ridge to the east, followed a little later by a chorus of wails and barks from farther to the northeast. The moose have never heard this sound during their lives in the willow thickets and lake marshes of Glacier National Park, but their ancestors of a few dozen generations before knew it well. The bulls are used to the wails of coyotes, but this is a deeper sound.

More silence, then two blackish-gray animals appear on the game trail that the moose have followed into the timber. The moose back up a little, rolling their eyes. The gray animals look and smell a little like coyotes, but are twice as big. The moose are curious, but they want to move away from this strangeness, stepping deftly over the deadfalls with long legs that only look awkward.

They actually have little cause for concern. The two wolves that have followed their scent down from the ridgetop lose interest in them immediately. These are healthy, mature bulls, not worth a moment's notice when the mountains are full of moose and elk calves and deer fawns. The wolves skirt the bulls, keeping an eye on them, wary of a sudden impulsive charge, then climb back up the ridge and head northeast toward the parents and siblings that answered their call earlier.

They don't hurry. They are still digesting their meal from the night before: the pack killed a sick elk and devoured it so thoroughly that only scraps of bone and hair remained. Even if they had not eaten for several days, they would be patient; they are well-fed wolves. Indeed, they are very possibly the best-fed wolves in the world. They are surrounded by thousands of square miles of big-game herds that have not seen a wolf pack in over fifty years.

Biologists call these wolves, which number about a dozen, the "magic pack." The name derives from their ability to elude trackers, but it may also reflect their achievement in being the first documented pack to take up residence in the western United States since the 1930s.

It is a typical pack, made up of a mated pair with two grown litters. The matriarch is named Kishnena because biologists trapped and radio-collared her near Kishnena Creek in the northwest corner of Glacier National Park in 1979. Kishnena came from Canada, perhaps from as far away as Banff National Park, 150 miles north of the American border. After the biologists released her, Kishnena's collar told them that she stayed mostly on the Canadian side, where she had her two litters in 1982 and 1984. There is much human disturbance and development on the Canadian side of the border, however—logging, strip-mining, oil exploration, hunting. In November 1985, Kishnena and her mate and offspring moved south, into the center of the 1,600-square-mile Glacier.

Achievement is perhaps not too anthropomorphic a term for the magic pack's return to a country that has been killing wolves assiduously during the past two centuries. The only substantial remaining population in the lower forty-eight states comprises roughly twelve hundred eastern timber wolves in Minnesota's North Woods. (Another population exists in Michigan's Isle Royale National Park, and a few individuals live in Wisconsin.) Americans shot, trapped, poisoned, and even dynamited some eighty thousand wolves in Montana alone in the thirty-five years from 1883 to 1918. Western wolves were big, about a quarter again as large as the eastern timber wolf; a hundred pounds was not an unusual weight for a male. A pack needed to kill a large animal every few days to live, and that need did not appeal to the livestock industry that replaced bison and elk with cattle and sheep on the Plains.

Given the vehemence and ingenuity of the American war on wolves, it's impressive that they lasted through fifty years of persecution in the Rockies and returned after fifty years of exile. They couldn't

WOLF ECOLOGY AND BEHAVIOR

The wolf is a major predator of hoofed mammals such as deer, moose, elk, and caribou. Remains of beavers and occasionally of snowshoe hares appear in wolf droppings and show these small mammals to be seasonally important. The wolf's role in regulating its prey is still the subject of much scientific debate. Most studies indicate that wolves prey mainly on young and aged animals. They tend to kill moose younger than a year old and older than seven years. In two major studies of moose and wolves, more than a third of the adult-moose prey showed evidence of disease—such as tooth infections, fat-depleted bone marrow, and arthritis.

Like other gregarious animals, wolves behave in highly developed and fascinating social patterns. Wolf packs consist of two to twenty animals and inhabit territories ranging in size from forty to one thousand square miles. A dominant, or alpha, mated pair leads each pack. Alpha wolves are responsible for the scent-marking that serves to demarcate the pack's territory, and defend the pack from any perceived dangers. The alpha male and female are thought to mate for life, although a survivor will seek a new mate whenever an alpha dies. One female at Isle Royale National Park remained in the alpha position for eleven years, during which time she had four mates in succession. Alpha wolves are commonly the parents of other wolves in the pack and usually are the only pair that successfully produces young.

Wolves commonly mate in February and bear young about sixty-three days later. Pups are born in early spring, usually in an underground den, abandoned beaver lodge, or hollow log. Adults move the pups periodically during their first summer through a number of homesites, or "rendezvous areas"; otherwise, the pups lead a rather sedentary life as adults bring back food for them. If pups are well-fed, they can reach adult size by September or October, when they begin the winter pattern of continuous travel within the pack's territory. Yearlings and two-year-old wolves commonly explore areas outside the pack territory on their own, and some disperse permanently as young adults.

Adapted from "Gray Wolf," by Rolf O. Peterson, *Audubon Wildlife Report*, 1986.

A pack of gray wolves feeds on an elk.

have done so without help from the mountains, however. Wolves were long gone from the Great Plains shortgrass prairies and the Great Basin sagebrush valleys when the last wolf was killed in the Rocky Mountains. If the last wolf ever was killed in the Rockies, that is. Wolves may simply have become so scarce as to be effectively invisible. Stories of large, wolf-like animals and deep, wolf-like howls never stopped coming out of the Rockies, and out of most mountain ranges in the West, and even some in the East.

Wolves persisted in the Appalachian Mountains long after pioneers dispatched their lowland counterparts. New York paid six bounties for wolves killed in 1897. In the Old World, wolves survived well into the twentieth century in the mountains of Wales, Ireland, Japan, and Sicily, and they still survive in the mountains of Spain, Italy, Greece, the Middle East, India, the Soviet Union, and China. None

CONSERVING THE WOLF

Fear of the wolf significantly hampers effective wolf conservation worldwide. While wolves may have killed and eaten humans in the past—for example, during the long-lasting, widespread wars in Europe after the Middle Ages—there are no records in North America of a healthy wild wolf attacking a human. Unfortunately, European settlers brought their traditional fears with them to North America. Such fears appear to be partly responsible for the negative attitudes toward wolves among some residents of Michigan, where, within a few months in the 1970s, humans killed a small group of wolves that had been introduced.

But the majority of citizens in states with wolves, such as Minnesota and Alaska, view the animals positively. And as more people have become aware of ecological principles, especially the important role predation plays in natural selection, millions of Americans have come to consider the wolf a symbol of wilderness and an important part of our wildlife heritage.

The status of wolves in both Alaska and Minnesota improved in the late 1960s as poison was banned, aerial gunning declined, and bounties were eliminated. North American wolf distribution is probably greater than at any time in the past fifty years, although significant regional declines have occurred. Wolves disappeared from Michigan's upper peninsula in the 1960s, and the red wolf (a small species that lived in southeastern forests) became extinct in the wild in the late 1970s. (In the winter of 1986 to 1987, plans for the reintroduction of red wolves into the wild were implemented in North Carolina. If successful, this would be the first time humans returned wolves to the wild.) In the face of soaring human population, wolves in Mexico have declined to just a few individuals and are expected to become extinct shortly. Wolf declines invariably have been linked to the role of man in their lives.

Adapted from "Gray Wolf," by Rolf O. Peterson, *Audubon Wildlife Report*, 1986.

Gray wolf.

of these countries left their wolves in peace. Conflict between wolves and humans became unavoidable after people stopped living like wolves—following game herds—and began raising livestock. Yet wolves persisted in some of the most civilized and heavily populated parts of the earth.

If forests and grasslands grew on level river basins or rolling interior plateaus, civilization might have tamed them all by now. The Earth would have to be a docile planet to allow this, however, and it is not. Tranquil as it may appear from an orbiting satellite, the Earth's surface has always been disturbed by powerful inner stresses. Terra firma is not really firm; rather it comprises a core of radioactive metal mantled with molten basaltic magma, of which only a thin crust has solidified. The rock mantle flows sluggishly in convection currents excited by "hot spots" in the core. Where these currents are strongest, the mantle's flow has cracked the planet's thin, solid crust into a jigsaw puzzle of vast plates which (over millions of years) push against and pull apart from one another as they move ponderously across the mantle.

Forests and grasslands lie on this uneasy foundation, not directly on the basaltic crust but on scattered areas of granitic, metamorphic, and sedimentary rock which we call continents. The continents drift on the crust rather as ice floes drift on an arctic sea. As mantle convection currents drive crustal plates together or pull them apart, continents bulge, split apart, collide, and (at speeds of a few centimeters a year) travel long distances across the planet's surface.

Continental drift was considered an improbable theory until the 1960s, but it has since become generally accepted as supporting evidence has accumulated. This evidence suggests that the continents are still drifting slowly—as much as two inches a year. India is in the process of colliding with Asia; Africa is splitting along the Rift Valley (the site, incidentally, of the earliest human fossils); southern California is moving northwestward, away from North America and toward the Aleutian Islands.

Mountains arise from these movements, in a number of ways. Where continents, or crustal plates bearing continents, collide, the force of the collision crumples the rock and uplifts it thousands of feet, at rates of a few centimeters a year. As a continental plate rides up over an oceanic plate, thousands of feet of sediments that once lay on the ocean floor may be scraped onto continental margins. Where plates slide against one another, continents crack and buckle, thrusting upward jagged walls of rock hundreds of miles in length. Where continents pass over hot spots in the core, molten mantle rock erupts through the thin surface to form volcanoes, covering entire regions miles deep, over thousands of years, with accumulated lava and ash.

A combination of these factors has contributed to the formation of most mountain ranges. The Rockies, for example, appear to have risen during crustal plate collisions in the Mesozoic era about one hundred million years ago. Volcanic activity has affected them throughout their history: many of the mountains around Yellowstone Park are of volcanic origin, and the area's geysers indicate that it presently lies over a hot spot. The jagged steepness of the Rockies' east slope, or "front range," indicates that present peaks have been uplifted during the past few million years by continental cracking and buckling (a process geologists call faulting, which is also responsible for earthquakes, of which the Yellowstone area has its share).

By wrinkling the earth's surface, mountain-building forces have affected life profoundly. Because climates are colder at higher altitudes, mountains act as barriers to the spread of warm-weather organisms and corridors for the spread of cold-weather ones. Many organisms have evolved special adaptations to their rugged conditions. Other mountain organisms are evolutionary relicts, restricted to the highlands by changing conditions on the plains. The worldwide drying trend that caused grasslands to expand pushed ancient forests to peaks and plateaus where rainfall remained more abundant. The conifer forests of today's Rockies once covered the Great Basin. Today's Rocky Mountain wolves are a recent example of relict organisms, pushed into the highlands not by changing climate but by the spread of civilization.

We know less about the evolution of mountain organisms than of lowland ones because mountains are shorter-lived than lowlands. Peaks such as the Rockies rise and erode away again in a few million years, while lowlands like the Mississippi Basin may accumulate layers of fossil-bearing sedimentary strata for hundreds of millions of years. Since fossils generally form in low-lying swamps and floodplains, fossils of mountain organisms are comparatively rare. In general, fossils found in mountains have originated in marine or lowland rock strata; the geological forces that formed the peaks also uplifted the fossils.

We also know less about the evolutionary relationship of humans to mountains than we do about their relationships to forests and grasslands. Footprints in volcanic ash indicate that more than three million years ago, hominids lived near active volcanoes of the African Rift Valley. We don't know if they climbed the volcanoes, however. Gorillas presently inhabit central African volcanic highlands, so early hominids might have, but there is no evidence of it. Highland climates may have been too cold for them. In any case, we may never know, because volcanoes that coexisted with early hominids have eroded away by now, leaving only ash deposits in the valleys below.

As *Homo erectus* spread north and east, hunting bands must have encountered mountain ranges again and again. They doubtless found the cliffs, peaks, and snows inconvenient, but many groups probably also found them useful. *Homo erectus* was a worker in stone, and there is no better place for finding stone than mountains. If they obscure their own evolutionary past by rising and eroding so quickly, mountains also expose an enormous amount of other geological history in the process—ancient seabeds, swamps, estuaries, even older mountains. Early craftsmen coveted the special stones that reveal this history—chert and flint from ancient seabeds, obsidian from ancient volcanoes—and found an ever-widening variety of uses for them.

Mountains are also often the sites of caves, and *Homo erectus* and his successors found these increasingly useful as glaciers scraped through Europe and Asia. Some older groups may have found the caves and the mountains useful not only against glacial cold but against newer bands that took over adjacent lowlands. Today, ancient hunting peoples still inhabit mountains where farming groups have usurped adjacent lowlands.

By the time humans began recording their thoughts in writing, mountains had become even more useful, not only as a source of new minerals, but for base and precious metals, gems, building and carving stones as well. Mountain grass stayed green after valley grass withered; herds driven to it got fat. Mountain trees grew slowly through cold winters, and their wood was accordingly tough; ships built of it stayed afloat. Mountain water flowed freely after valley streams had dried to summer trickles; fields irrigated with it stayed productive.

But mountains also harbored inconveniences and dangers for a civilization that grew more elaborate. They stood as barriers to travel and trade. Wolves or bears fed on herds driven to summer pastures. Human predators lived in the mountains also—brigands or resentful tribesman like the Bedouins and Berbers who periodically attacked ancient Middle Eastern and North African civilizations. Even the mountain streams that filled irrigation ditches so obligingly in summer could turn into raging dragons in winter and spring, bursting dikes, flooding whole valleys. Furthermore, all of this unruliness was often within view of the greatest cities; bears and wolves roamed Italy's Appenines throughout Rome's imperial heyday.

Attitudes toward mountains varied. In the Far East, painters and poets celebrated alpine wildness and loneliness as early as the seventh century A.D. In the European Middle Ages and Renaissance, painters seldom rendered mountains except as a distant background to civilized subjects, and literary descriptions emphasized their dangers and discomforts. When the fourteenth-century poet Petrarch climbed Mount Ventoux in southern France, he tried not to pay attention to the

THE EASTERN TIMBER WOLF

The United States Fish and Wildlife Service has been responsible for wolf management in Minnesota for the past decade, with federal control agents taking a few dozen wolves each year where

Gray or timber wolf.

depredation on domestic animals has occurred. The Minnesota Department of Natural Resources has maintained that it should initiate a limited sport hunting and trapping season, reasoning that this would reduce depredation of livestock and illegal killing of wolves, and decrease the animosity directed toward the wolves by local citizens.

The Minnesota proposal found a sympathetic ear in the U.S. Department of the Interior in the early 1980s. But in 1984 and 1985, a coalition of environmental groups filed suit in United States courts and succeeded in blocking the Interior Department's move to return management authority to Minnesota. The courts determined that management of the eastern timber wolf in Minnesota, where the species is federally listed as threatened, could not be turned over to the state.

The Fish and Wildlife Service uses a zone system to manage Minnesota's estimated 1,200 wolves, giving full protection within designated habitat zones but controlling wolves in buffer zones and agricultural zones if they prey on livestock.

Adapted from "Gray Wolf," by Rolf O. Peterson, *Aububon Wildlife Report*, 1986.

scenery. Eighteenth-century court ladies are said to have had their carriage window blinds pulled down when passing the Alps, to spare them the distressing sight of the peaks.

Whether early attitudes toward mountain wildness were approving or not, the mountains stayed wild because taming them was too inconvenient. This began to change with the growth of industry. Vastly increased manufacturing called for more raw materials, not only traditional ones like metals, stone, and wood, but relatively new ones like coal. Industrialists put mountain streams to work propelling complicated machinery, and once-lonely valleys in central Europe and western Britain filled with towns and slag heaps. As industrial wealth accumulated, so did the power of central governments.

One might have expected this new power over mountains to

generate an increased distaste for their remnant wildness. Yet this didn't happen, perhaps partly because people newly able to travel safely in mountains began to see their good points. Artists and scientists began to make alpine journeys with pleasure rather than trepidation, seeing wildflowers, cloud formations, and waterfalls where their predecessors had seen bare rock, dead horses, and graves.

Throughout much of Western history, mountains seemed evidence of some primeval cataclysm, even to scientific minds. God created the world smooth, according to a common theory, but the vast waves of the biblical flood pushed up the mountains. Theorists offered petrified sea shells and fish skeletons on mountaintops as evidence. The travelers of the Enlightenment and Romantic eras tended to see mountains quite differently, however, not as relics of divine wrath but as examples of natural order.

Geologists tried to understand mountain origins as manifestations of harmony rather than discord, as the result not of a flood but of gradually operating physical laws. If mountains did not arise, they reasoned, the continents would erode completely into the seas: mountains were a natural mechanism for regenerating land. Sea shells and fish skeletons had not been washed to the mountaintops by tidal waves, but gently uplifted from ancient oceans. Dizzying cliffs and gorges were not threatening reminders of earthly mortality, but invitations to the comprehension and appreciation of an order beyond that of civilization, what the Romantics called "the Sublime."

In the New World, where mountain wilderness was more daunting than in the Old, the romantic appeal of cliffs and waterfalls was particularly strong. Of course, that mountain wilderness posed challenges for Western civilization in America. The Appalachians had stopped colonial expansion into the interior for centuries. Yet the very effectiveness of the barrier reinforced a tantalizing promise. It seemed to many colonists that almost anything might lie beyond the mountains—fabled beasts, lost tribes, El Dorado. After the Revolution, American trappers and traders scurried out across the prairies reserved by the British Crown for its Indian clients, and men like Jim Bridger soon returned with tales that might have come from Coleridge's *Rime of the Ancient Mariner*—wonderingly describing valleys where the earth smoked, mountains of glass and trees of stone.

The tales were so fabulous that few believed them, and the western mountains remained mysterious for a few decades more as settlement spread across the Mississippi Valley and westward. Then Sutter's big gold strike in the Sierra Nevada foothills fulfilled their more tangible promise extravagantly in 1849, and mountains not only in California but throughout the West swarmed with miners. Ranchers, loggers, and merchants followed quickly. As they crossed every ridge in search of useful things, the romantic promise began to come true as well.

In 1854, a party of California militia in pursuit of Indians wandered into a Sierra Nevada valley of extraordinary beauty, walled on three sides by sheer, two-thousand-foot cliffs of shining granite with waterfalls cascading down from their rims. The Indians called the valley Yosemite, which was also their name for the California grizzly bear, then abundant in the vicinity. News of the fabulous place quickly spread and in 1859, the influential newspaper magnate Horace Greeley visited Yosemite and urged the state to protect it and the giant sequoias nearby.

Concern for wilderness had been escalating for several decades. Explorer and artist George Catlin urged that parts of the Great Plains be declared a sanctuary for bison and the Indian cultures that depended on them, and Henry Thoreau proposed later that each town set aside a virgin forest reserve. Neither idea found much favor, but that of protecting an incomparably beautiful valley and unbelievably big trees in remote mountains in a thinly peopled state did not seem so impractical. In 1864, President Lincoln signed a bill granting Yosemite Valley and the Mariposa Grove of giant sequoias to the State of California "for public use, resort, and recreation." The alternative would have been to grant the land to homesteaders, railroads, or some other private interest for commercial exploitation.

Five years later, three Montana businessmen found another fabled place, one very similar to Jim Bridger's preposterous stories, at the headwaters of the Yellowstone River. It was a rolling plateau the size of a small eastern state, ringed by ten-thousand-foot peaks. On it were lakes, geysers, hot springs, petrified forests, obsidian mountains, and almost every species of game that was already disappearing from the Plains.

A larger group that visited Yellowstone in 1870 was so impressed that its members voted not to file personal claims on the region, but to work for its preservation instead. They wrote letters to eastern newspapers and launched speaking tours. An even larger expedition the next year included an artist and photographer, and their pictures of Yellowstone hung in the Capitol rotunda in Washington that fall. By March of 1872, President Grant had signed a bill establishing a Yellowstone National Park protected "from settlement, occupancy, or sale under the laws of the United States, and dedicated and set apart as a public park or pleasuring ground for the benefit and enjoyment of the people." The bill stipulated "the preservation, from injury or spoliation, of all timber, mineral deposits, natural curiosities or wonders within said park, and their retention in their natural condition."

Yosemite and Yellowstone were something of landmarks for civilization, because they were the first places that a government set aside purely (*almost* purely, railroads interested in promoting tourism having done much of the lobbying for the parks) as *wild* places. European monarchs had preserved lands for hunting, and Asian ones had done so for Buddhist religious reasons, but the concept of wildness as we know it had not really been developed yet. It took the industrial revolution's increasing separation of civilization from wild nature to establish wildness as a distinct, positive value.

Americans liked the idea of Yellowstone and Yosemite parks so much that they quickly created other new national parks under the messianic urgings of romantic naturalists such as John Muir and mountaineering groups such as the Sierra Club. California ceded Yosemite back to the nation in 1890 along with two other Sierra parks, Sequoia and General Grant (later Kings Canyon). Congress created Mount Rainier in 1899, Crater Lake in 1902, Mesa Verde, Glacier, Rocky Mountain, and Lassen in the next dozen years. That all but one of these parks—and most later parks—were in high mountains was no accident.

Creating parks proved easier than preserving their wild condition, however. Some frontiersmen did not stop at the borders of Yosemite or Yellowstone simply because the president had signed a bill. Homesteaders already occupied Yosemite in 1864, and publicity surrounding Yellowstone Park's establishment actually attracted squatters, poachers, commercial fishermen, and herders. Early legislation did not provide funds for the parks' protection, and unscrupulous businessmen schemed to get private control of tourist attractions. The situation quickly became so bad that the U.S. Cavalry had to come to the rescue. The army administered the parks for thirty years, until passage of the National Park System Organic Act in 1916 established for the Park Service that, under the Department of the Interior, cares for the parks today.

Even with a Park Service, wildness continued to dwindle because unadulterated wildness was unacceptable even to many naturalists and conservationists. The Rocky Mountain wolf is a case in point. Wildlife conservationists' chief concern in the early twentieth century was the welfare of big game that was being decimated everywhere in the West except the national parks. They perceived natural predators as threats to big game, and wolves were the supreme predators. The Yellowstone administration began a formal extermination campaign against wolves, and in 1922 the park superintendent observed, "It is evident that the work of controlling these animals must be vigorously prosecuted by the most effective means available." By 1926, the Yellowstone campaign had trapped, shot, or poisoned at least 136 wolves, including eighty pups, and had effectively extirpated the species from the park by the 1950s. Similar campaigns liquidated wolves in other parks and killed thousands of coyotes and mountain lions as well. Mountain lions remain scarce in Yellowstone to this day.

Early park managers fought wildness in a variety of other ways. They suppressed the lightning fires, an important part of the forests' cycle, even though park forests were not a source of commercial timber. Parks were remote and seldom visited then, so they actively encouraged tourism, busily constructing roads and allowing concessioners to build elaborate resort facilities with park timber. Park managers also conducted a number of recreational activities more suited to circuses than to natural areas—flinging bonfires off Half Dome at Yosemite in a kind of woodsy fireworks display and setting up bleachers in Yellowstone so tourists could watch bears feeding at garbage dumps. Powerful economic interests sometimes forced major commercial developments such as the damming of Hetch Hetchy Valley in Yosemite National Park, an area John Muir considered equal in beauty to Yosemite Valley.

Policies began to change in the 1930s, however. The Depression lowered the demand for commercial development of parks. Decades of predator killing and wildfire suppression were having unexpected and ominous results. On the Kaibab Plateau adjacent to the Grand Canyon, where over six thousand wolves, coyotes, mountain lions, and bobcats had been killed, mule deer numbers had increased in two decades from four thousand to a hundred thousand. Deer and livestock overgrazed the Kaibab severely. Without wildfires, trees grew to obscure the views that had made parks famous. More important, the spread of forest into meadows and marshes reduced the food supply of many wildlife species that depended on grasses, berries, herbs, and roots.

The Park Service created a Wildlife Division in 1932 under the direction of biologist George M. Wright. He stopped predator-killing programs under a government policy that stipulated every species should be left to carry on its struggle for existence unaided, as being to its greatest ultimate good, unless there is real cause to believe that it will perish if unassisted. Such policies were slow to penetrate to the local level, however, and predator killing resumed in Yellowstone after Wright's death in 1936. Commercial development of parks continued to increase during and after the Second World War.

In the 1950s, elk became so numerous in Yellowstone that it was

Wyoming bull moose wading in slough.

necessary to reduce the herd by shooting. Public outcry led to the creation of an advisory board to deal with wildlife management problems. In 1963, the board issued the influential "Leopold Report," which strongly affirmed laissez-faire policies toward wildness, recommending that parkland be maintained "as nearly as possible in the condition that prevailed when the area was first visited by the white man." To a large extent, park managers have become committed to this policy, allowing insects and fires to kill forests and predators to kill big game. There still are plenty of forests and game, as well as evidence of elk overgrazing in the Yellowstone backcountry.

A laissez-faire approach has problems, too, of course. Parklands were not untouched by human hands when the white man arrived. Indians managed places such as Yosemite Valley, burning woody undergrowth to promote food plants for game and for themselves. To approximate conditions when the white man arrived, the Park Service must manage such places as the Indians did. It has begun to do so, with encouraging results in Yosemite. Controlled burning of dense, second-growth fir is restoring the open, parklike conditions that the militia found in 1854. Indian techniques can be adapted to modern purposes too. For example, giant sequoias seem to need fire for reproduction, because faster-growing fir and cedar shade out sequoia seedlings. In parts of the Mariposa Grove recently burned by the Service, tiny sequoia seedlings are growing for the first time in years.

Another problem will prove much more difficult to handle. When the white man arrived, the land surrounding today's national parks was wild. Today, most of it is tamed in some way—as farmland, ranchland, timberland, mines, or second-home developments—and park wildlife generally suffers at the hands of commercial development. The Rocky Mountain wolf is again a good example. Much of the pressure to exterminate wolves even in parks came originally from livestock interests concerned that wolves would spread out of such protected areas. These groups are no more enthusiastic about wolves today, although the general public's attitude has become much more favorable to these predators.

Proposals to restore wolves to Yellowstone or other parks still meet resistance, although the Rocky Mountain subspecies is on the endangered list and federal agencies are required to restore it. Evidence gathered from studies of the eastern timber wolf suggests the danger to ranchers outside the parks would be slight. Minnesota wolves coexist with 325,000 cattle and sheep belonging to 12,230 farms, but only about one in every 640 farms loses an animal to wolves in a given year. In Isle Royale National Park in Lake Superior, the only other wolf population in the east coexists with thousands of backpackers and campers who see the wolves only rarely, but can frequently hear their howling.

A laissez-faire policy toward wolves in parks would have its limits. Biologists, having introduced individuals into a park, would monitor them with radiotelemetric collars and use a zone method to manage them and their offspring—different levels of protection would apply to different zones. Biologists would emphasize the maintenance of a viable wolf population in Management Zone One, for which federal lands with little livestock grazing would be suitable. Management Zone Two would be a buffer zone, where maintenance of wolves would be an important, but not primary goal, and where state and federal agencies could control wolf predation on livestock. Management Zone Three would be devoted principally to established human activities and would contain developed land and livestock. State and federal agencies would monitor wolf activity carefully and would exercise controls as needed.

Free from persecution, wolves would probably thrive in large western parks. The magic pack grew from two wolves to over a dozen in two years. There is some concern that they will thrive too much and threaten vulnerable prey species. Wolf populations might grow quickly in the beginning, taking advantage of unoccupied space and abundant prey, but they would probably level off fairly soon because of their own social organization. A wolf pack is a hierarchy in which a dominant pair does not permit other members to breed. Packs claim a lot of territory and exclude strange wolves, so once packs establish themselves, the number of breeding wolves in parks would remain quite small.

Another supremely wild animal may have more trouble surviving in the western mountains than the wolf, even though it is presently more numerous. Between six hundred and nine hundred grizzly bears live in three or four of the lower forty-eight states, although the big bears (adult males average approximately 490 pounds in Yellowstone National Park) have disappeared from most of their former range. Once dominant from the Pacific to the Great Plains and south into Mexico's Sierra Madre, grizzlies survive only in Montana, Wyoming, and Idaho, with a possible small population in Washington's North Cascades. (Like wolves, grizzlies remain fairly common in Canada and Alaska.)

Hunters and stockmen shot grizzlies on sight in national park lands during the early days, but park predator extermination campaigns included neither grizzlies nor black bears. Both were perceived as big game rather than predators (although past and recent studies have shown that individual grizzlies can be efficient and frequent killers of large mammals), and their antics at park dumps amused visitors. They became a major attraction at Yellowstone, second only to geysers, and dump spectators might see dozens of grizzlies in an evening.

Their very popularity ultimately proved bad for the grizzly, however. Bears became accustomed to the human presence at dumps, and to human foods. Because dumps were near visitor-use areas, conflicts between bears and people increased, and when the Park Service tried to resolve them, the bears usually suffered. Rangers stopped the feeding spectacles at dumps in 1942 because visitor use dropped during World War II, and in the year after they had to shoot twenty-eight grizzlies and fifty-five black bears; the animals had become so partial to garbage that they sought it in cabins and campsites once their accustomed supply had ended. When the park closed all dumps in the late 1960s and early 1970s, rangers had to kill many more grizzlies or transplant them out of the park for the same reason. In 1970 and 1971, they "removed" eighty-eight grizzlies from the greater Yellowstone area: killed them or sent them to zoos or Canada.

Outside parks, grizzlies face dangers resulting not from popularity,

"HE IS ABSOLUTELY AT THE MERCY OF THOSE WHO KNOW NO MERCY"

Grizzly bears may have been more numerous than the smaller black bears in Wyoming and Montana before the advent of civilization. Lewis and Clark encountered them regularly while exploring the Missouri River in Montana in 1905. They found so many grizzlies in the vicinity of present day Great Falls, Montana, in fact, that they did "not think it prudent to send a man alone on an errand of any kind."

White settlement brought a very rapid decline in grizzly numbers. Livestock associations and individual ranchers often hired predator control agents specifically to kill all the grizzlies and wolves in their areas. By 1929, naturalist and artist Ernest Thompson Seton, who had studied grizzlies extensively in the Rockies, expressed doubts about the species' survival: "Each year the number of hunters increases; each year more deadly traps, subtler poisons, and more irresistible guns are out to get the Grizzly. He has no chance at all of escape . . . he is absolutely at the mercy of those who know no mercy; and before five years or more, I expect to learn that there are no Grizzlies left in the United States, except in the Yellowstone National Park." The grizzly disappeared from Texas in 1890, California in 1922, Utah in 1923, Oregon in 1931, New Mexico in 1933, and Arizona in 1935. A grizzly killed in Colorado's San Juan Mountains in 1979 may have been the last survivor in that state. Two years of intensive field work failed to find evidence of another Colorado grizzly.

The present verified range of the grizzly bear in the coterminous United States encompasses about twenty thousand square miles in four ecosystem areas: the Yellowstone ecosystem in Wyoming and Montana; the northern continental-divide ecosystem in northern Montana (including Glacier National Park); the Cabinet Yaak ecosystem in northwestern Montana and northeastern Idaho; and the Selkirk Mountains ecosystem in northern Idaho and extreme northeastern Washington. Grizzly populations may exist in two other lower-forty-eight areas: the North Cascades in Washington and the Selway-Bitterroot ecosystem in Idaho.

Adapted from "The Grizzly Bear," by Chris Servheen, *Audubon Wildlife Report*, 1985.

Grizzly.

but from a lack of it. They have learned to avoid people in the last century and a half of persecution. But because they are so large, they have no innate fear of other animals, even humans; they attack instinctively on occasion, and so they inspire great fear. Thus people kill grizzlies every year, although the federal endangered species list has identified the species as threatened since 1975 in the coterminous United States. Montana still allows sport hunters to kill grizzlies in limited numbers, but there and elsewhere the illegal kill is much greater. Black-bear hunters kill some grizzlies through error, and other people undoubtedly kill them deliberately, simply from dislike or because the hides and paws are valuable on the black market. Cars hit bears, some bears eat poison baits, and still more meet other accidental ends.

At least 179 grizzlies died from human-related causes in the Yellowstone ecosystem (that is, the park and the wildlands around it) from 1970 to 1984. If the grizzly were a numerous and fast-reproducing species, this would not seem a great many, but the Yellowstone ecosystem's grizzly population numbers only about two hundred. Female grizzlies don't start to breed until they are about six years old; then they bear an average of 1.9 cubs every two to three years, many of which die from various causes before they reach breeding age. Biologists fear that continued uncontrolled mortality may mean a gradual slide into oblivion for the Yellowstone grizzlies.

As with other threatened species, there is a good deal of disagreement about the grizzly's plight and what should be done about it. In 1979, the United States Fish and Wildlife Service proposed to designate "critical habitat" for grizzlies (that is, habitat that the agency would manage, to promote grizzly restoration), but quietly dropped the proposal after it met extensive opposition at public hearings. The agency presently manages grizzlies with a zone system similar to that described for wolves.

Biologists have been studying grizzlies intensively since the Craighead brothers pioneered radiotelemetric tracking of wildlife during a Yellowstone bear study in the 1950s and '60s. They have learned much about how grizzlies live: how they mate and raise their young; where they den; what they eat. Yet the size and ruggedness of the range, and the complexity of grizzly behavior, have made study difficult.

Researchers will need to study further before they learn enough about grizzly habitat needs to allow land managers to identify and protect the main feeding areas. After human-caused mortality, getting enough food is the main problem grizzlies face. The bears must eat enormous amounts to lead their strenuous lives and to accumulate fat for winter hibernation, which lasts from October to April. Although

LIVING WITH GRIZZLIES

Human-related disturbance of grizzlies can take two forms. One is habitat and ecological disruption caused by logging, oil development, housing subdivisions, developed campgrounds, and livestock grazing. The other is behavioral disruption resulting from helicopter flight patterns, recreational use of grizzly habitat, roads, and such. Ecological disturbance changes the availability of resources, while behavioral disturbance changes the bear's use of resources. Ecological disturbance can be a long-lasting or permanent change, while behavioral disturbance is usually transient.

At present, we know little about grizzlies' abilities to change learned habitat-use patterns in response to disturbance. Some evidence suggests that bears living in disturbed areas have learned to adapt their own activity so that they avoid humans. They are most successful at doing this if human activity is predictable. Grizzly mothers living in disturbed areas may teach their cubs behaviors that tend to reduce conflict with humans.

Grizzlies can also adapt to humans in a harmful way, becoming used to finding food in dumps, camps, and cabins. Such bears lose their wariness of man, which not only endangers people, but usually leads to the death of the bear.

Adapted from "The Grizzly Bear," by Chris Servheen, *Audubon Wildlife Report*, 1985.

This grizzly family appears unperturbed as visitors watch from shuttle buses.

they eat almost anything edible, from insects and wildflowers to moose and other grizzlies (roots, berries, grasses, rodents, and fish are the staples), they may struggle to find enough even under wilderness conditions. Most bears travel long distances every year to a wide variety of seasonal food sources, learned from their mothers or from individual experience. Some of these sources are in parks, some outside. More than half of the Yellowstone ecosystem is outside the park. When oil-exploration teams, strip mining, second-home developments, clear-cutting, and road building disturb the feeding habitat (48 percent of national-forest land adjacent to Yellowstone is currently leased or under lease application by oil companies), individual bears may find their ranges insufficient.

In one sense, it is a good thing that the grizzly situation is so complicated. It would be simpler, after all, if grizzlies survived only in Alaska. Still, the situation places a heavy burden on conservation agencies, which must try to educate the public and regulate its use of bear habitat at the same time they try to learn what grizzlies need to survive. The Park Service must maintain bear habitat *and* make that habitat accessible to the public as well as the bears. The situation is worst in the greater Yellowstone area, because the grizzly population there appears to be isolated, unlike the population in Glacier National Park. If the Yellowstone grizzlies die, none will come from Canada to replace them.

Because they too are surrounded by development, other national parks suffer problems similar to Yellowstone's grizzly situation. Grizzlies were extinct in California national parks by the 1920s, but conflicts between visitors and black bears remain a problem. Bears that have lost natural timidity rob camps with a reckless bravado that would be comic if not for its potential for tragedy to bears and humans. In eastern parks such as the Great Smoky Mountains, black bears survive precariously on shrinking and isolated habitats, while visitors are so numerous that they regularly cause traffic jams on park entrance roads.

Like bears, national parks are threatened by their very popularity. Annual visits to Park Service-administered areas increased from 30 million in 1950 to 280 million in 1984, and people increasingly come from Europe and Japan to see American parks. Of course, the system has also grown, presently comprising 334 areas, yet only forty-eight of these are designated national parks. The rest are national monuments, recreation areas, preserves, seashores, or historic sites, areas which generally are smaller and enjoy less protection than parks. Creating new parks in the lower forty-eight states is much harder than it was in the nineteenth century because there is less suitable land. The land for Yellowstone and Yosemite was in the public domain; it belonged to the government. New parks must be purchased, which is difficult even in the best of times and more so in times of budget deficits.

In 1980, the Park Service published a report that listed seventy-three kinds of threats to the units it administers, including air pollution, water pollution, wildlife loss, overcrowding, and mismanagement. A survey found that every unit in the system was subject to many threats, an overall average of twenty-three per unit, to be exact. The most popular parks, such as Yosemite and Yellowstone, had twice the average number of threats.

Threats to park wildness don't always come from outside the parks. At Yosemite, the park concessionaire tried to turn Yosemite Valley into a convention center in the 1970s, advertising as follows: "This

HIGH-COUNTRY HIBERNATORS

The grizzly bear is one of two brown-bear subspecies native to North America: the other subspecies is the Kodiak bear of Kodiak, Shuvak, and Afognak islands off the Alaskan coast. Brown bears also live in Europe, North Africa, and Asia. The grizzly is characterized by a humped shoulder, a somewhat concave face, and long, curved front claws. Color varies, but the long guard hairs often are lighter at the tips, giving the bear a silvery or grizzled color, and thus its name.

A grizzly bear's home range may be among the largest of any land mammal. In exceptional cases, adult males may range over some 1,100 square miles. Home ranges typically include spring, summer, and autumn feeding habitat, and winter-denning sites. Food and habitat availability determine movements between parts of the range. In mountainous areas, grizzlies often use low elevations for spring and late-autumn feeding, and high elevations for summer feeding and winter denning.

Grizzlies hibernate in winter. Lower-forty-eight bears don't eat, drink, urinate, or defecate during the entire four and a half to five months they spend on average in their dens. While hibernating, they undergo reductions in heart and metabolic rates and slight reductions in body temperature. Bears are sensitive to noises and changes in their surroundings throughout hibernation, and are easily aroused. They usually dig their own dens, but some individuals use natural caves. In Montana and Wyoming, den sites usually are above 6,500 feet, facing north, where enough snow lasts throughout the winter to cover and insulate the den entrances. Females give birth in the den in January. The cubs spend the next few months nursing on the hibernating mother, then emerge with her in spring. Cubs usually stay with the mother for two full summers, and den with her twice. They learn many of the food habits and behaviors they will use throughout

GRIZZLY BEAR RANGE

■ Present distribution
□ Historical distribution

GRIZZLY BEAR RANGE IN THE LOWER 48 STATES

North Cascades
Cabinet Yaak
Selkirk Mountains
WASH.
Northern Continental Divide
OREGON
Selway Bitterroot
MONTANA
IDAHO
Yellowstone Nat'l Park
WYOMING

isn't No Man's Land. Or Primitive Wilderness. This is Civilization." Public opposition stopped the convention center, but Yosemite Valley already contains a level of urbanization that many find excessive. At Yellowstone, a seven-hundred-unit, three-restaurant hotel complex called Grant Village sits in the heart of the park, on Yellowstone Lake,

adulthood during this period. There is much speculation about how dependent young grizzlies are on maternal training for such critical information as habitat use and response to humans.

Adapted from "The Grizzly Bear," by Chris Servheen, *Audubon Wildlife Report*, 1985.

Three-month-old grizzly-bear cub.

Grizzly-bear sow and five-month-old cub.

near important trout-spawning streams, a source of grizzly food.

Park wildness does have legislative allies. As with the Forest Service, the 1964 Wilderness Act allows the Park Service to propose, and Congress to designate, large areas as off-limits to development. The 1965 Land and Water Conservation Fund provides funds from the sale of offshore oil leases for the purchase of private holdings in existing parks and land for new ones. The 1906 National Antiquities Act allows the president to create by proclamation national monuments or historical areas on government land. Congress, which alone can create parks, created some of our greatest—Grand Canyon and Glacier Bay, for example—by upgrading them from national monuments.

Such laws can do little about the kinds of outside pressures that threaten Yellowstone's grizzlies, however. As a result, there has been some re-evaluation of the national-park concept. Parks originally were conceived as museums, in a sense, places where the wild past could be preserved. Even the forward-thinking Leopold Report had a curatorial side in its insistence that parks be kept in or restored to a pre-settlement condition. Parks aren't museums, though. The organisms in them are alive, and never remain quite the same.

Living ecosystems always evolve in response to environmental changes, and national parks are no exception. They change as their surroundings change; thus we cannot maintain park wildness without maintaining some wildness outside parks. This isn't easy to do, because it goes against the legal, political, and economic habits of civilization, which has prospered by dividing land into separate, often mutually exclusive uses. Yet the only alternative is to allow human influence to gradually destroy the most valued aspects of parks. The effects of that influence may be indirect and unintentional, but are as harmful as deliberate vandalism in the long run. Within decades, Yellowstone could be without either geysers or grizzlies, as bear-killing and geothermal developments outside the park drain off the regenerative capacities of both.

Conservationists increasingly are trying to manage parks not as separate museums but as parts of larger ecosystems. The zone system of protecting threatened species such as wolves and grizzlies is an example of this approach. A phased transition from full protection in a park through partial protection in buffer zones to little or no protection in exterior zones allows more scope for natural wildlife dispersal than a single boundary line. Yellowstone National Park lends itself particularly well to the ecosystem approach because millions of acres of national-forest wilderness buffer it on the east, north, and south, providing year-round range for much (if not all) of its wildlife.

Yet even the Yellowstone ecosystem is somewhat isolated, and it may not be enough to support grizzlies indefinitely. Certainly, the Yellowstone grizzlies would benefit if bears from the larger population farther to the north could migrate there; this would avert inbreeding. In the long run, parks will work best not as separate blocks of wildness, but as particularly beautiful and interesting spots along corridors of wildness that run throughout the land. (Unfortunately, this concept comes too late for Yellowstone's grizzlies: if they are to maintain genetic vigor, we need to augment their population with intentional transplants.)

This really is what parks have been all along, particularly pristine spots in corridors of mountains or other wildlands that run through tamed country. We just haven't noticed it, because the other parts of the corridors—the national forests, BLM lands, and private rangelands—have remained wild enough to minimize conflicts between wildlife and civilization. This is less and less the case, however, and only a good deal of work will keep park ecosystems intact. Some of this work is being done already: conservation agencies have cooperated to an unprecedented degree on grizzly-bear management, and at least one oil company has hired a biologist to try to avert habitat destruction during oil exploration.

Despite its weaknesses, the national-park idea is very popular with conservationists worldwide. Other countries began borrowing it almost immediately: Australia, Canada, and New Zealand had parks based upon the American model by 1900, and Sweden and Switzerland established the first European parks in 1909 and 1914. Many countries started park systems in the 1930s, and after the Second World War the movement accelerated as former colonies showed an interest in preserving their native flora and fauna. From 1972 to 1982, thirtynine countries started park systems, and the number of parks and protected areas worldwide increased from 1,584 to 2,618.

As in the United States, many or most of the world's parks are in mountains, for similar reasons—the romantic impulse to set aside "sublime" scenery, and the economic impulse *not* to set aside arable land. Almost every major mountain range in the world contains national parks today. In the more populous temperate countries, parks tend to be in mountains simply because those are the only places that don't have settlements in them. This has led to an over-representation of peaks, snow, and conifers in parks overall, but in most countries mountains support at least some of the wildlife that has disappeared from adjacent lowlands. As in the United States, bears are conspicuous inhabitants of temperate mountain parks: European and Asian brown bears (close relatives of grizzlies), Asian black bears, and, best-loved "bears" of all, the giant pandas of western China's Hsifan Reserve.

In tropical countries, mountains sometimes are better suited to settlement than disease-ridden lowlands. Historically, most of the populations in countries such as Guatemala, Peru, and Mexico have lived in highlands. This makes the establishment of mountain parks in the tropics even more important, because some of the most beautiful and threatened tropical wildlife live in mountains. The only South American bear, the spectacled bear of the Andes, has become quite rare. The cloud forests of Central American volcanoes contain many endangered species such as the resplendent quetzal, a long-tailed green and red bird sacred to the ancient Maya. In Africa, equatorial volcanoes harbor the mountain gorilla. In Asia, the Himalayas are the last refuge of the snow leopard.

National parks worldwide face the same threats as American ones. In older countries of Europe and the Far East, much mountain terrain has already suffered from centuries of logging, overgrazing, mining, and wildlife decimation. Extractive uses may be so firmly established that nations must continue to tolerate them after establishing parks. For example, mountainous but overpopulated Japan has more than twenty national parks that take up a larger percentage of its land surface as compared to the land-park ratio in the United States, but only a small percentage of Japanese parklands meet United Nations criteria for protection from human activities. A walk through one of Japan's larger parks reveals much beautiful scenery, but also high-rise resort hotels, dams, and such a high level of visitor use that trails may be impassably muddy or crowded. Many countries are trying to restore damaged ecosystems, however, by terminating inappropriate uses and restoring extirpated wildlife.

Younger countries have an advantage in that more of their land is closer to being pristine. But they must move quickly to maintain it and to convince rapidly growing populations of the need for parks. In times of worsening economic conditions for much of the Third World, most countries simply don't have the money to establish park services equivalent to those of the United States, and parks without staff or facilities aren't really parks. Even new parks, when developed and protected, face the danger of becoming wild islands constantly eroded by encroaching development.

The universality of such threats has caused a greater emphasis on a global approach to park conservation. Mountain ranges don't stop at national borders; nor do air, water, or wildlife. Because national borders often correspond with thinly populated regions such as mountains, adjacent countries have many opportunities to coordinate park systems, as the United States and Canada have begun to do with the Wrangell-Saint Elias and Kluane complex on the Alaska-Yukon border. Of course, not all nations are on as generally cordial terms as are Canada and the United States. Still, no nations have gone to war over national parks as yet, and human populations as well as wildlife benefit from the open spaces of buffer zones.

THE
DESERTS

THE GRANITE SLOPES above the canyon look bare from a distance, and bone dry even in the cool of the morning. Closer, plants become visible—spiky ocotillos and cholla cactuses that look more like torture instruments than green growing things—but the ground between them is bare except for a few dead grasses and wildflowers. It is late April in Arizona's Sonoran Desert, but it hasn't rained for a month, so the spring flowering is over.

Cactus wrens make harsh, grating calls that seem appropriate to the chollas in which they perch. Black-throated sparrows sing sweetly, however, and mourning doves and mockingbirds calling from farther down the canyon suggest that this might be somebody's backyard instead of a desert. Their presence here seems reasonable, for of course the birds can fly; the canyon still appears too harsh for any four-legged creature except a lizard or kangaroo rat. Then the illusion of desolation dissolves as a group of sand-colored mammals appears at the rim of the canyon.

They are bighorn sheep, two lambs and three ewes. They pause awhile, looking into the canyon, but see nothing threatening. They start down the slope, even the two-and-a-half-month-old lambs jumping from boulder to boulder with complete assurance, as though they have suction cups on their hooves. (In fact, bighorn hooves are slightly concave, allowing the sheep to run up precipitous slopes.) What they want in the apparently barren canyon is hard to see. They seem to wander at random, but wild animals seldom do that. The bighorns are moving toward the most important thing in their daily lives.

Desert bighorn.

It doesn't look like much when they reach it: an algae-clogged pool of tepid rainwater trapped in a deeply shaded granite basin. Yet the pool, which formed during winter rains and will probably continue to hold water until late summer thunderstorms replenish it, is the only water within two day's walk, and the bighorns cannot live without it for more than a couple of days in the heat of spring and summer. It is central not only to their lives, but to the lives of every kit fox, bobcat, and jackrabbit in the vicinity, not to mention birds, insects, and other creatures. The sheep can get adequate moisture from green vegetation during rainy times, so they need the pool less than the predators. They cannot metabolize water from dry seeds, however, as kangaroo rats can, or spend hot months dormant underground as do desert tortoises, so they have to drink.

The ewes are tired after hours of scrambling over boulders, so they stand and rest awhile before drinking. The lambs are not tired, and they butt each other playfully and make absent-minded attempts to nurse, which the ewes evade stolidly. They have been living on dry fodder for weeks now, and their milk is giving out. It is time for the lambs to learn to eat what desert bighorns eat in summer: prickly pear, yucca, saltbush, brittlebush—plants with names that describe their texture aptly. Few animals can survive on poorer forage than sheep. The only other large mammals in the area are wild burros, whose ancestors served prospectors in the old days, and a small herd of prong-horns, which seldom ventures into rocky canyons.

Desert bighorns are the best-adapted native hoofed animals in North American deserts. A herd lived in virtually every desert range on the continent when Europeans arrived. Yet desert bighorns belong to the same species as bighorns that inhabit the lush Rockies and Sierra Nevada. The desert sheep are smaller and lighter-colored than others, and their habits and diet are quite different. If a Rocky Mountain herd were transported to the Sonoran Desert, it almost certainly would not survive, and vice versa. Still, the two could interbreed easily (bighorns can also interbreed with domestic sheep), indicating that they are very similar genetically, that relatively little separate evolution has occurred.

The basic similarity between desert bighorns and mountain big-horns says something essential about deserts, the roughly 12 percent of the world's land where fewer than ten inches of rain fall annually. Life adapts to deserts with surprising ingenuity, but only up to a point. Desert bighorns get water differently than mountain bighorns, but they don't use it differently. They use about as much water to carry on the basic cellular processes of life as a sheep in a lush mountain meadow. In this, desert bighorns are like every other desert organism, from cacti to kangaroo rats. Desert organisms *cannot* use less water for basic bio-chemical cell processes than nondesert ones, because water is the basic compound of earthly life. Exposed to full desert heat, most desert ani-mals die quickly; they survive by evading heat and conserving moisture.

There probably have been deserts since life began, but desert organisms do not have the long evolutionary pedigrees of forest life, or even grassland life. Most desert plants and animals today, like bighorns, have ancestors and relatives in nondeserts. Species of cacti live in tropical forests; species of kangaroo rats live in grasslands. There always is something marginal about desert life, because an absence of water *is* life's margin. Toward the centers of the Earth's driest deserts, the Sahara and Atacama, there is very little life at all.

Deserts have existed since life began because the physical causes of deserts have existed that long, although erratically. The planet's turbulent atmospheric and geological movements generate deserts as inexorably as they do mountains. Indeed, mountains are among the major causes of deserts because they act as barriers to the movement of moisture-laden oceanic air over continents. Air holds less moisture as it cools, and mountains force air upward, cooling it and making it lose moisture as rain, snow, or mist. After crossing mountains, the descending air warms and loses little moisture, so desert may result, as it has west of the Rockies and east of the Sierra Nevada.

Most, but not all, of the world's great deserts lie behind mountains. The normal movement of the Earth's atmosphere also creates dry places. Solar energy heats air at the equator, making it rise and lose moisture, creating tropical forests. Then this air fans out to the north and south and descends, causing belts of low rainfall just outside the tropics. The hottest and driest deserts lie along these belts; even within this zone, however, desert formation usually requires some other factor, like mountains. Some deserts exist because deep ocean trenches (caused by movements of the Earth's crustal plates) lie just offshore of lands within the subtropical arid belts: deep ocean is much colder than shallow seas, and cold water evaporates less than warm water. The coastal desert of Baja California is an example.

Because deserts depend considerably on mountains and ocean trenches for existence, they tend to be short-lived by evolutionary standards. Our knowledge of their past is correspondingly limited. Ancient desert fossils exist (including those of dinosaurs caught in sandstorms and mummified so perfectly that their skin texture is preserved), but there is no continuous fossil record of desert evolution as there is of forest or marine evolution. As with mountains, the desert environment discourages formation or preservation of fossils.

Contemporary deserts are surprisingly recent. Fossil evidence shows that the American Southwest was covered with grasslands, pine forests,

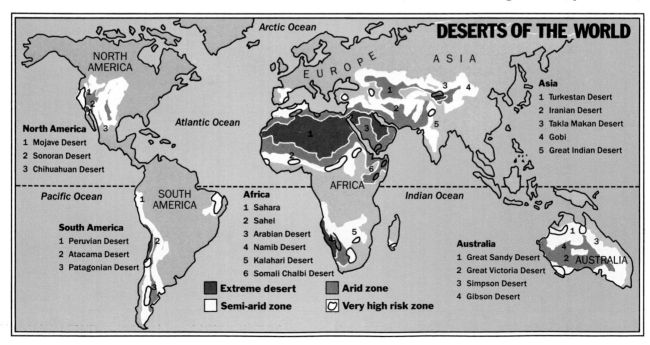

DESERTS OF THE WORLD

North America
1 Mojave Desert
2 Sonoran Desert
3 Chihuahuan Desert

South America
1 Peruvian Desert
2 Atacama Desert
3 Patagonian Desert

Africa
1 Sahara
2 Sahel
3 Arabian Desert
4 Namib Desert
5 Kalahari Desert
6 Somali Chalbi Desert

Asia
1 Turkestan Desert
2 Iranian Desert
3 Takla Makan Desert
4 Gobi
5 Great Indian Desert

Australia
1 Great Sandy Desert
2 Great Victoria Desert
3 Simpson Desert
4 Gibson Desert

Extreme desert   Arid zone
Semi-arid zone   Very high risk zone

and huge freshwater lakes a mere fifteen thousand years ago. Eight-thousand-year-old rock paintings in the presently almost lifeless central Sahara show giraffes, ostriches, and antelope, indicating that the area was once savanna. Of course, specialized desert organisms such as cacti and kangaroo rats probably couldn't have adapted to aridity in only fifteen thousand years, so there must have been deserts long before the present ones. We may never know much about them.

Deserts probably existed during early human evolution, and small hominid populations perhaps lived in or around them. Humans don't have much physiological adaptation to severe water scarcity, and they must drink large amounts to maintain normal body temperature in desert conditions. Still, grassland adaptations such as the ability to cool the body by sweating would have made desert life more feasible for hominids than for apes. By historical times, at least, hunting-and-gathering peoples inhabited many deserts.

Like Arizona bighorns, early humans adapted to desert largely by knowing their home ranges so well that water, shelter, and food sources were always available, no matter how severe the climate. During World War II, Australian aborigines proved more effective at finding downed airmen in desert than search planes. Humans also made technological adaptations, of course. Kalahari bushmen carried and stored water in ostrich eggs. Domestication of livestock allowed herding peoples to survive in deserts by ranging even more widely in search of water and forage. After 500 B.C., increased use of camels opened the driest parts of North African and Middle Eastern deserts to nomads.

Hunting and herding peoples could adapt to desert as they found it, but farmers could not. Yet the richest of early agricultural civilizations eventually developed in desert or semidesert regions. Desert soils often are quite fertile, because rains don't leach nutrients away and winters in the subtropical arid belts are mild. Deserts can bear abundant crops if watered, and people began to discover this as the Sahara was drying out six thousand years ago. Egyptian civilization began at roughly the same time, based on crops both irrigated and fertilized (with silt from yearly floods) by the Nile. Similar farming civilizations also developed in the Tigris, Euphrates, and Indus valleys, and in Mexico and Peru.

Irrigation produced unprecedented amounts of food, enough to support leisure classes of aristocrats as well as specialists such as artisans and priests. It also required an unprecedented control over nature. Humans had to maintain irrigation canals, dikes, and ditches carefully, working harder to maintain them the more elaborate and efficient they became. In premechanized civilizations, large populations of laborers did the work, requiring large bureaucracies to keep them in order.

NATIVE AMERICAN DESERT CROPS

The Hopi, Papago, and other Southwestern Indian tribes grew a variety of crops in the desert with little or no irrigation. These included desert-adapted varieties of corn, beans, potatoes, peppers, melons, and squash, as well as other plants: Sonoran panicgrass, amaranth, and devil's claw. The Papago tribe of southern Arizona alone grew at least nineteen kinds of domesticated plants and, as late as 1926, were cultivating fourteen thousand acres by traditional methods.

University of Arizona botanist Gary Nabhan has studied the ways Indian crops survive in their harsh environment. Like desert wildflowers, most mature quickly, passing through their reproductive cycle while moisture from infrequent rains remains in the soil. Some corn and bean species germinate so vigorously that farmers can plant them deep in sandy soil, where the sun's heat doesn't desiccate them. Some plants can carry out photosynthesis and respiration under conditions so dry that most other crops lose their leaves, wilt, or wither. During extreme drought and heat, these plants rotate their leaves to reduce the chances of sunburn.

Although Native American agriculture has dwindled under the influence of modern civilization, many gardeners, farmers, and scientists have revived interest in it. Much of the interest is stimulated by the recognition that modern crop varieties require too much water to be economical in the Southwest. In the last dozen years, farmers have abandoned 20 percent of Arizona's cultivated land because of the high cost of pumping irrigation water.

Adapted from "Saving the Bounty of a Harsh and Meager Land," by Noel Vietmeyer and Terrence Moore, *Audubon*, January 1985.

Such a system has considerable vulnerability to natural and social disruption. Destruction of canals during spring floods may result in the loss of a year's harvest, which may mean that not enough grain remains both to feed laborers and to plant next year's crops, giving rulers a choice between famine and revolt. More insidiously, continued irrigation can destroy soil fertility. With traditional methods, most of the irrigation water applied to a field evaporates in the desert sun, leaving dissolved salts in the soil. If farmers allow these to accumulate—and only proper drainage methods will flush them out—the soil eventually becomes too salty for crops.

Irrigation civilizations thrived for thousands of years and produced large cities, Ur and Babylon for instance. By the beginning of the Christian era, however, mercantile powers of the temperate zone had largely superceded them. Babylon and Ur were in ruins, victims of soil salinization and foreign conquest. Egyptian cities persisted because

Nile floods maintained soil fertility, but they were vassals of Rome. Despite cultural and political resurgence under the Arabian and Ottoman empires, the desert civilizations never really regained economic supremacy, perhaps because irrigation methods remained essentially unchanged.

In the nineteenth century, industrialization began to revolutionize irrigated farming, particularly in the American Southwest, where desert valleys, never irrigated heavily, retained fertility. The Hopi, Papago, and other native tribes were skilled farmers, but on a small scale, working village plots individually or cooperatively. American pioneers tried to settle desert valleys on a similar small scale at first. Highly cooperative groups such as the Mormons succeeded, but the average homesteader lacked the skills and capital to practice irrigation farming on the few hundred acres granted by Congress.

Desert farming fell into the hands of large landowners, and because even large landowners didn't have the capital to build reservoirs and canals to supply water, government subsidy increased. In a way, this was a return to the ancient system, but the technology of modern governments was vastly superior to that of ancient ones. After the 1902

Dumont Dunes in California.

Newlands Act authorized a Reclamation Service to provide irrigation water to farmers, it rebuilt natural drainage in the West into a water-supply system of dams, reservoirs, canals, wells, and pipelines. This rebuilding accelerated during the New Deal projects of the 1930s, and in the two decades from 1950 to 1970, the system grew so fast that it doubled the amount of water available to Southwestern communities.

Providing water and electricity for urban as well as agricultural growth, federally subsidized water development created what amounts to a new form of civilization. Ancient desert cities had to stay close to rivers and oases, but with the automobile and with electric power pumping water from hundreds of feet underground or over mountain ranges, modern cities have spread across the desert as never before. They simply draw water from farther and farther away as they grow: Los Angeles extended its pipes first to southern California's Owens Valley, then to the Colorado River, then to northern California's rivers. With irrigation costs subsidized (farmers paid about a fifth of the costs of their water in 1982), farmers continually irrigate more land. Growing cities attract factories and energy-development projects, like the power

Feral burros in Death Valley, California.

BIGHORNS AND LIVESTOCK

Competition for forage and water between livestock and desert bighorns began with the arrival of the Spanish in the Southwest in the late 1700s, and it reached a peak about 1900, following rapid development of ranching. Feral burros were introduced in the same period. Although domesticated for thousands of years, burros originally evolved in arid regions. When domesticated burros escaped, or when prospectors released them into the wild, they thrived, having managed to survive for thousands of years in the presence of humans and diseases of other livestock species.

Extensive field studies support the view that competition from burros for food and water can be detrimental to desert bighorns.

plants that burn coal strip-mined in Arizona and Utah and sell the electricity to Los Angeles.

The effects of this unprecedented growth on desert wildlife have also been unprecedented. Although ancient irrigation civilizations exterminated crocodiles, lions, and hippopotamuses and other big game in valleys, they did not affect outlying desert ecosystems greatly. Wolves, leopards, and many species of antelope remained common in the Middle East. Civilization's new mobility has made the most remote desert vulnerable to change.

Most desert organisms are so specialized for survival in arid surroundings that they cannot hang on along the edges of irrigated land, as forest or grassland wildlife live along fence-rows or field margins. They simply disappear. Crops, lawns, and golf courses have completely replaced Joshua trees, saguaro cactuses, elf owls, and kit foxes on thousands of square miles of the Southwest. In other areas, development has preempted or destroyed water resources on which wildlife depended. Stream diversion and groundwater pumping have turned riparian thickets and spring-fed wetlands into dry gulches and salt flats.

Burros can be quite destructive of native desert vegetation, particularly shrubs and small trees such as paloverde. In one study, vegetation within a burro-free enclosure in Death Valley National Monument had 73.8 plants per square meter, compared to 26.7 outside. The ratio of dead shrubs outside to dead shrubs inside was 27 to 1.

Competition for forage between desert bighorns and domestic or feral animals is especially intense during summer, when bighorns confine themselves to ranges within a few miles of water. If livestock or burros remove preferred forages, they force bighorns to eat less nourishing plants. Competition for water is also most severe during the dry summer months. Desert bighorns in midsummer may wait for more than an hour for other sheep to leave before getting a drink at a spring. If domestic livestock or feral burros also are competing for this water, the effects can be detrimental.

Adapted from "The Desert Bighorn," by Allen Cooperrider, *Audubon Wildlife Report*, 1985, and "Horses, Asses, and Asininities," by Ted Williams, *Audubon*, September 1985.

Sonoran desert vegetation in bloom.

Many native desert fishes are extinct or endangered; the droll little pupfish, for instance, which survived the drying up of ancient lakes by adapting to pools and streams as salty as seawater or as hot as bathwater.

Desert wildlife may be threatened even where civilization's effects appear negligible. The remoteness of a desert bighorn herd's range may not be sufficient to protect it, for the meagerness of the herd's water supply makes it extremely vulnerable to disturbance. A single miner or flock of domestic sheep may be enough to exterminate a bighorn herd by cutting off its summer water or forage supply. The herd would have to cross dozens of miles of unfamiliar country to find another source, and highways, pipelines, canals, and fences make such journeys increasingly difficult.

Even before the modern boom in the Southwest, relentless hunting and susceptibility to the diseases of domestic livestock threatened desert bighorns. Although they began to be protected from hunting around 1900, the population was down to no more than 8,100 by 1960, a small fraction of the estimated 500,000 to 1 million that once had inhabited the Southwest. Bighorns still have a wide distribution, from Mexico to Nevada and Utah, but many desert ranges that once supported them are empty.

Motorized civilization has overrun southwestern deserts so completely that not only wide-ranging big game is threatened. The desert tortoise, one of the commonest small desert animals, has shown alarming population drops in the past thirty years.

Desert tortoises are especially well-adapted to their environment: they once occurred in densities of several hundred per square mile over much of southern California, Utah, Nevada, and western Arizona. In a few places, as many as two thousand tortoises inhabited a single square mile; pioneers and prospectors saw twenty to thirty tortoises in half an hour while crossing such areas.

Tortoises have adapted to desert by being slow. They spend the cold winter and the hot summer months asleep in burrows they dig in sand or loose earth. They are active in spring and fall, when winter rains or late-summer thunderstorms foster the grasses and wildflowers they mainly eat. During these feeding times, they store water and fat on which they live during dormant periods in their burrows. Their storage system is so effective that tortoises can live through occasional drought years, during which they virtually never emerge from their burrows because there is nothing to eat. Their leisurely lives may last sixty to eighty years, in the course of which they reach a maximum length of fourteen inches.

Being slow has its drawbacks, however. Tortoises are slow breeders, reaching sexual maturity only when fifteen to twenty years old. Females lay at most a dozen eggs a year, and only two to five hatchlings in a hundred survive to breeding age. This was a good arrangement as long as tortoises were abundant, but more and more vehicles crisscrossed the desert, including General Patton's tank corps during World War II training maneuvers, crushing many tortoises or burying them alive. Livestock ate much of the forage on which tortoises depend, and thousands of tortoises also ended in pet shops and collector's backyards.

Tortoises have disappeared from some areas today. In others, their density has fallen so low that probably too few breeding females remain to maintain the population. Many of these populations will probably die off within a few decades. Utah's tortoises have been listed as threatened under the Endangered Species Act, and other populations may not be in any better shape.

Even cacti are disappearing from the desert in places. Not only did development and overgrazing destroy many, but self-proclaimed plant lovers have decimated the bizarre plants. Cacti became fashionable ornamentals in the 1970s, and a profitable international trade in rare and unusual species developed. Many state and federal laws protect cacti from illegal collecting, but such laws are difficult to enforce because cacti live in remote areas; moreover, rare plants are not a high priority with law enforcement. In fact, judges tend to be lenient toward most wildlife offenders, even though poachers and other offenders occasionally murder rangers and wardens.

The contraband cactus boom seems to have declined in the 1980s,

Desert tortoise eating wildflowers, Joshua Tree National Monument, California.

but at its peak it was enormously destructive. Japanese and European enthusiasts stripped hills and islands bare of rare species and smuggled specimens home by the thousands. A California nursery was reported to have illegally received sixteen thousand plants of one threatened species. In the Big Bend region of Texas, dealers collected half a million plants a year from one stretch of private ranchland; an estimated ten million cacti were shipped from Texas alone in 1977. Most died before they even got to nurseries and department stores.

The Smithsonian Institution recommended listing seventy-two species of cacti as endangered or threatened. The Endangered Species List now includes some species, but the protection this gives them is limited because rare cactus populations are tiny and scattered, probably known best by the very collectors who threaten them. Survival of such species will probably continue to depend as much on the goodwill of plant fanciers as on conservation laws. Collectors have shown an increased willingness to buy nursery-propagated specimens instead of wild ones, however, and projects for restoring some decimated wild populations are under way.

Having contributed to the decline of tortoises and cacti, the new desert civilization has begun to show some vulnerabilities of its own. Until quite recently, new reservoirs and canals continued to increase the water supply in the Southwest, allowing it to keep ahead of problems, like soil salinization, that plagued ancient civilizations. Problems grow more complex, however. Unless properly disposed of, pesticide residues and other modern pollutants in groundwater can come to the surface along with salts if the water table rises.

Civilization is now using most of the water in the Southwest. The best dam sites are already developed, and the major water source, the Colorado River, is so heavily exploited that it sinks into the ground miles short of its former mouth on the Gulf of California. At least river water is renewable, descending from melted Sierra Nevada and Rocky Mountain snows. Desert groundwater is often a remnant of the more humid climate of fifteen thousand years ago. Once pumped out, nothing replaces it, and ground level sinks in consequence, dozens of feet in parts of the Southwest.

Even where water is left for development, there may not be money. Inflation has made dams and canal systems many times more expensive than they were in the 1950s and '60s, and the taxpaying public is increasingly reluctant to subsidize them. Not only is the federal government deep in debt, but the northern industrial region that generated much of the tax money for Southwestern water development has declined, partly because so much industry has moved to the subsidized Southwest.

If it is to avoid the fate of its ancient predecessors, modern desert civilization might follow the tortoise's example—it might learn to slow down and use water more efficiently. The only time a tortoise wastes water is when someone frightens it by picking it up. Then it voids the water in its bladder; otherwise it retains the water until dry times, when the body reabsorbs it. The tortoise also conserves water by spending most of the day in its burrow, where humidity is high and it loses little moisture through evaporation.

Humans can't hope to imitate the tortoise's physiological adaptations, however convenient that might be, but they can adapt technology to conserve water. Industry now finds recycling water cheaper than meeting Clean Water Act standards for water discharged into the environment. United States industry already recycles water an average of three times during manufacturing processes, and it may use less water by the year 2000 if it meets pollution-control goals. Reclaimed wastewater still represents only 0.2 percent of annual United States water use, however. Most towns and cities do not recycle wastewater, but use conventional sewage treatment and disposal methods.

If towns can't use water as efficiently as tortoises, they can at least conserve water by adapting behavior to desert realities. Having begun to do so in the past decade, Tucson, Arizona has reduced per capita water consumption by over 20 percent. In the 1970s, projections of customary water use showed that the city would not be able to meet peak summer demands in the 1980s unless it invested 145 million dollars in new pipes and wells. Instead of simply building to meet demand, however, the city decided to manage its appetite for water. It asked residents not to water lawns more often than every other day, and not during the hottest part of the day. It also encouraged landscaping with native plants as an alternative to lawns. Combined with water-price increases, these measures reduced peak-period water use by 26 percent from 1976 to 1984. Tucson's average daily per capita water-consumption rate is about 140 gallons, whereas that of another Arizona big city, Phoenix, is about 220 gallons.

Farming uses water even less efficiently than towns because much irrigation water simply evaporates. Flooded-field irrigation, an ancient method still in wide use today, may lose over 50 percent of water to evaporation. But more precise ways of delivering water to crops can increase efficiency: drip irrigation, which makes use of perforated plastic pipes at or below ground level, can reduce water use to 40 to 60 percent less than traditional methods. It is not without problems though; it flushes soil less effectively than sheet irrigation, for example, and may allow buildup of salts.

Although increasingly used, drip irrigation still serves only a small proportion of United States farmland. Installation is costly, and as long as farmers get government-subsidized water at a fraction of cost, they have little incentive to change over. Conservationists are exploring ways to encourage them to use water more efficiently. Among the more promising ideas are allowing farmers to sell water they don't use to cities and allowing cities to pay for improved irrigation systems in exchange for water, as long as the cities use the water in an environmentally sound manner.

Modern desert farmers could also conserve water by adapting the techniques of native Americans, who farmed successfully with little or no irrigation by taking advantage of every natural moisture source. They planted their crops in washes or other places where occasional rainwater would concentrate, built small dams and dikes to channel and retain rainwater, disturbed soil as little as possible to minimize evaporation, and left some plots fallow every year so moisture would accumulate in the soil. Now, wheat yields increase dramatically when farmers leave fields fallow every other year and when they minimize tilling, and agronomists can engineer fields to channel and retain moisture.

Native Americans also planted varieties of corn, beans, squash, and peppers that were drought-resistant, and here once again is a lesson for modern farmers: conserve water by growing crops that use less. Modern breeding techniques can increase plant tolerance to desert conditions—dryness and salt. Some crop plants that probably evolved in arid regions are already resistant to salt and drought, like the Saudi Arabian barley, beets, cotton, spinach, asparagus, and date palms that grow in water too salty for drinking. Wild desert plants have potential to become valuable new crops. Guayule, a Southwestern shrub, has been a source of synthetic rubber for decades; more recently, farmers have grown another desert plant, jojoba, to produce an industrial lubricant of such high quality that it replaces the oil of the endangered sperm whale.

Water conservation reduces demands on surface- and groundwaters so that springs and streams keep flowing, to the benefit of bighorns, quail, pronghorns, and other game. Wildlife also benefits more directly from the efforts of wildlife agencies, which have developed backcountry springs and pools to provide a more reliable water supply. The agencies can build small concrete dams to create seasonal rain pools, and make the collected water last even longer by letting it flow into metal tanks that supply water to drinking troughs. With such techniques, these agencies can cause springs, once seasonally dry, to provide year-round water. A half-inch of rain can supply a year's water to bighorns.

Even municipal wastewater can benefit wildlife. In the late 1960s, water from a treatment plant near Las Vegas was made available to the local bighorns, and their population increased from 80 to 240 in a few years, allowing managers to transplant some of the herd to abandoned ranges. Partly because of such water conservation developments, the United States desert bighorn population has increased to about nine thousand in recent years.

Water conservation doesn't automatically help wildlife, however. To the extent that conservation allows civilization to keep expanding, it may be just as harmful to desert flora and fauna as cross-country motorcycle races and dune buggies. So far, cities that conserve water, like Tucson, have not changed the patterns of uncontrolled growth that forced them to conserve. Water and wildlife conservation must be integrated, and this is a complicated thing to do. Desert aquifers

THE LIMITS TO TUCSON

The Tucson Chamber of Commerce expects that city to roughly double in size within the next twenty-five years. Tucson depends on a groundwater aquifer for its municipal water supply, and it is pumping more of that water from the ground than is being replaced by natural recharge. It has been doing so since 1940, and at current rates of depletion, the aquifer will be gone in about a century.

Conservationists are concerned that Tucson's recent emphasis on water conservation is directed more to sustaining its rapid industrial and residential growth than to consideration for the long-term quality of life in the region. They fear that Tucson will someday be a huge city without trees or gardens, because all the water will have been committed to new growth instead of to the needs of existing residents.

Tucson hopes to ameliorate its water supply problems by importing water from the Colorado River, 330 miles away, for which purpose the massive Central Arizona Project is designed. Yet Colorado River water is already heavily diverted, and there is growing opposition to the Central Arizona Project because it will cost 3.5 billion dollars to finish (only 40 percent is completed). Even if the project is completed, overdrafts of Tucson groundwater will continue. Meanwhile, the intimacy with a highly diverse desert landscape of saguaro cactuses, ocotillos, and paloverdes that made Tucson attractive to many newcomers is gradually disappearing.

Adapted from "The Tucson Paradox," by James R. Udall, *Audubon*, January 1985.

The desert landscape surrounding Tucson, Arizona is gradually disappearing as the area is urbanized.

are far-reaching and unpredictable phenomena: drilling irrigation wells in a valley can cause distant mountain springs to dry up. In deserts as in other places, wildlife conservation generally requires leaving as much land as possible in an undisturbed state.

Parks and refuges came late to deserts, not, as with prairie, because they were considered too valuable, but because they were considered too worthless. Most of the American desert was never even homesteaded: when Herbert Hoover tried to give it to the states in 1929, they refused. As one governor said, they already had enough desert. Yet desert "worthlessness" proved advantageous to conservationists, as

---

AN ENDANGERED CACTUS

The Knowlton cactus is a tiny plant, its globular, gray-green stems ranging from 0.3 to 2 inches in height. Cloaked with white spines, the plant blends with surrounding rocks and scarcely protrudes above soil level for most of the year. From mid-April to early May, however, it bears yellow-centered pink flowers, generally bigger than itself, which make it more conspicuous. The only known viable population of Knowlton cactuses in the world is on a single hill in northwestern New Mexico, an area of about twelve acres covered with pinyon pines, junipers, and sagebrush.

The Knowlton cactus is named after its discoverer, F. G. Knowlton, who brought it to the attention of science in 1958. From 1965 to 1979, cactus fanciers collected the Knowlton cactus so enthusiastically that the number of individual plants dropped to one hundred. Plants that grew in a few other localities may have been completely wiped out. By the late 1970s, some collectors thought that the species was extinct in the wild. As collectors turned to propagation, pressure on the wild population is thought to have lessened. Seeds in the soil germinated, and the species recovered to an estimated nine thousand individual plants by the mid-1980s.

In an attempt to ensure that collecting or other factors will not decimate the species again, public and private conservation organizations are cooperating to establish other populations of Knowlton cactus in protected areas.

Adapted from "The Knowlton Cactus," by Peggy Olwell, *Audubon Wildlife Report*, 1986.

Knowlton cactus.

notions of natural beauty expanded beyond the mountain lake and snowy peak—most desert remained in the public domain.

Using the 1906 National Antiquities Act, various administrations proclaimed millions of acres of the finest desert scenery and vegetation as national monuments, including Death Valley, Joshua Tree, Saguaro, and Organ Pipe Cactus. Congress created a smaller number and acreage of national parks such as Grand Canyon, Big Bend, and Capital Reef; and various governmental entities set aside sizable wildlife refuges, largely for pronghorns and bighorns, such as Kofa, Cabeza Prieta, and Charles Sheldon. There is potential for sizable new parks in the desert. A 174,000-acre Great Basin National Park has been proposed for Nevada, which contains the largest proportion of federal desert land. A new Mojave Desert National Park has been proposed for California, and Death Valley and Joshua Tree national monuments may be enlarged and upgraded to park status.

The Bureau of Land Management is responsible for most desert land, and it has historically favored livestock and mining interests over wildlife. Although the 1976 Federal Lands Policy and Management Act directed the BLM to manage land for wildlife conservation as well as other uses, funds available for such management have been a small fraction of the bureau's budget. The 1976 act also required the BLM to inventory its lands for possible protection under the Wilderness Act, an enormous potential considering that such lands encompass 284 million acres, an eighth of the United States. By 1983, however, the BLM had recommended only about 24 million acres for study as possible wilderness. Like the national forests, BLM desert lands are under growing pressure for various kinds of development.

Volunteers have done much of the wildlife conservation work on BLM lands. A southern California group contributed over 11 thousand person-days of labor and 170 thousand dollars' worth of other goods and services to bighorn conservation from 1969 to 1982. Also in southern California, concerned citizens and a private conservation group, The Nature Conservancy, have cooperated with the BLM in establishing a preserve for desert tortoises on land that supports the highest density of tortoises known to remain, about two hundred per square mile.

The BLM built a woven wire fence around some thirty-eight square miles of public and private land in the Mojave Desert, which kept livestock and off-road vehicles out while allowing tortoises and other wildlife to come and go. Residents helped to develop visitor-use facilities, including self-guided interpretive trails and a small nature center. The Nature Conservancy is trying to assure the preserve's viability by purchasing private inholdings. On a spring morning in the preserve, when tortoises are active, one can see a dozen or so in a few hours' walk, as well as burrowing owls, zebra-tailed lizards, antelope ground squirrels, Le Conte's thrashers, and other desert creatures.

The idea of desert preserves came to the rest of the modern world even later than it did to America. Traditional desert cultures did have conservation systems for water and grazing land. In Arabia, the hema system, which had existed since before the time of Mohammed, set aside areas where controlled grazing assured forage for military and royal camel herds, and protected reservoir systems. After motor vehicles replaced camels, however, the hemas were opened to general use. Within a decade, overgrazing and resultant soil erosion caused silting and flooding of ancient dams and water conservation channels. At the same time, hunters pursued desert wildlife such as the white-and-black banded Arabian oryx (a large species of antelope) in jeeps with mounted machine guns, exterminating that species in the wild.

When the United Nations published international lists of parks in the 1970s, few desert areas were included. The Arabian countries had no parks at that time, and the few parks in the Saharan region were in coastal mountains. Israel had a number of small parks, mostly

Sand Dunes National Monument in Colorado.

located in the well-watered north of the country. South American countries such as Argentina and Chile had parks in the Andes, but not in their extensive desert regions, although very significant desert organisms live there. Only Australia had made a substantial commitment to desert conservation, having placed thirteen million acres of its central desert in parks and preserves. One of these, the Tanami Desert Sanctuary, contains over nine million acres and is four times as large as Death Valley National Monument.

Desert parks may seem redundant at a time when desertification of grasslands is a spreading problem. Desert wildlife doesn't necessarily benefit from desertification, however, as the fate of cacti, bighorns, and tortoises in North America shows. The overgrazing that causes desertification is just as destructive to desert plants and animals as it is to grassland ones. Today, moreover, overgrazing is usually combined with development involving heavy motor-vehicle use, from which desert vegetation is particularly slow to recover. The roads, spoil heaps, and garbage of the past century of mining remain conspicuous in deserts throughout the world. And modern, large-scale mining pollutes and depletes desert water and even air, as the Four Corners strip mine and power plant complex, which has clouded once-crystalline air in the Navajo country, demonstrates.

Traditionally, of course, people have seen deserts as undesirable wastelands. In the climate of technological optimism following World War II, many expected them to disappear rapidly, transformed by irrigation water from ocean desalinization projects or the diversion of arctic rivers. This largely hasn't happened; the energy and construction costs of such grandiose developments may be beyond the means of even the richest nations, and environmental costs would also be high. The Aswan Dam allowed Egypt to greatly increase its irrigated land, but like many other vast projects that have been completed, it had an undesirable side effect: it ended the Nile floods that had fertilized fields automatically for six millenia.

Meanwhile, desert parks have become vastly popular with the highly mobile population of the American Southwest. This hasn't always been to the benefit of deserts crisscrossed by off-road vehicles and marred by vandals and illegal collectors. It does show that the future of deserts may rest in their recreational, scientific, and aesthetic values. Desert nations such as Saudi Arabia have shown increasing interest in establishing park systems in the past decade. Recently, a herd of Arabian oryx, which had been maintained in the Phoenix, Arizona, zoo since the species became endangered in the wild in 1962, was returned to its native habitat in the Arabian peninsula.

T H E
POLAR REGIONS

ALTHOUGH IT IS EARLY JUNE, there are still patches of snow in shady spots among the low range of hills. The snow isn't left over from the winter, though; it fell in mid-May. The hills are a few miles from the Arctic Ocean in Canadian tundra, and spring snow is common. Despite the snow, grasses and wildflowers cover the stony ground, and stunted willow bushes are leafing out in moist places. Since the hills are above the Arctic Circle, it never gets dark in June, and plants can grow all the time once spring sunlight thaws the upper inches of soil.

At first, the place seems devoid of animal life, then there is a flash of white against a gravelly slope and a stout, robin-sized bird appears. It has evidently descended from the sky, but so quickly and quietly that it seems to have come out of nowhere. The bird has a pale orange breast like a robin's (although its bill and wings are longer), and it begins to run over the gravel as self-assuredly as a robin explores a backyard. The bird appears so familiar with the desolate hills, in fact, that it is hard to believe it has just arrived from the other end of the earth, ten thousand miles to the south.

This is a red knot, one of the fourteen species of North American shorebirds that nest in the Arctic and winter in the Southern Hemisphere. A few days before, he was on Delaware Bay, where he had gorged for two weeks on the eggs of spawning Atlantic horseshoe crabs, replacing the fat he had burned during a five-thousand-mile oceanic flight from the southern Brazilian coast. That flight had taken him thirteen days, five days of flying and eight days of rest stops; in that time, his weight had dropped from eight ounces to four. Even Brazil wasn't the beginning of his migration: he started over a thousand miles south on the eastern shore of Tierra del Fuego, a desolate place somewhat like this Canadian tundra.

If the knot is exhausted by his epic journey, he doesn't show it. He gives a low, two-syllable whistle and teeters over the rocks, looking for caterpillars and fly larvae. He doesn't find many; most of the insect hordes that will cloud the tundra in a few weeks haven't hatched yet. But after the horsehoe crab eggs, he isn't excessively hungry anyway.

There is a certain urgency about the knot's movements though. He is in peak breeding condition. He has about two months to find a female, attract her, mate with her, and then help her incubate the four eggs she will lay in a leaf-lined nest among the pebbles. When they hatch, he will lead the chicks to the shores of a valley lake where there is abundant food, and he will guard them for the two to three weeks they need to learn to fly. Then it will be time to fly south again, and the knot will leave the chicks alone behind him, their mother having already flown south herself.

Abandonment of inexperienced young would of course be extremely cruel in human parents, but one can't blame the knot, because that is exactly what his parents did to him two years before, and what all knot parents do. He lingered with the other fledglings at the lake for another two weeks after his father's departure, until early frosts began to reduce the food supply. Then one day he simply began to fly south himself, along with the other fledglings, eventually following roughly the route across two hemispheres that his parents had taken, even though they had given him no instructions (at least, none that we know of) on how to do it.

This completely instinctual intercontinental migration is one of the greatest mysteries of animal behavior, and it is linked to one of the most mysterious environments on Earth. The birds' migrations halfway around the world to nest or winter on barren northern or southern coasts seem likely to have originated at least partly because those coasts are uninhabitably cold for insect-eating birds most of each year. Yet we know very little for certain about how those coasts got that way or how the tundras and glaciers that presently cover about 20 percent of the continents originated.

We take for granted that the north and south poles are ice-covered, and that the lands around them are so cold that subsoil is permanently frozen. This is a fairly recent state of affairs by evolutionary standards, however. Fossils indicate that before about ten million years ago, temperate forests of sequoia, Norfolk Island pine, and southern beech covered the Antarctic continent. Temperate forest also grew from Alaska

FUELING A LONG MIGRATION

Red knots make some of the longest migrations known to science, and in recent years they have been intensively studied in both the New and Old Worlds. Some knots fly nonstop across two to three thousand miles of water at high altitudes, crossing these distances in an estimated fifty to eighty hours. Other shorebird species also make world-wide migrations to get from traditional wintering grounds in the Southern Hemisphere to suitable breeding habitat in Alaska and the Canadian Arctic.

The majority of shorebird species migrating between North and South America tend to congregate in enormous numbers at relatively few staging areas along their routes. In some cases, up to one-half a species' population may gather at a single site, attracted by predictably abundant but ephemeral food sources. While at stopover areas, shorebirds feed intensively, sometimes doubling their weight in less than two weeks. The accrued fat then metabolizes during flights to successive staging areas, sometimes a thousand or more miles away. Estimates suggest that half, and in some cases perhaps 75 to 80 percent, of individuals of ten to twelve species use one or the other of two major North American spring stopover areas—a single site at Cheyenne Bottoms in Kansas and a scattering of feeding places on the mid-Atlantic coast. Similar places exist on the West Coast. These areas will need protection if large numbers of shorebirds are to survive.

Vast numbers of shorebirds depend on an area on Delaware Bay, where millions of horseshoe crabs come ashore in spring to lay their eggs. As the crabs move over the sand, males scrambling over females, the knots, sanderlings, turnstones, and other shorebirds hurry to fatten on the eggs so they can be on their way north in time to establish nesting territory. Bayside development is moving southward fast from Atlantic City, however, and the state of New Jersey, interested companies, and birding organizations are working to acquire the area so the shorebirds can be saved.

Adapted from "Red Knot," by Brian A. Harrington, *Audubon Wildlife Report,* 1986.

Red knots.

to Greenland and Siberia, and the Arctic Ocean was open water. Even two million years ago, the northern polar regions were at least much warmer than they are presently, since polar bears and other specialized arctic fauna hadn't evolved yet.

The poles then are not cold simply because they are at the ends of the Earth, but for another reason or reasons of which we are unsure. We do know that the past few million years' polar cold are not unprecedented in the Earth's history. Fossil and geological evidence suggests that there were major glacial periods over two billion years ago, and that there has been one such period roughly every two hundred million years for the past billion. This periodicity suggests to some scientists that polar cold may have a cosmic origin, occurring when our solar system is farthest from the center of the galaxy during some two-hundred-million-year rotation cycle. Others think polar cold may arise from changes in solar radiation, from wobbling of the Earth's orbit, from changes in ocean temperatures, or from changes in the Earth's atmosphere because of increases in volcanic ash particles or decreases in carbon dioxide gas. Yet none of these theories has been proved.

Whatever its origins, polar cold has had profound effects on life during its latest occurrence. (As with desert life, we know almost nothing about cold-adapted organisms that might have existed during previous episodes.) On the Antarctic continent, wholesale glaciation virtually extinguished land life, except for invertebrates, lichens, and mosses. The only large animals able to breed inland in the Antarctic are emperor penguins, which trek for miles to reach nesting colonies. They refrain from eating for months, as they incubate their eggs on their feet to protect themselves from subzero air and ground temperatures. The penguins do not eat, of course, because there is nothing for them to eat away from the coast.

In the Northern Hemisphere, the effects of polar cold were equally catastrophic, although more varied. At least four times in the past two million years, vast ice sheets advanced and receded over the continents. Land life was extinguished wherever these ice sheets extended, but the sheets didn't cover as much land as they did in the Antarctic, so life adapted. Animals either migrated south every year to avoid frozen winters, as shorebirds did, or evolved ways to survive the winters, as did snowshoe hares, lemmings, ravens, snowy owls, wolves, caribou, musk oxen, and a surprising variety of other creatures, some of which live everywhere in arctic lands except on the remaining ice sheets.

Even where ice covered everything, as in Antarctica, life adapted to chilly surrounding waters, often extremely rich with nutrients from upwelling currents. Unicellular marine algae bloomed abundantly during long polar summer days and fed great swarms of small marine animals. Emperor penguins could incubate their eggs without feeding for months because they were so well-nourished on fish and krill (shrimp-like crustaceans) from offshore waters. Flightless penguins seem comically awkward on land, but swim gracefully through water with flipper-like wings. They spend long periods on the open ocean and can leap from the water as nimbly as dolphins to escape the killer whales and leopard seals that prey on them. Dozens of other bird species adapted to the Antarctic margins—fulmars, petrels, skuas, albatrosses—an estimated hundred million birds in all.

Whales, seals, and other marine mammals attained unprecedented diversity and specialization in the rich polar waters and occupied every niche of marine and coastal environments. In the Antarctic, crabeater seals and baleen whales fed on krill; Weddell seals, fur seals, elephant seals, dolphins, pilot whales, and sperm whales fed on fish and squid; and leopard seals and killer whales fed on penguins, fish and smaller seals. In the vicinity of the Arctic Circle, northern species and subspecies of whales and fur seals lived similarly, while walruses and sea otters probed the sea bottom for molluscs and sea urchins, Steller's sea cows munched kelp, and penguin-like auks and auklets fished the open North Atlantic. Many species of hair seals (the same group as the Antarctic crabeater and leopard seals) frequented the ice floes, where the largely aquatic polar bear hunted them. The white bears spent most of their lives on the pack ice of the Arctic Ocean, even bore young there, females digging dens in floes and spending winters suckling their tiny cubs as the ice drifted.

Land plants had more difficulty adapting to polar cold than animals because they could not keep from freezing by metabolizing the tissues of other organisms. They had to photosynthesize their own food, which is difficult in an environment where the sun doesn't shine for many months of the year. As long as the poles were temperate in climate, large trees presumably survived sunless winters by going dormant, but they could not survive permanently frozen soil or constant below-zero temperatures. The plants that survived had shallow root systems and adapted chemically to resist frost damage—small conifers, willows, and alders, a wide variety of low shrubs, herbs, and grasses. They survived in the Arctic, that is. The Antarctic continent has only two species of terrestrial higher plants today. Aquatic algae such as kelp and diatoms flourished in the long summers, however, and provided the photosynthetic base for animal food chains.

This land of big animals and tiny plants was far from humanity's biological origins in tropical forest and savanna, and humanity came to it very late. There is no evidence of people living in the polar regions before the last glaciation, which began about eighty thousand years ago. Humans crossed into Alaska on a Bering Strait land bridge as long as forty thousand years ago, but most of them seem to have hurried south, if the rapid occupation of the rest of the western hemisphere is any indication.

Native peoples we associate with the Arctic today, such as the reindeer-herding Chuckchees and Lapps of Siberia and Scandinavia, and the seal-hunting Inuit (or Eskimo) of North America and Greenland, may have developed their unique cultures only in the past ten thousand years. The kayak- and dog-sled-using Inuit culture, which has fascinated Western civilization since discovery of the New World, didn't become prevalent across the western Arctic until the twelfth century A.D. Inuit colonization of Greenland succeeded where medieval Scandinavian colonization failed: the Inuit had a much better polar technology than the Europeans at that time.

Of course, humans became acquainted with polar cold long before they colonized the shores of the Arctic Ocean. Not by choice, however: the cold came to them in the form of continental ice sheets. Northward spread of *Homo erectus* and early *Homo sapiens* must have been stopped many times by glacial episodes, as warm grassland and woodland turned into cold steppe and muskeg. Cultures gradually adapted to the cold and so, to some extent, did physiology. The stocky, massive Neanderthal subspecies of *Homo sapiens* probably was cold-adapted: all animals lose less heat as they become more massive, because large bodies have much lower ratios of surface to volume than small ones of similar shape. Neanderthals certainly hunted animals typical of the Arctic—reindeer and musk oxen—although they lived in what we today call central Europe. The cave-painting cultures that followed the Neanderthals specialized even more in reindeer.

Yet polar cold seemed distant and alien to the civilizations that developed after the ice sheets receded. The Arctic was little more than legend to people of the classical world—a realm of darkness, ice, and strange beasts. But at least they had evidence that it existed: traders occasionally brought walrus ivory, polar-bear skins, and other goods southward. The Antarctic was completely cut off from other continents by a belt of open ocean, where gales were more or less the norm because there was no land to slow winds and currents (these latitudes are known now as the "roaring forties" and the "filthy fifties").

As trade and industry expanded in the late Middle Ages and Renaissance, however, civilization discovered the wealth of polar wildlife. Explorers sought a northwest passage through the New World to Chinese markets, and returned with stories of beaches covered with seals and walruses, rocks covered with birds and their eggs, and bays crowded with whales. Europeans had exploited whales commercially since Basque fishermen had learned to catch plankton-feeding right whales in the thirteenth century. (Plankton are floating swarms of tiny crustaceans, fish fry, and other small marine animals.) By the sixteenth century, Dutch and English fleets caught whales as far north as Greenland, rendering their blubber into oil to light the lamps and lubricate the machines of mining, textile, and other enterprises. When right whales became scarce, the fleets turned to seals and walruses, which were even easier to catch, though smaller. All sealers had to do was find the colonies where the marine mammals congregated in the hundreds of thousands to breed and raise their pups. There the seals were quite helpless and unwary, having no natural predators on land; sealers could herd and club them, and easily load a ship to the gunwales with oil. Such voyages were immensely profitable because captains did not even need to carry many provisions. A stop at one of the islands, where great auks nested, provided eggs and salted carcasses; when the sailors reached the breeding colonies, they ate seal meat.

As whales, seals, and auks disappeared from the North Atlantic, the fleets followed explorers elsewhere. Vitus Bering discovered Alaska in 1741, and its fur seals and sea otters quickly became new commodities, for the fur trade which was opening up with China. In the late eighteenth century, the voyages of Captain Cook and other explorers finally began to open up Antarctic waters, where southern fur

Fur seal bull and harem of cows.

seals, right whales, and elephant seals quickly followed their northern counterparts into pelt bales and oil barrels.

The exploitation of the polar regions was probably the single greatest spectacle of commercial wildlife slaughter in history, surpassing in brutality and wastefulness even the bison's swift demise. Hunters killed great auks and Steller's sea cows remorselessly, causing their extinction; they very nearly extinguished sea otters, elephant seals, and fur seals as well. Sealers killed an estimated three to five million fur seals in the Southern Hemisphere alone before the turn of the nineteenth century. First the Russians, then the Americans almost wiped out north Pacific fur seals, whose population fell from about three million to a tenth of that in the first half century of American control of Alaska. As civilization penetrated into Arctic land masses in the late nineteenth century, the slaughter was visited on furbearers and big game, although less systematically, since inland wildlife had less profit potential than seal and whale herds. Even so, trappers, miners, and whalers managed to extirpate caribou and musk oxen from various regions.

Hunters also slaughtered polar-region wildlife far from the poles, during migration. They carried on much fur-seal killing not in breeding colonies, but on the open sea, an especially wasteful practice because they shot females and males indiscriminately, and many simply sank out of sight. After the passenger pigeon's demise in the 1880s, sport and market hunters decimated arctic-nesting shorebirds and waterfowl as the birds concentrated in feeding areas such as Delaware Bay during fall and spring flights. Migrating red knots had been so numerous along the Atlantic Coast before 1850 that nobody ever dreamed of counting them, but by the 1890s they had become hard to find. A species that had been even more abundant, the eskimo curlew, was virtually exterminated, its numbers reduced so much by constant persecution all along its migratory route that its population has never recovered, even though a few individuals may survive.

Despite extinction of some species, however, large animals did not disappear from the polar regions as completely as they did from many lower-latitude forest and grassland areas. Hunters destroyed millions of animals, but not their habitat. Ice-covered lands obviously were unfit for agricultural settlement; so were lands covered with spruce bogs or dwarf birches, although less obviously. There have been many unsuccessful attempts to farm parts of Alaska and northern Canada and Siberia. Endless summer days can produce good harvests of hardy vegetables in Alaska's southern coastal areas and interior valleys, but many factors work against successful agriculture in the far north. Growing seasons are short, soils are thin and acidic, not to mention permanently frozen a foot or so below the surface, and rainfall is scanty.

Much of the polar region would be actual desert if permafrost did not hold moisture in the soil, for very much the same meteorological and geological reasons that produced the Sahara. Air that has risen and lost moisture over the humid temperate zones descends as it passes over the polar zones, and thus produces little precipitation. Two inches of precipitation fall over the Antarctic interior in a year, and that over the Arctic Ocean is not much higher because the cold Arctic waters evaporate little moisture. Areas such as Antarctica and Alaska are ringed with mountains, further excluding moisture-bearing air from their interiors.

The only kind of farming that has been practiced for very long in the Arctic is nomadic reindeer herding on a subsistence basis. The tundra vegetation on which reindeer feed is slow-growing, and thus vulnerable to overgrazing, which is always a danger when animals are concentrated in domestic herds. Eurasian reindeer herding tended to undergo boom and bust cycles of herd expansion and shrinkage because of overgrazing and other factors such as bad weather. When charitable Americans gave reindeer to Alaskan Inuit whose whale and walrus food supply had been commercially destroyed, the herd quickly increased to over a million animals, but then dwindled away because of overgrazing, predation, and interbreeding with native, wild caribou. More recently, entrepreneurs have tried to tame musk oxen and raise them for their high quality wool. The shaggy creatures tame easily enough, but it remains to be seen if trade in their wool will be a financial success.

So polar regions remained largely wilderness, in which wildlife survival usually succeeded commercial exploitation and decimation. Once their numbers fell below a certain point, the survivors of most species simply became too hard to find, although frustrated trappers and fishermen looked very hard for them, surprised by the sudden "departure" of creatures that once had been so easy to kill. Eventually the boats went away, and the survivors began the slow process of restoring their populations on deserted rocks and beaches and in remote ocean waters. Thus elephant seals, fur seals, otters, penguins, and right whales survived in the late nineteenth and early twentieth centuries.

Of course, they wouldn't have survived long if commercial exploiters had descended on them again as soon as their populations had expanded enough to become visible. Civilization changed, however. Petroleum products proved much more efficient industrial fuels and lubricants than oils rendered from whale and seal blubber. Commercial exploitation remained profitable in some trades, like fur, but the old days of unrestricted slaughter were ending: governments slowly realized that conserving wildlife, rather than exterminating it, would yield more revenue in the long run.

This realization first took effective form in a fur-seal treaty signed by the United States, Great Britain (for Canada), Russia, and Japan in 1911. Intended to protect the northern fur seals of the Pribilof Islands off Alaska, the treaty outlawed the pelagic (open ocean) sealing that had decimated the herd, set yearly kill limits, and divided the proceeds among the nations involved. It also limited the kill to nonbreeding males, which reversed the herd's decline; the seals' numbers increased into the millenia again. Unfortunately the nations have not renewed the treaty, and the fur seals are declining again, for reasons that are not well understood. Human depletion of ocean fish stock may be reducing their food supply, and thousands are known to die annually by becoming entangled in commercial fishermen's drift nets.

Unfortunately, the fur-seal treaty was more the exception than the rule for many years. Migratory-bird treaties created in the 1920s helped waterfowl and shorebirds, but the difficulty of getting at most polar species constituted their principal protection. If a commercial exploiter really wanted to get at a particular kind of wildlife, as the Norwegian whaling fleet with its new explosive harpoons wanted to get at Antarctica's blue, sperm, humpback, and fin whales, polar remoteness remained more a hindrance to conservation than a help. Conservation came particularly late to remote Antarctica because no nation really controlled it, although several claimed parts of it. Nobody lived there, and few cared what happened in the region in the first half of the twentieth century. Even after nine nations signed an agreement to regulate Antarctic whaling in 1937, whalers killed 46,039 whales there in the next year alone, the largest number ever.

Conservation was a little easier in the Arctic, at least on paper, because national sovereignty was recognized. Theodore Roosevelt established migratory bird refuges on the Alaskan coast in 1909, and ensuing decades saw the creation of Mount McKinley National Park (now Denali National Park), and Glacier Bay and Katmai national monuments. Canada and the Scandinavian countries set aside Arctic areas, and the Soviet Union established a system of nature reserves in the early 1920s. Yet there was a certain futility about the drawing of park boundaries on largely empty, sometimes even blank, maps. Most of the areas were too remote for either the public to visit or the governments to protect. More important, such areas had the same problem as southerly parks and refuges in being chunks of (supposedly) protected land surrounded by unprotected land.

In 1917, when Congress established Mount McKinley National

Park, such a problem must have seemed highly unlikely. The land outside the park was just as remote as the land inside it. Yet Mount McKinley had even more potential for degradation from outside its boundaries than Yellowstone, because of the harshness of northern ecosystems. Alaska's vegetation is sparser and slower-growing than northwest Wyoming's, so a moose, grizzly, or wolf needs more land for support there. The original park excluded much of the best bear and wolf range around Mount McKinley.

The days of polar remoteness were numbered anyway. Gold miners followed whalers and trappers in ransacking every corner of Alaska and of Canada's Yukon and Northwest territories after the Klondike and Nome strikes around the turn of the century. Copper and tin miners were not far behind. But what really attracted twentieth-century industrial civilization toward the poles was the same thing that had attracted its eighteenth and nineteenth century counterparts—concentrated energy. Coal, petroleum, and natural gas are obviously very different from seals and whales, but for industrial purposes, all are treasure troves of photosynthetically stored solar energy. Geologists discovered every kind of fossil fuel in Alaska early in the twentieth century, and by 1924, the government had already established the Indiana-sized Naval Petroleum Reserve Four on the North Slope.

As long as there was plenty of oil in more accessible places, there was little incentive to seek it among the permafrost and ice floes. Reaching the polar regions kept getting easier, however, and making big oil strikes in the south kept getting harder. During World War II, the AlCan Highway linked Alaska to the lower forty-eight states by land for the first time. In the 1950s, a large oil strike was made on Alaska's Kenai Peninsula; although the area had been a national wildlife refuge since the 1930s, the oil was exploited. In 1968, oil companies made another big strike on the North Slope at Prudhoe Bay, east of the Naval Petroleum Reserve.

Bordering the Arctic Ocean, the North Slope had remained without roads, making it the last truly remote arctic wilderness in the United States. Now oil companies proposed to build a pipeline across the entire state to bring oil from Prudhoe Bay to the port of Valdez, where tankers would take it south. Conservationists feared a repeat in Alaska of the wildlife slaughter that had coincided with the building of railroads through the Great Plains. If a pipeline and the road necessary for its maintenance could be built across the entire state, what would stop pipelines, roads, and other developments from subjecting the entire state to the environmental hazards that made grizzlies and wolves scarce in the rest of America?

Oil companies built the pipeline after Vice President Spiro Agnew cast a deciding vote for it in the Senate, but the surrounding controversy had a positive effect. It brought conservationists together in an unprecedented way around the issue of preserving Alaska's wilderness. An Alaska Coalition—with fifty-three member organizations, including labor and business groups as well as conservation ones—advocated new parks, wildlife refuges, and wilderness areas in the state.

In 1971, two years before final authorization of the pipeline, conservationists succeeded in adding a provision to a bill settling native land claims (claims made during Alaska's passage to statehood). The provision required a study of up to eighty million acres of the remaining federal lands in Alaska for possible inclusion in parks, refuges, preserves, and other national conservation units. The Park Service and the Fish and Wildlife Service had been making surveys in Alaska for decades, with an eye toward saving its most scenic and wildlife-rich parts in the national interest.

Conservationists had created an unprecedented opportunity: to take a preventive, instead of remedial, approach to protecting wilderness. Rather than wait for wildlife destruction to begin and then try to stop it, they could put together a conservation system that would endure as mining, logging, and other development proceeded in the rest of the state.

The Native Claims Settlement Act, under Section 17 (d) (2), gave Congress six years to pass legislation establishing new parks and refuges. This turned out to be a complicated and arduous task that eventually took two years beyond the original deadline. The political climate in the early-to-mid-1970s was unfavorable to large Alaskan parks, so conservationists bided their time, drafting legislation and building a national activist and lobbying network. They were ready when the 1976 elections brought a favorable change in that climate. In 1977, Congressman Morris Udall introduced a conservationist-supported bill to set aside some 115 million acres of Alaska for ecological purposes. Congressional hearings produced a large majority of public testimony in favor, and the House of Representatives passed the bill by a vote of 277 to 31 in 1978. The Senate still had to pass similar legislation, however; that required two more years of debate and legislative maneuvering, as well as presidential invocation of the 1906 National Antiquities Act. (In 1978, President Carter set aside more than fifty million acres of the lands in question as national monuments, to demonstrate his administration's support for the bill.)

President Carter finally signed the Alaska National Interest Lands Conservation Act into law on December 2, 1980. The act placed over one hundred million acres of Alaska under various forms of protection. It established or substantially enlarged sixteen national wildlife refuges and fifteen parks, monuments, and preserves. Denali National Park and Preserve alone gained 3.7 million acres of scenery and crucial wildlife habitat. The act also placed all or parts of twenty-four Alaskan rivers in the National Wild and Scenic River System, and placed over fifty-six million acres of national parks, refuges, and forests in the National Wilderness Preservation System.

The scale of the new Alaskan conservation system created under

ALASKA'S GRIZZLIES

An estimated ten thousand grizzly bears still inhabit most of Alaska, from the arctic North Slope to the relatively mild climate of the southeastern panhandle. This mild, humid climate and an abundance of food allow southern coastal grizzlies to reach enormous size: adult males sometimes weigh as much as a ton. These coastal bears are also called Alaskan brown bears because their fur may lack the grizzled appearance of bears living in the interior.

During salmon runs on coastal rivers, one can sometimes see large numbers of the huge brown bears.

As many as eighty-five, of all ages and sizes, have congregated in a single summer along the McNeil River on the Alaska Peninsula.

Bears as large as these once lived along the Pacific Coast from Puget Sound to southern California, but are now extinct. Establishment of national monuments and national forest wilderness areas along Alaska's coast will help to protect these magnificent mammals. But increased clear-cutting planned for the Tongass and Chugach national forests in the area could have an adverse effect on the bears through direct loss of habitat and silting of salmon spawning streams.

Alaskan brown bear.

the 1980 act is a little hard to comprehend. One could spend a lifetime just getting acquainted with the various land units, which contain highly significant archaeological and geological features as well as ecological ones. The thirty-five land units also contain an enormous variety of ecosystems, from spruce and hemlock rain forest on Admiralty Island National Monument in the southeast, to enormous glaciers in Wrangell-Saint Elias National Park, from vast marshes in the Yukon Delta and active volcanoes in Lake Clark National Park, to sand dunes in Kobuk Valley National Park.

The northernmost unit is the Arctic National Wildlife Refuge, which encompasses over eighteen million acres. Bordering the Arctic Ocean, the refuge is the summer calving ground of the Porcupine caribou herd, which numbers some 170,000 animals. The herd's spring migration from wintering grounds in spruce forests southeast of the refuge is one of the greatest wildlife spectacles in North America. Dozens of shorebird, waterfowl, and songbird species also breed on the coastal tundra, and several hundred thousand snow geese visit the area during fall and spring migrations. Musk oxen, wolves, Dall's sheep, grizzly and black bears, moose, wolverines, arctic foxes, and other species inhabit the refuge year round. A few polar bear females den on the coast (most do so on the pack ice).

Despite its size and distance from civilization, the Arctic Refuge still has potential problems. Most of the Porcupine caribou herd winters outside refuge boundaries. In fact, it winters in another country—

Adélie penguins on iceberg.

NORTHERN WILDLIFE PRESERVES

Alaska and northern Canada are the last places in North America where large populations of wolves and grizzlies can survive. Even there, growing pressure from population growth and commercial development threatens to fragment and reduce wildlife. The sheer size of the parks, wildlife refuges, and preserves set aside under the Alaska National Interest Lands Conservation Act of 1980 makes protection and administration of the areas a problem. Poaching, inappropriate development, and a host of other problems plague the new reserves.

Similar pressures affect Canada's northern wilderness. Massive hydroelectric projects in northern Quebec and northern Alberta threaten to encroach on thousands of square miles of wildlife habitat, including the 17,300-square-mile Wood Buffalo National Park in Alberta, nesting ground of the whooping crane and home of the last wood bison herd, as well as wolves, bears, caribou, and a reported 226 other bird species. The great size of Canada's arctic holds considerable potential for expansion of its national parks system.

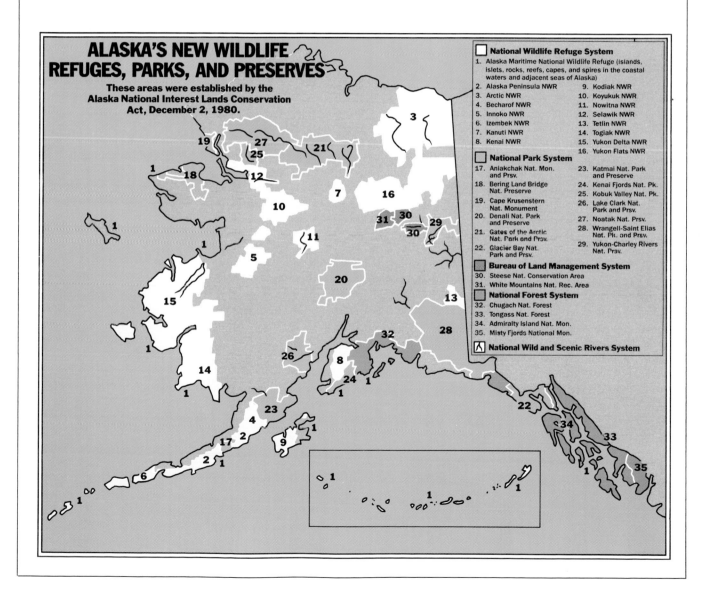

ALASKA'S NEW WILDLIFE REFUGES, PARKS, AND PRESERVES

These areas were established by the Alaska National Interest Lands Conservation Act, December 2, 1980.

National Wildlife Refuge System
1. Alaska Maritime National Wildlife Refuge (islands, islets, rocks, reefs, capes, and spires in the coastal waters and adjacent seas of Alaska)
2. Alaska Peninsula NWR
3. Arctic NWR
4. Becharof NWR
5. Innoko NWR
6. Izembek NWR
7. Kanuti NWR
8. Kenai NWR
9. Kodiak NWR
10. Koyukuk NWR
11. Nowitna NWR
12. Selawik NWR
13. Tetlin NWR
14. Togiak NWR
15. Yukon Delta NWR
16. Yukon Flats NWR

National Park System
17. Aniakchak Nat. Mon. and Prsv.
18. Bering Land Bridge Nat. Preserve
19. Cape Krusenstern Nat. Monument
20. Denali Nat. Park and Preserve
21. Gates of the Arctic Nat. Park and Prsv.
22. Glacier Bay Nat. Park and Prsv.
23. Katmai Nat. Park and Preserve
24. Kenai Fjords Nat. Pk.
25. Kobuk Valley Nat. Pk.
26. Lake Clark Nat. Park and Prsv.
27. Noatak Nat. Prsv.
28. Wrangell-Saint Elias Nat. Pk. and Prsv.
29. Yukon-Charley Rivers Nat. Prsv.

Bureau of Land Management System
30. Steese Nat. Conservation Area
31. White Mountains Nat. Rec. Area

National Forest System
32. Chugach Nat. Forest
33. Tongass Nat. Forest
34. Admiralty Island Nat. Mon.
35. Misty Fjords National Mon.

National Wild and Scenic Rivers System

Canada. That nation has shown a strong interest in protecting the region, having established a three-million-acre Northern Yukon National Park adjacent to the refuge, but this shows that refuges can never really be big enough for complacency. Conservationists also see threats from the American side of the border.

When Congress passed the Alaska Lands Act, it excluded the 1.4 million acres of the Arctic Refuge's coastal plain from the National Wilderness Preservation System. No one knows for sure whether oil exists on the coastal plain, but the area is thought to have the greatest potential for discovery of a major commercial oil field anywhere on-shore in the United States. Oil and gas industries have applied considerable pressure for development there. The roads, pipelines, buildings, air traffic, and human population increases attendant to oil development could have an adverse effect on the Porcupine caribou, the refuge's major wildlife species. Exploration activities in 1984 and 1985 caused some damage to tundra vegetation and disturbed wildlife.

Far-northern wildlife would not be completely safe even if all the area's parks and refuges were inviolate, because many of the animals migrate away for part of the year. When shorebirds such as red knots leave tundra nesting grounds and head south, they face a gamut of

Caribou bulls crossing the Porcupine River on fall migration, near the village of Old Crow, Yukon Territory, Canada.

WOLVES AND WILDLIFE MANAGEMENT

The most controversial aspect of wolf management in Alaska and Canada today is wolf control, the aim of which is to increase big game populations for sport and subsistence hunters. Research in the 1970s indicated that wolves maintain prey populations at relatively low densities, and since then, state and provincial wildlife agencies have carried out expensive and large-scale wolf control programs.

In the past decade Alaska has spent about a million dollars to kill wolves, a cost that exceeds one thousand dollars per wolf killed. Even though reports show that more young moose have survived in some areas, wolf control for the purpose of increasing game species has met heated opposition from conservationists and many professional biologists. Opponents say the policy raises biological as well as ethical questions because research indicates that not only wolves, but also hunting pressures, maturation of forest, weather, and other factors cause low moose populations.

Wolf control programs have often been based on poor data, undermining public confidence in wildlife management. Control methods that managers consider "efficient," such as aerial gunning and poison, are unacceptable to a majority of the public, and wolf control in Alaska is likely to remain a major point of contention.

Adapted from "Gray Wolf," by Rolf O. Peterson, *Audubon Wildlife Report*, 1986.

Arctic wolves.

environmental threats: industrial pollution and condominium development on the coasts of the United States, sport and subsistence hunting in the Caribbean, tourism development in southern Brazil, offshore oil development in Argentina. Almost everywhere, shorebirds face the danger of oil spills from tankers or drilling platforms. Crude oil contaminates their food supply and causes their plumage to lose its insulating properties. The number of places where shorebirds can gather to feed during migration has dwindled steadily over the years as beaches and marshes have been developed.

No drastic decline of shorebirds has been confirmed in recent years, but some water fowl species have declined precipitously. Figures compiled by the U.S. Fish and Wildlife Service show significant losses among several goose species that nest in western Alaska's 19.6-million-acre Yukon Delta National Wildlife Refuge. In the 1960s, there were 140,000 emperor geese, 150,000 Pacific black brant, nearly 500,000 white-fronted geese, and 380,000 cackling geese. By the 1980s, populations of the four species had dropped to about 70,000, 120,000, 100,000, and 35,000 respectively. In the case of the white-fronted and cackling geese, the drop was disastrous. Studies indicate that the geese were being hunted too hard by sport hunters in Alaska, the lower forty-eight states, and Mexico during fall and winter, and by subsistence hunters during the spring and summer breeding season. Mortality was too high for them to maintain their numbers, no matter how much breeding habitat was set aside for them. Continued loss of critical wintering habitat in the West Coast states also contributed to the problem.

Migration to more heavily populated temperate zones isn't the only threat to polar-region wildlife. Polar bears mainly migrate north from arctic lands and spend most of their lives on the Arctic Ocean pack ice in search of hair seals, their main food. The bears are vulnerable in the water, and whalers and sealers shot many in the early days. Until the 1970s, trophy hunters used planes to find them on the ice. The impact of subsistence hunting by the Inuit and other natives has increased since hunters equipped themselves with motorboats, high-powered rifles, and snowmobiles. In the 1950s and '60s, the annual polar-bear kill averaged twelve hundred of an estimated global population of forty thousand bears, a high mortality rate for such a thinly distributed, slow-reproducing species. (Hunters mostly killed large males, however; this is less threatening to the species than if females had died.)

The past two decades have shown that extraordinary creatures such as polar bears don't have to decline before the spread of civilization. Recognizing the growing threats to the bears, the five nations within whose boundaries they occur—the United States, the Soviet Union, Canada, Norway, and Denmark (Greenland)—signed an International Agreement for the Conservation of Polar Bears in 1976. This treaty and the independent actions of these countries have reduced the killing of polar bears. The Soviet Union ended polar-bear hunting

ARCTIC-NESTING WATERFOWL

The vast and remote tundra wetlands of Alaska and northern Canada have long provided secure breeding habitat for a host of swans, geese, and ducks. Well over thirty waterfowl species nest in various parts of the north. Alaska's four species of nesting geese, including seven subspecies, are of particular interest because of their popularity with sportsmen, subsistence users, and other wildlife enthusiasts.

Although most waterfowl habitats in Alaska and northern Canada are still in essentially pristine condition, the future of arctic-nesting geese is becoming precarious. Like other waterfowl, they are limited to specific breeding, molting, migration, and wintering habitats. The demands of growing numbers of people are accelerating the loss of these habitats to drainage, reclamation, and pollution. Meanwhile, the birds are becoming more vulnerable to mounting hunting pressure throughout their ranges.

Adapted from "Arctic-Nesting Geese," by David Cline, *Audubon Wildlife Report*, 1985.

ABOVE: *Whistling swan on nest with cygnet catching mosquitoes off its back, Cape Churchill, Manitoba, Canada.*

LEFT: *Canada goose at nest.*

in 1955, and Norway banned it in 1973. Denmark permits only subsistence hunting of Greenland bears, and requires hunters to use traditional methods. Canada has imposed a quota system, allowing each native village to kill only a certain number of bears each year.

The United States is attempting to manage polar bears under the Marine Mammals Act of 1972, which allows coastal Indians, Aleuts, and Eskimo living within the bears' range to kill polar bears for subsistence purposes only. The act does not regulate subsistence hunting, as Canada and Greenland's laws do, unless the polar bear population can be shown to be depleted. This was appropriate when native populations were small and impoverished, but is not now that industrialization of the Arctic is changing the situation. Snowmobiles, motorboats, and airplanes increase the mobility of hunters and so increase the pressure on bears, especially females, that live closer to coastal areas where most hunting takes place. The annual kill has

MASTERS OF THE POLAR ICE

The polar ice cap is a plate of frozen sea floating 2,500 miles across the north of Alaska, Canada, and Eurasia. The ice cap is not solid: it splits into slabs of a few feet or many miles under the influence of winds, currents, and changing temperatures. The slabs collide until their surfaces are littered with ice rubble. In summer, freshwater lakes spread across the surface of the ice, and larger stretches of open water (called leads) open up between the floes.

Polar bears are the overlords of this ever-moving expanse, occupying the entire sea-ice covered portion of the northern hemisphere. While adult females weigh from three hundred to seven hundred pounds, depending on the season and their reproductive status, adult males are often twice that. A large male polar bear is commonly eight feet or more from nose to tail, stands more than twelve feet tall on its hind legs, and leaves a footprint ten inches wide.

Polar bears evolved from the predecessors of today's brown and grizzly bears between 100,000 and 250,000 years ago, a brief time in evolutionary terms. Although recently evolved, they have changed substantially from their ancestors. Long, gently curved claws—previously used for digging up roots, insects, and small mammals—became short, strongly curved, and very sharp, for clinging to ice and catching seals. Flat cheek teeth—formerly used for grinding vegetation—became sharper and more pointed, for shearing meat, blubber, and hide. Fur density increased, and individual hairs became hollow, providing better insulation against cold.

Adapted from "Polar Bear," by Steven C. Amstrup, *Audubon Wildlife Report*, 1986.

Polar bears.

declined since the 1960s, but Alaskan bears are still the object of concern: arctic industrialization spreads, and the killing of females and their cubs continues without regulation.

Despite such worries, which will probably always attend the protection of such huge but vulnerable animals, the polar-bear treaty shows that there is great potential for international coordination of wildlife conservation in the Arctic. Wildlife will not be conserved at all in the Antarctic without international cooperation, as the nineteenth-century sealers' and whalers' free-for-all showed. Nineteenth-century sealing captains were so unwilling to cooperate with *anybody* that they sometimes marooned their own men on seal islands while they sailed away to market their cargoes of skin and oil. They feared the men would tell other sealers where to find breeding colonies, and they preferred abandoning their employees to months of isolation and semistarvation to the prospect of sharing the seals with other ships.

Fortunately, scientists and adventurers, not market hunters, undertook most of the later Antarctic explorations. These explorers were highly competitive—the Scott and Amundsen expeditions, for example, first reached the pole within weeks of each other in 1912—but they also embraced a strong cooperative ethic when it came to sharing vital supplies. After establishing precedence, these men were willing to acknowledge each other's accomplishments and share scientific knowledge.

Researchers declared an International Polar Year for scientific studies as early as 1882, and another in 1932. During the International Geophysical Year of 1957 and 1958, twelve nations agreed to set up fifty-five scientific observation stations on and around Antarctica, some of them deep in the interior. International staffs manned several of the posts, such as the Antarctic Weather Station; Americans set it up, but scientists from Argentina, Australia, France, New Zealand, South Africa, and the Soviet Union also used it.

In 1962, the cooperative spirit of the IGY led all the nations that had participated, along with several others, to sign an Antarctic Treaty. The treaty nations agreed to use Antarctica and its waters south of sixty degrees latitude for peaceful purposes only, to conduct scientific research freely and to share it openly, to freeze all political claims pending a treaty review in thirty years, and to ban nuclear explosions and disposal of radioactive wastes. The treaty also included recommendations for the protection of wildlife and the setting aside of special natural areas. Further agreements have augmented these recommendations. The Conventions of 1972 and 1980, for instance, concerned management of seals and of marine-living resources (meaning fish, crustaceans, molluscs, and birds).

The Antarctic Treaty has worked pretty well so far, but it hasn't really been tested yet. Pressure for commercial exploitation has not been great except in the case of whales, which Japanese and Soviet factory ships depleted despite the treaty. Commercial pressures continue to increase, however. Antarctica is thought to be rich in petroleum and natural gas: the U.S. Geological Survey estimated in 1974 that accessible continental shelves could contain forty-five billion barrels of oil. The treaty nations, which meet secretly, are believed to be negotiating changes that will permit commercial exploration for fossil fuels after a treaty review in 1992.

If rich deposits exist, how will we determine which nations are to control and benefit from them? Such questions could become difficult. Beyond them, conservationists fear that exploration and oil drilling in the severe Antarctic climate could cause major environmental damage. High winds and icing of superstructures could destroy tankers and drilling rigs, resulting in massive spills. Oil spills anywhere are threatening to wildlife; in icy Antarctic waters, one could be catastrophic. We don't know what the effects would be, since a spill has never occurred. But we do know that a spill would be much harder to clean up in so remote a place, and that bacteria would break down the spill more slowly in such cold water. Much oil might even freeze permanently into pack ice. A tanker spill on the Ross Sea, where much of the oil activity would probably occur, might adversely affect a million square kilometers.

The days of wildlife exploitation in Antarctica are by no means over. Now that most of the great whales are gone, commercial fleets have been turning their attention to the whales' primary food, the shrimp-like krill that feed on marine algae and thus form the basic

Arctic krill from the Bay of Fundy.

link between plants and animals in the Antarctic food chain. Although individually small—the commonest species reaches a length of three inches—krill form dense swarms hundreds of feet across and dozens of feet deep, through which seventy- to ninety-foot-long blue whales graze like cows in rich pasture. One especially large krill swarm occupied more than a square mile of water and extended six hundred feet below the surface. Its weight was estimated at ten million metric tons, about one-seventh of the 1981 global catch of *all* fish species.

Some people have envisioned krill as a major new food source for humans, although nobody seems entirely sure just how people will consume them. We know relatively little, also, about the details of krill life cycles and distribution, which clouds the prospects for their mass exploitation. How much krill we can catch without decimating the swarms is a matter of considerable debate. Nevertheless, nations with large distant-water fleets, such as the Soviet Union and Japan, already catch millions of tons of krill.

If, like other Antarctic fisheries, a krill industry reduces the numbers of its prey drastically, the ecological impact could go beyond anything yet seen there. Because krill are the basic link between plants and animals, their depletion would affect all Antarctic wildlife disastrously, both species that feed directly on krill and those feeding higher up the food chain. The danger would be especially great for threatened baleen whale species—the blue, humpback, fin, and right. Mass starvation would be possible among the minke whale, crabeater seal, and penguins. Observers have noticed further declines in the already shrinking numbers of southern fur seal in krill fishing areas.

Commercial fishermen have exploited the Antarctic since the 1960s, although fish grow relatively slowly in the icy water along its coast. Half of the hundred or so species that live south of the Antarctic Convergence (where warm and cold southern waters meet) don't reach more than ten inches in length. Commercial catches in some areas are already declining, an indication of overfishing.

Resumed exploitation of seals and penguins is also possible. Krill-eating crabeater seals have become so abundant since the depletion of whales (they number thirty million, according to estimates, half the population of all seal species) that some nations are considering possible economic uses for them. Not having rich coats like fur seals or great masses of blubber like elephant seals, crabeaters were never a major commercial species. Commercial possibilities for penguins were dubious, although hunters killed hundreds of thousands for the small amount of oil they provided during the sealing days. In the early 1980s, one Japanese company reportedly considered making gloves from penguins.

Considering the potential for environmental havoc and international strife, one wonders if the rapid, wholesale commercial exploitation of Antarctica would be worthwhile. An alternative does exist. Conservationists have sought for some years to make Antarctica the first world park, thus carrying the international implications of the national-park concept to a logical conclusion. If the local environments outside park boundaries affect the management of parks, then in the long run, the global environment affects their management as well. Antarctica, which astronauts say is the most striking feature that an outer-space view of Earth provides—a great white lantern illuminating the Southern Hemisphere—seems an excellent place for the first application of this principle.

Many nations might have to forego some economic benefits if Antarctica is allowed to return to its original abundant, if frigid, wildness, but none would really be harmed because Antarctica is outside their boundaries. The benefits of scientific research and tourism could continue unhindered by oil spills or strip mines; so could Antarctica's highly significant role as a monitoring station for the global effects of pollution and exploitation elsewhere. In a sense, Antarctica *has* been the first world park since signing of the 1962 Antarctic Treaty. And this arrangement has worked very well.

Representatives of eighty nations attending the 1972 Second World Conference on National Parks called on governments to establish Antarctica as a world park under United Nations auspices. In 1975, New Zealand, one of the countries with territorial claims in Antarctica (the others are Australia, Argentina, Chile, China, France, Norway, Poland, the Soviet Union, the United Kingdom, and South Africa), indicated a willingness to drop its claim if the Antarctic Treaty nations establish a world park there. The other nations never responded formally to the proposal, however, so New Zealand withdrew its offer. In 1982, delegates attending the Third World Conference on National Parks in Bali raised the possibility of a world park in the Antarctic, and the Nairobi Conference on the Environment passed a resolution calling on the treaty countries and the United Nations to consider creating such a park.

Of course, a world park would be a novel episode in a world history of almost uninterrupted international squabbling. If it should prove impossible, the treaty nations might establish an international environmental protection agency to oversee development and regulate pollution. The agency might also take on some of the functions of a park service, searching for areas with ecological and scenic value, recommending their protection from development, and then managing them. Although the treaty designates all of Antarctica as a Special

Conservation Area, it sets aside only a few small areas for special protection. Antarctic development would require a considerable increase in the number and size of such areas, which would probably prove much more difficult and expensive than making the whole place a park.

International cooperation will not protect wildlife automatically, of course, any more than water conservation will. Nations cooperate to exploit wildlife as well as to conserve it, and there is often a thin line between the two. A recent example is the controversy surrounding the killing of baby harp seals in the North Atlantic. Canada and the countries to which it sells the skins have maintained that the killing does not threaten the population and is not excessively cruel, while critics, of course, have maintained just the opposite. Nations resolve such problems through various forms of political maneuvering rather than by appeal to international standards of wildlife management, because no such standards exist.

Despite controversies, polar wildlife is a fairly remote concern to many people today. It is likely to become less so in the near future, as expanding technology brings increasing numbers of people into contact with it. Technology already gives civilization almost absolute power over the most distant animals: wolf packs on the tundra are virtually sitting ducks for aerial gunners. In the distant future, polar wildlife may become a more immediate concern, indeed, especially if another glaciation spreads across Eurasia and North America. There is no reason to believe that it will *not* happen eventually. If it does, and places like France and New Jersey become too chilly for cattle and cornfields, our distant descendants may have occasion to thank us for conserving caribou and polar bears. A glaciated world will be lonely and sterile without them.

T H E
RIVERS

PRECEDING PHOTO: *Emerald River, Yoho National Park, British Columbia, Canada.*

I N ITS LOWER REACHES, the Connecticut River doesn't look like the kind of place where one would expect to find a salmon. The large relatives of trout thrive in cold, swift waters, and the lower Connecticut is warm and slow, particularly in late spring and summer. Yet the lower Connecticut has one advantage, from a salmon's viewpoint, that many rushing mountain streams lack today. It isn't dammed, so salmon can swim up it. Consequently, there is at least one Atlantic salmon in the Connecticut between Hartford and Middletown one muggy afternoon in May.

The salmon rests in a tree-shaded hole beneath a bluff. The water is cool there, although not as cold as the North Atlantic waters off Greenland, where she has lived for two years. That water is cold enough to make a man unconscious a few minutes after he falls into it, but the salmon thrived in it, feeding voraciously on herring and amphipods, and growing from less than a pound in weight to over ten.

Despite the comfort and ample food of the Greenland waters, the salmon abandoned them a few months before. She traveled southwest looking for the Connecticut's mouth—we have no idea, though, exactly how salmon navigate. Somehow, perhaps from the water's taste, she recognized the Connecticut as the river from which, as an eight-inch-long smolt, she began her journey to the Greenland feeding grounds.

She left the saline water of Long Island Sound and started swimming upriver. She was sexually mature, ready to breed; salmon spawn not in the ocean where they grow to maturity, but in rivers and streams.

This fish is unlike most of the salmon she has fed with in the North Atlantic, however. She was not spawned in a river, but in a fish hatchery nearby. She is not descended from a long line of Connecticut River salmon, but from the sperm and roe of salmon that biologists brought southward from rivers in northern Maine. Several million young hatchery salmon were released into the Connecticut with her, but she is one of only a few hundred who returned. Accidents, pollution, starvation, disease, and a wide range of predators—fishes, birds, marine animals, and fishermen—killed the rest.

Of course, the salmon isn't aware of how unusual she is. She

THE ATLANTIC SALMON

The Atlantic salmon is an anadromous species, living in the sea as an adult but breeding in freshwater rivers and creeks (*anadromous* comes from the Greek words for running upwards and refers to the upstream migrations that salmon make to reach their spawning areas). While in the sea, Atlantic salmon are silvery on their sides, silvery white underneath, and blue on their backs (as most pelagic, or ocean-dwelling, fish are). In rivers, they gradually lose their silvery color and become darker, taking on a bronze-and-brown coloration as spawning approaches. Many fishermen refer to postspawning adults as "black salmon."

Individual Atlantic salmon have weighed as much as seventy-nine to one hundred pounds. Specimens this large undoubtedly were older salmon that had spawned a number of times and then returned to the sea after each spawning. Salmon returning to rivers usually are between three and six years old. Connecticut River spawning takes place in the spring. As spawning begins, the head of the male salmon elongates and the lower jaw enlarges, curving upward at the tip. The exact biological function of this characteristic is not known.

The female chooses the nest site, or redd, usually a gravel-bottomed riffle area above or below a pool, and with her strong caudal fin digs a pit into which she deposits the eggs. Males then fertilize the eggs by depositing their sperm, or milt, on them. The female lays from two thousand to more than fifteen thousand eggs, depending on her body weight. Only a small percentage of Atlantic salmon, usually females, return in later years as repeat spawners.

Water temperatures below fifty degrees are desirable for normal egg development. The alevins, or newly hatched salmon, remain buried in

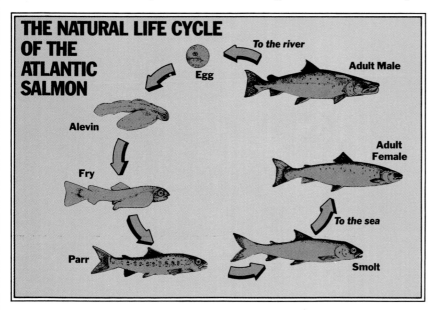

THE NATURAL LIFE CYCLE OF THE ATLANTIC SALMON

Egg
To the river
Adult Male
Alevin
Fry
Adult Female
To the sea
Parr
Smolt

Atlantic Salmon generally spend half of their life in freshwater (reproduction and nursery phases) and the other half in the oceans (growth and maturation phases).

follows her instincts, which prompt her to rest in deep water during the day and move upstream at night. They also prompt her to stop feeding while she is in the river. She will not feed again until she returns to the ocean after spawning—unlike Pacific salmon, Atlantic salmon don't always die after spawning—if she does return to the ocean. The odds are heavily against that, though. Having returned to the river in breeding condition, she is too valuable to be allowed to follow her instincts to their natural conclusion.

She is part of an arduous effort to return salmon to a river from which they had been extinct for over a century, and her role is a

the gravel until they absorb the yolk sac. Emergence of the alevins, now called fry, from the gravel may occur from March through June. The fry disperse and rapidly assume the coloring of the life stage referred to as parr, which have from eight to eleven narrow, vertical pigmented bands on their sides with a single red spot between each band. Parr remain in rivers from one to three years in New England. At a size of five to eight inches, the parr undergo preparations for the transition from a stream-bottom animal to a free-roaming ocean fish. As smolts, they run to the sea, where they grow to adulthood and return to spawn in their native streams.

Adapted from "Atlantic Salmon," by Lawrence W. Stolte, *Audubon Wildlife Report*, 1986.

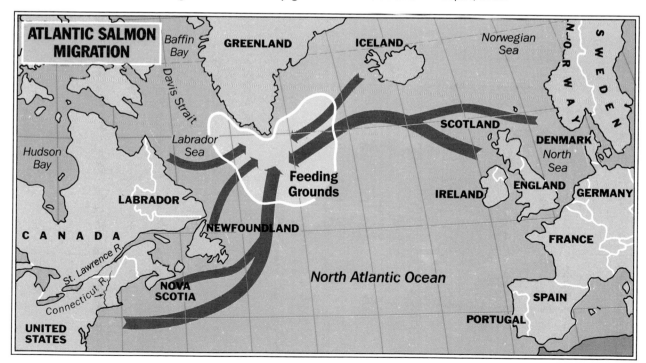

The Atlantic Salmon is native to the northeastern United States, eastern Canada, and northern Europe. Many Atlantic salmon follow these routes to and from the icy waters off Greenland. Some remain close to their home streams in Europe or North America.

precarious one. Because so few salmon return to the river, she is unlikely to find a mate even if she makes it all the way upriver to the cold-water spawning habitat of Vermont. If she survives the gill nets of shad fishermen and other hazards, she will probably be trapped and brought to a hatchery, where her eggs will be fertilized artificially. That would be best, from a conservation standpoint, because then her unusual predilection for returning to the non-ancestral Connecticut might pass on genetically to the young salmon that would hatch from her eggs and gain release in the river later. From those thousands of eggs, perhaps two or three mature fish might someday return to the river.

Yet no one can predict any of this with any certainty as the salmon rests in the shade of the bankside cottonwoods and willows, because nobody knows she is there. The river hides her completely and might continue to do so past the dams, fish ladders, and fish elevators she will encounter upstream, and perhaps even until she reaches a clean gravel bottom somewhere, encounters an equally anomalous male salmon, and spawns naturally. Then the river, rain-swollen in autumn, might conceal her passage back to Long Island Sound.

Despite heavy human use and scrutiny, such unlikelihoods may still occur in rivers. Giant, ancient fishes and reptiles may survive in the shadow of high-rises and freeway overpasses. We may rediscover species we believe to be extinct. Rivers are so changeable, with their floods and shifting channels and hidden holes, that they are never altogether predictable.

Indeed, rivers might be said to epitomize the principle of changeability in the biosphere, because they are always in the rapid process of becoming something else. Raindrops become ridgetop rivulets, which become creeks, which become tributaries, which become forks, which become main stems, which become estuaries, which become oceans. As rivers change, they change everything around them, tearing down mountains, leveling valleys, filling harbors with silt. Powered by gravity, running water is a force to match the tectonic stresses that uplift mountains: it erodes them almost as quickly as they rise. The faster land rises, the faster rivers cut through it, as the Colorado River has cut a mile-deep gorge through the surrounding plateaus in the geological instant of a million years. With their loads of sand and silt (and, during floods, rocks and boulders), rivers not only push and pull, but scour and scrape land.

In the beginning, running water must have been even more powerful, because no land vegetation or organic soil cushioned its force, no leaves stopped raindrops, no roots held banks. Massive deposits of sand and gravel at the fossil mouths of Paleozoic rivers attest to this. Floods then must have been of truly biblical proportions.

Yet rivers must also have been among the main corridors along which life spread from oceans to continents. On their quieter, lower reaches, they offered new habitat for crowded ocean life, once it adapted to fresh water. Many enormously ancient creatures still survive in rivers. Lampreys, probably the descendants of the earliest, jawless fishes, still move from oceans and lakes to rivers for spawning, as do ancient bony fishes such as sturgeon. The oldest reptiles, turtles and crocodilians, still live in rivers; they have been doing so uninterruptedly for hundreds of millions of years.

As life climbed higher into steeper, faster waters, more specialized, streamlined forms developed: salmon, for one, which are thought to have evolved in northern temperate-forest streams around fifty million years ago. As it colonized rivers, life changed them as they changed it. With watersheds stablilized by forests and grasslands, streams probably flooded less than formerly and kept more to established beds and channels. Forest shade and plant- and animal-nutrient cycling affected water temperature and chemistry.

Some river animals have adapted in extraordinary ways. One can hardly imagine a mountain or desert animal changing its environment as dramatically as the beaver changes streams. Somehow, these large aquatic rodents evolved the ability to build dams, canals, and artificial islands, and to do so with a skill that has been compared favorably to that of the Army Corps of Engineers. Beavers lived on most of the streams in the Northern Hemisphere, and their effects on hydrology were important. They turned what must have been rocky, rather sterile postglacial torrents into meandering complexes of meadows, ponds, and marshes that provided habitat to a great variety of other wildlife. They didn't do this on purpose, of course: by flooding land with dams, they gained easier access to their tree-bark food supply and greater security for their stick lodges. As they consumed poolside trees, they built canals and series of check dams on small tributaries, thus gaining access to farther ones. Nevertheless, the dams regulated stream flow in ways that benefited many other creatures. Waterfowl and wading birds found nesting and feeding habitat around ponds. Moose, deer, and other mammals found forage in beaver marshes and meadows.

Beaver lived in the Great Plains and Southwest as well as in more humid areas. With their rich riparian biotas, rivers were corridors of aquatic life in regions of water scarcity. Fostered by seasonal floods, gallery forests extended far into grasslands; desert rivers supported lush

A beaver feeds on chips it has cut from a tree.

growths of mesquite and willows. Large fish like the Columbia River chinook salmon traveled far into dry continental interiors along these corridors. Migrating waterfowl, wading birds, and shorebirds used them as feeding and resting places.

In the great humid lowland basins of the world, the Mississippi, Amazon, Zaire, Ganges, Yangtze, and Danube, rivers were the dominant force of nature. In flood, they spread for miles beyond their banks and created a world where forests and streams mingled strangely, where fish habitually swam out in floodwaters to feed on the forest floor, and where most land animals were aquatic to some degree. Riparian life reached staggering abundance.

The world's greatest river, the Amazon (which discharges eleven times more water from its mouth than the Mississippi), contains an estimated two thousand fish species, perhaps a tenth of all the fish species in the world. These include what may be the world's largest freshwater fish, the arapaima, which reaches fifteen feet, as well as lungfish, electric rays and eels, and most of the colorful little tropical fish we keep in aquariums. The second-largest river, the Zaire (formerly the Congo), has around six hundred fish species, and so many resemble those of the Amazon that scientists believe both may have been part of a single giant river system before continental drift separated South America and Africa some two hundred million years ago.

Tropical river basins played a part in human evolution. The great apes evolved in the rain forests that covered the river basins of Africa and Asia. Early hominids may have had close contact with rivers as they moved out of deep rain forest into savanna. In that hot environment, they needed to be near a water supply, and the gallery forest growing along savanna rivers offered food and shelter. As hominid food-gathering methods diversified, fish, frogs, mollusks, and crustaceans proved easy to catch in river shallows.

Homo erectus dispersed through Europe and Asia along river-valley corridors. In the process, early humans encountered the mass spawning migrations of salmon, sturgeon, and other anadromous fish that characterize Eurasian rivers. Since fish may pack themselves into shallow streams, humans probably took a lesson from bears and other predators and spent spawning runs camping by rivers and living on a salmon-and-caviar diet that would be wildly luxurious to their distant descendants. Fish bones in fossil campsites indicate that salmon were an important food even in the Paleolithic period, when big-game hunting was at its height. In the later Neolithic, after big game had dwindled, fish became a staple source of protein. Probably, humans first began fishing with boats and nets then.

The reliability of fish as food contributed to the rise of permanent settlements. Villagers could depend on fish to run into the same rivers and lakes every year, and could dry and salt the surplus catch for later consumption. Neolithic villages on the shores of central European lakes were fishing communities. The early settlements of the mound-building Mississippi Valley Indian cultures were built on enormous piles of freshwater mollusk shells.

As civilization evolved, it generally followed river valleys. The first cities of Egypt and Mesopotamia grew up beside rivers that were the source of irrigation water. As urbanization spread into more humid areas, cities stayed close to rivers because they depended on trade for their wealth, and rivers were they only avenues for transporting large quantities of vital goods, like grain, across continents.

Civilization began changing rivers as soon as it appeared, for very much the same reason that beavers change rivers: to secure homes and food supplies. Human methods of river control are so similar to those of beavers, in fact, that one wonders if some neolithic genius got the idea of dams and canals from watching the rodents at work, just as a paleolithic counterpart may have learned to catch salmon from watching bears.

There is an important difference between human and beaver river

Beaver dam.

Grand Coulee Dam in Washington.

control, however. Beaver live in rivers, and most of their activities are directed to expanding the river's influence over the landscape. They are the river's allies, in this sense. Rivers are not home to humans, on the other hand, but unruly sources of various goods and services; that tends to make us their adversaries instead of their allies. We want river water in our bathtubs and irrigation canals, but not our living rooms and streets, so we try to restrict a river's influence on the land with our dams, dikes, and canals. Instead of enriching riparian life, this tends to impoverish it.

The river-control projects of early civilizations may seem small-scaled in proportion to today's high dams, but they are impressive in that they were built largely by hand. The Sumerian network of canals brought so much water from the Tigris and Euphrates rivers that overwatering of fields was a problem, the high water table bringing salts to the surface. The Chinese imperial canal system, developed in the first millenium A.D., ran for hundreds of miles throughout the country, connected the Yangtze and Yellow rivers, and accommodated grain barges weighing many hundreds of tons. River flooding once had distributed silt across valleys, but the Chinese built levees that controlled rivers effectively enough to confine silt to river beds, which gradually rose several feet above the elevations of surrounding fields. (When levees broke, the raised rivers caused disastrous floods.)

Industry eventually joined agriculture and transportation as a reason for controlling rivers. The pressure of falling water on wheels could power all kinds of machinery, from flour mills to looms. Engineers soon discovered that simply putting a wheel in a river is less efficient than damming the river and diverting the impounded water down a chute, so it would hit the wheel as fast as possible.

By the eighteenth century, humans had developed the basic technology of river control. We haven't changed it essentially since, but have simply applied it on a continually larger scale with larger machines. Dams provide water power to electrical turbines instead of mill wheels, concrete-lined canals bring water to fields hundreds of miles distant from the original river, riprapped stone levees rigidify hundreds of miles of banks. Giant dredges and draglines not only dig canals and navigation channels, but also turn entire rivers into canals, straightening meanders and destroying riparian vegetation. Needless to say, technological growth has resulted in corresponding shrinkage of river wildlife.

The development of North America provides a particularly clear picture of the drastic changes rivers have undergone in the past two centuries. When Europeans arrived, American rivers were essentially in a natural state. Indians used them for transportation, and to some extent for irrigation in the Southwest, but there was no extensive system of riparian works north of the Aztec and Mayan civilizations. This natural state was abundant. An estimated three hundred thousand Atlantic salmon spawned in New England rivers each year, crowding some streams so thickly that colonists caught them with pitchforks.

*Red salmon attempt to jump Brooks
River falls in Alaska.*

Salmon also thronged rivers throughout eastern Canada, as well as
Lake Ontario. They didn't get above Niagara Falls, but the other Great
Lakes were full of white fish and lake trout almost as big as salmon.
Sturgeon were quite a bit bigger, nine feet long at maximum, big
enough that no one caught them with a pitchfork; settlers managed to
land them by hitting their heads with axes in the shallows.

South of the Great Lakes, the Mississippi drainage contained not
only sturgeon, but alligator gars of equal size (if not equal palatability)
and six-foot paddlefish, an ancient species named for the elongated
snout with which it apparently locates swarms of the zooplankton on
which it feeds. The Mississippi and its tributaries contained more than
300 fish species, nearly half of the 750 species that inhabit the continent
as a whole.

On the West Coast, the several species of Pacific salmon filled mountain streams in numbers that seem incredible today. Fresh, dried, or smoked salmon was the year-round staple for Northwestern Indians. The Columbia-basin tribes alone are estimated to have caught from eighteen to forty-two million pounds of salmon every year without seriously depleting fish populations. The original run of Pacific salmon and steelhead (a seagoing rainbow trout) in the Columbia basin may have been between eleven and sixteen million fish a year.

Perhaps the first important change that European civilization brought upon North American rivers was the decimation of beaver; the animals were extremely valuable because their fur made a particularly choice grade of felt for the fancy hats that were *de rigueur* in European society. Trappers had virtually exterminated them from the East by the late eighteenth century, and from the West by the mid-nineteenth. With beaver gone, the ponds, marshes, and meadows they had created all along the waterways began to grow up into forest, greatly reducing habitat for much riparian wildlife.

It's hard to say what the exact effects of beaver extirpation would have been, however, because greater changes followed quickly. As settlement spread, settlers cut forest for cropland or timber, rain eroded denuded soil, and river siltation increased greatly. Many river organisms need clean sand or gravel bottoms. The eggs and newly hatched fry of some, like salmon, cannot breathe without them; adults of other species, for instance, bottom fishes and freshwater clams and mussels, need clean substrates for feeding and respiration. Clouds of mud from fields, pastures, and roads buried millions of them. Dozens of fresh-water-stream mollusk and fish species are presently on endangered lists.

Towns and factories quickly followed settlers. Their builders usually transported construction materials either on rivers or on canals, the construction of which brought more changes. In 1798, the Upper Locks and Canal Company of Turner's Falls, Massachusetts, built a sixteen-foot dam across the Connecticut River, effectively ensuring that Atlantic salmon could no longer reach upstream spawning beds. The salmon disappeared from the river so completely in the next few decades that a shad fisherman couldn't identify one he caught in his nets in 1815.

Nineteenth-century Americans regarded rivers (and every other natural phenomenon) as inexhaustible. After filling them with topsoil and felled trees, civilization proceeded to employ rivers simultaneously as reservoirs and sewers. By the close of the nineteenth century, most rivers in the industrializing Northeast and Midwest reeked of raw sewage, slaughterhouse wastes, and factory effluents. When pollution near a city became too unpleasant, authorities simply moved inlets for municipal water supplies farther upstream, where other cities were doing the same thing. When the Chicago River began distributing raw sewage on the lawns of Lake Michigan mansions, the city simply reversed the river's flow so that it carried the pollution toward the Mississippi instead of the lake.

The fate of wildlife in and around such gross pollution was obvious. In rural areas, threats to riparian life were less blatant, but still deadly. Increased runoff from denuded forest and prairie lands caused floods that devestated downstream towns and crops. People reacted by trying to cure symptoms instead of causes: they built levees to keep flood water out. As in ancient China, the heavy silt load in the contained rivers built up their beds above the level of surrounding lands. When levees broke, floods became catastrophes. Spring floods had once risen gradually into floodplain forests, fertilizing trees with silt and feeding fish with forest fruits and insects; man-made floods tore away trees and soil.

Even where industry and agriculture were less influential, as in the upper Great Lakes and Pacific Northwest, commercial fishing and trapping decimated river life. Salmon canneries built contraptions at the mouths of western rivers that automatically scooped up the fish as they moved upstream to spawn. Commercial exploitation of chinook

THE PACIFIC SALMON

The silver, chum, pink, dog and other salmon species spawn in the rivers of western North America. The largest, and perhaps the most economically, culturally, and politically important is the chinook or king salmon, which spawns from southern California to Point Hope, Alaska, and also from Hokkaido, Japan, to the Soviet Union on Asia's Pacific coast. Chinook also have been transplanted to places such as the Great Lakes and New Zealand.

All Pacific salmon are gravel-nest builders. The female constructs the nest, or redd, by rolling on her side and violenting flexing her tail against the gravel bed. This motion creates currents that lift the gravel into the flow of the stream, which in turn deposits the material downstream. When the redd is about a foot deep, the female lies in it and lays part of her eggs, which attendant males fertilize immediately. The female then moves slightly upstream and begins the redd-building process again, which flushes gravel downstream to cover the previously laid eggs.

Chinook salmon spawn in the fall and early winter. Both males and females die after a single spawning. The eggs hatch in the spring. Some young chinooks remain in their natal rivers until the second spring after their emergence from the gravel, then move seaward in the next few months. Other young chinooks remain in freshwater only a few months or weeks, then move seaward slowly, growing quickly as they migrate. Most chinook remain in the Pacific from two to five years before returning to their native rivers to spawn. The size of mature chinooks varies according to the amount of time they have spent in the ocean. Twelve to thirty pounds is the usual range today, although individuals weighing up to one hundred pounds have been known in the past.

Adapted from "Chinook Salmon of the Columbia River Basin," by Lloyd A. Phinney, *Audubon Wildlife Report*, 1986.

salmon on the Columbia River began in 1866, reached a peak of one and one-half million fish caught a year at the turn of the century, then declined steadily as the numbers of spawning fish decreased. By the 1960s, fishermen caught fewer than three hundred thousand chinooks a year. As the fish declined, canneries exploited other species—coho, sockeye, and chum—until they too became scarce. Then the industry moved to Alaska, where the same cycle of peak and decline occurred.

Since American rivers were in as bad shape as American forests in 1900, it would have made sense to begin treating them as Americans began to treat forests: to protect the remaining undamaged ones and to restore the rest. Forest protector Theodore Roosevelt expressed similar sentiments when he urged preservation of the Colorado River's Grand Canyon. "Leave it as it is," he said. "You cannot improve it. The ages have been at work on it and man can only mar it."

Yet rivers proved to be more like prairies than forests: they simply were too useful, and people would not leave them in peace to regenerate themselves. Instead, Americans tried various artificial methods of restoring rivers to productivity and quiescence, while continuing to use them even harder than before. Despite his Grand Canyon sentiments, Theodore Roosevelt was a dam proponent. Artificial restoration combined with increased use, not surprisingly, changed rivers even more than they had been changed before.

The fate of inland fisheries is typical of this approach. Fish had already declined so much by 1871 that Congress appointed a commission to investigate the problem and make recommendations for solving it. Although less was known about fisheries biology then, the reasons for the decline—overfishing, dams, destruction of spawning habitat—were evident to observers. Instead of addressing them, however, Congress established fish hatcheries throughout the country to restock streams. Fish hatcheries are a valid way of restoring depleted stocks or of providing put-and-take fish for sportsmen, but they do nothing about dams, habitat destruction, and pollution. As a result, the Federal Fish Commission and its successor, the Bureau of Sport Fisheries, as well as various state and private hatcheries, spent ensuing decades pouring millions of fish into rivers too polluted or otherwise degraded to support them. Worse, they put a great many non-native fish such as carp into rivers, and competition from these often sped or completed decline of native species.

Meanwhile, other federal agencies made rivers even harder for fish to live in. The Army Corps of Engineers was assigned to solve the problems of flooding and harbor and channel siltation that had arisen from forest destruction and soil erosion. Stoutly ignoring causes, the corps addressed symptoms with massive engineering works that have effectively turned America's greatest rivers into strings of dammed pools. The Mississippi, Missouri, and Ohio are now series of long reservoirs formed behind corps flood-control structures. Locks and dredged channels allow oil tankers and freight barges to ascend the former rivers. There are no such provisions for sturgeon and paddlefish, which have largely disappeared, along with many other creatures that inhabited the rivers' natural floodplain habitats, their oxbow lakes, yazoo channels, tupelo swamps, and cottonwood groves. The corps has also dammed many of the country's smaller rivers, adding the sometimes-questionable benefits of water supply and flatwater recreation to its basic flood-control rationale. The acquisition of land around reservoirs sometimes "mitigates" the impact on wildlife, but river wildlife doesn't usually thrive in reservoirs, which lack the emergent vegetation, spawning beds, floodplains, and other features of riparian habitat.

In the twentieth century, the Bureau of Reclamation—which President Roosevelt created as part of the Reclamation Act of 1902—joined the corps in the river-control business. The bureau addressed a problem somewhat the opposite of the corps': too little water, rather than too much. Since rain is scanty west of the one-hundredth meridian (which runs through the middle of the Dakotas south to central Texas), Western states wanted federal help in bringing river water to fields. The bureau's approach in the West was pretty much the same as the corps' in the East, however: it dammed rivers, again, and again. Sometimes the corps and the bureau got together in areas where floods *and* drought caused problems. Fearful that the federal government would create another agency to supercede them as they quarreled over damsites on the Missouri, they eventually cooperated to build seven dams on that river in twenty years.

The bureau has also prospered on its own. It has dammed the Colorado River eight times since the construction, in 1935, of Boulder Dam, the first on the river. It would have dammed the Grand Canyon in the 1960s, if not for massive public opposition. As of 1980, the bureau administered an empire of 329 storage reservoirs and 346 diversion dams, as well as thousands of miles of canals and pipelines, and fifty hydroelectric powerplants. The effects of these improvements on western fisheries have been even more severe than those of corps dams on midwestern ones. In the Pacific Northwest, dams closed thousands of river miles to Pacific salmon spawning, and hatcheries and fish ladders have not stopped yearly runs from dropping to a fraction of original numbers. In the Southwest, dams have driven native fishes—

like the squawfish, or white salmon, a Colorado species reaching a length of six feet—nearly to extinction.

Two other federal agencies, the Soil Conservation Service and the Federal Energy Regulatory Commission, also dam rivers. Without doubt, the massive bureaucracies employed by these four agencies have carried out their assignments to control floods and provide irrigation water and hydroelectric power. There is often some question as to whether traditional economic benefits outweigh environmental costs. One proposed Bureau of Reclamation project, the Garrison Diversion Unit in North Dakota, became notorious because its canals would have destroyed or degraded thousands of acres of wetlands and wildlife habitat, including some on national wildlife refuges, to bring Missouri River irrigation water to 250 thousand acres of private farmland that are already productive.

The long-range viability of our present river-control system is open to much more serious question. It costs billions a year, and it is not going to get cheaper. The trouble with engineering solutions to ecological problems is that they are never really finished: we must continually maintain them and eventually rebuild them. Levees crumble, canals erode, reservoirs fill with silt, river water may become saline and unusable downstream. The costs of projects soar while the benefits become more questionable.

No amount of maintenance and rebuilding will solve some of the river-engineering problems that lie farther down the road. When dams on the scale of Boulder or Hoover fill with silt, as they will within centuries, they will be useless. More immediately, the southwestern reservoirs are supposed to save water, but lose vast amounts of it by evaporation because they expose so much surface to the desert sun. Evaporation from Lake Mead and Lake Powell on the Colorado amounts to more than 8 percent of the river's flow, enough to provide water for two hundred cities the size of Flagstaff, Arizona. The only way to stop the loss would be somehow to build a top on the reservoirs, which would not be popular with water skiers and houseboaters.

While federal agencies kept busy wringing ever-increasing amounts of transportation, irrigation, and electricity out of rivers, towns and factories continued to dump more wastes into these rivers. Some industrial-area rivers became empty not only of fish but of all life. By the 1950s and '60s, things had become bad enough that Congress passed a variety of water-quality legislation. By 1972, three years after Cleveland's Cuyahoga River had caught fire along several industrially polluted miles of its length, things had become so bad that Congress amended the 1956 Federal Water Pollution Control Act to give the

RIVERS AND WATERFOWL

Seasonal flooding along rivers provides important habitat for migrating ducks, geese, and swans, which find protection from predators in the flooded land, as well as foods such as nuts, invertebrates, and waste grain. River-bottom forest also provides vital nesting habitat for the magnificent wood duck, which nests in treeholes.

Reduction of seasonal flooding by Army Corps of Engineers flood-control projects is removing much of this habitat, particularly on the lower Mississippi River basin, where vast numbers of waterfowl spend their winters. A fifteen-year flood-control project on the Yazoo River basin north of Vicksburg, Mississippi, for example, could wipe out habitat for many of the almost two million mallard ducks that winter there each year. A reduction in wintering habitat may cause crowding or food scarcity in the remaining habitat and reduce the number of ducks that breed.

The Army Corps of Engineers plans to build hundreds of control structures that will drain farmland along the upper Yazoo. The United States Fish and Wildlife Service

Wood duck drake.

wants to acquire control "easements" over these structures during the winter months, so that they can flood the land to provide wintering habitat for waterfowl. In this way, a federal flood-control drainage system might help to maintain habitat for wildlife instead of destroying it. Agricultural interests oppose such measures, however, for fear the winter flooding might hinder their operations.

federal government preeminence in directing water-pollution-control programs throughout the country. The 1972 amendments (commonly called the Clean Water Act) set national goals for the achievement of fishable and swimmable waters by 1983 and the cessation of all polluting discharges into the nation's waters in 1985. They required factory and city dischargers to adopt stringent technological controls and to conform to federal standards for the concentration of pollutants in discharges. The amendments also increased federal funding for sewage-plant construction significantly. Discharge permits, civil and criminal penalties, and citizen lawsuits provided means of enforcing the law.

The water quality of many streams has improved significantly, but obviously, the discharge of pollutants into waters did not stop in 1985. The building of new sewage-treatment plants, and the upgrading of others, did much to clean up sewage in rivers, but little about other pollutants. Liberal use of chlorination in sewage treatment actually added to chemical pollution of rivers. And some federal funds were not used to clean-up existing pollution, but to finance new sewage plants on as-yet unpolluted streams near where developers wanted to build.

The problem of keeping pollutants out of the nation's streams is more complicated than regulating the contents of factory or sewage-plant drainpipes, unfortunately. Much water pollution comes from the surface of the ground, from roads, parking lots, and farm fields in the form of silt, oil, manure, pesticides, and herbicides. Legislation has so far been less than effective in dealing with these "nonpoint" pollution sources. Toxic pollutants also get into streams from below and above the ground as they corrode barrels and holding tanks and seep into groundwater, or rise into the air as dust and smoke and return to Earth in raindrops. Toxic rain has caused higher levels of pesticide and PCB contamination in apparently pristine lakes of Isle Royale National Park than exist in the Lake Superior waters surrounding Isle Royale. Pesticides such as DDT may be banned in the United States, but they arrive here from Mexico and Central America in atmospheric dust, and their levels are rising in fish and birds again.

The disappearance of clean, free-flowing rivers from most of the American landscape has at least increased the value of clean, free-flowing rivers in the minds of many Americans. Healthy rivers do not have to be cleaned up and maintained with tax money, and they provide recreational and aesthetic amenities that become even more visible as our streams disappear behind concrete.

Migratory birds become increasingly visible as habitat shrinkage concentrates their populations. During the month of March, for example, a half-million sandhill cranes congregate on an eighty-mile stretch of the Platte River in Nebraska. The cranes once could rest and feed along three hundred miles of the Platte during their migration to Canadian nesting grounds, but man has so modified most of the river (having diverted 70 percent of its water for agriculture) that the cranes can no longer use it. They need a wide, shallow channel in which to roost at night. Seasonal floods used to provide such a channel by scouring the bed of silt and vegetation, but willows grow in the bed now that flooding is controlled.

Heightened visibility doesn't benefit the cranes, of course. Crowding in the remaining suitable habitat increases chances of crane mortality from disease and stress. The spectacle of the crane concentration may at least encourage people to try to save the remaining crane habitat, however. Crane habitat clearly will continue to deteriorate if more water is diverted from the Platte. If cranes are to survive, at least part of the river will have to remain as it was during the millions of years cranes have roosted on it. The National Audubon Society and the Platte River Whooping Crane Trust have begun to address the problem by establishing crane sanctuaries on the Platte.

The importance of rivers to wildlife is reflected in the multitude of refuges and preserves established on them. Even before the Bureau

AMERICA'S BEST KEPT SECRET

Tall, stately sandhill cranes have inhabited North America for more than ten million years. Each year, the gray, red-capped cranes fly from wintering grounds in Texas, New Mexico, and Mexico to breeding grounds in Canada, Alaska, and the Soviet Union. About five hundred thousand cranes stop for several weeks in the Platte and North Platte river valleys of Nebraska during this spring migration. There they rest and feed on waste grain, aquatic invertebrates, and other foods before resuming their journey north.

The concentration of so many thousands of cranes in one region is one of America's best kept secrets. It is unparalleled in North America, yet it has received relatively little attention. In Europe and Japan, on the other hand, migrating cranes are a popular spectacle, drawing tourists from afar.

Sandhill cranes on the banks of the North Platte River.

of Sport Fisheries merged with the Bureau of Biological Survey to form the U.S. Fish and Wildlife Service, the federal government had established refuges on the upper Mississippi and other streams important to migratory birds. River refuges are vital to both water and land wildlife, yet they have the same problems as national parks and other nature preserves: they are only parts of river ecosystems, vulnerable to adverse impacts from the other, unprotected parts.

Clearly, the best way to protect a river's wildlife is to protect the river. In the past few decades, conservationists have developed one of the newest kinds of nature preserves—the wild and scenic river. The idea grew out of the controversies surrounding dam-building projects in the scenic Canyonlands region of Utah and Arizona in the 1950s and '60s, and was contemporaneous with the Wilderness Act.

In 1960, the National Park Service proposed to Congress that some of the last free-flowing rivers be preserved in a natural state. Congress authorized the departments of Agriculture and Interior to study the matter, and they identified 650 rivers as still free-flowing. A Wild Rivers Committee from both departments eventually selected twenty-two of these rivers for possible preservation. This still had to be approved by Congress. Introduced into the Senate by Frank Church, legislation passed by a vote of 71 to 1, but a similar bill ran into trouble in the House because some congressmen thought it was too strong while others thought it too weak. A compromise bill eventually passed the House by a vote of 267 to 7, and President Johnson signed the National Wild and Scenic Rivers Act into law in October 1968.

The act established three protected categories for rivers: wild, scenic, and recreational. Wild rivers are undammed, undiverted, unpolluted, inaccessible by road, and generally pristine; scenic rivers may have some inconspicuous development; recreational rivers may have impoundments and considerable development. The act also prohibited federally funded or licensed water projects on any river in the system or under consideration for it. This was critical because it kept the corps and bureau at bay.

Passage of the act put segments of eight rivers in Idaho, California, New Mexico, Oregon, Minnesota, and Wisconsin under protection— 789 miles of river in all. In the next decade, Congress added another sixteen in the lower forty-eight states as well as those included in the Alaska National Interest Lands Conservation Act of 1980. Some states took advantage of a Wild River Act provision that allowed governors to add rivers to the system by applying to the secretary of the interior. The system presently includes rivers in every part of the country: 95 miles of the Allagash in northern Maine; 56.9 miles of the Chattooga on the Georgia-South Carolina border; 191.2 miles of the Rio Grande in Texas and 52.7 miles in New Mexico; 149 miles of the Missouri in Montana; 157 miles of the Skagit in northern Washington; 286 miles of the Klamath on the Pacific coast in California and Oregon.

Recently the Park Service proposed to extend the concept of river preservation even further by creating a river national park. Such a park, ideally, would encompass the watershed and tributaries, main stem, and mouth of some particularly scenic and pristine river, giving visitors a chance to experience an intact riparian ecosystem. The Smith River was one possibility; its mouth is in the California redwoods, and it winds into the Siskiyou Mountains of southern Oregon. The Smith is already a designated wild river. Another candidate is the Suwannee, which begins in Georgia's Okefenokee Swamp and flows 272 miles to a wild delta on the Gulf of Mexico. The Suwannee is presently under study for wild designation.

In 1986, the Park Service removed the Smith River from its list of river national park candidates, perhaps partly because a Canadian company has plans to strip-mine for nickel in the Smith River watershed. This raises a basic shortcoming of a wild-river system. Since it gives fairly effective protection against river development, conservationists have a lot of trouble getting wild rivers designated. When the Wild Rivers Act was passed, Congress intended that the number of rivers in the system would increase to one hundred by 1978, and to two hundred in 1990. The system has fallen short of its goal because a cumbersome designation process makes keeping a river out of the system easier than getting it in. Congress first must pass a law to study the river, and after study, must pass *another* law to designate it. The process takes years, allowing opponents plenty of time to lobby and to propose amendments that would make the act even less effective.

The difficulty in designating wild rivers parallels the difficulty in designating wilderness areas. Legislation protects against commercial overdevelopment, but because of industrial and bureaucratic opposition to wilderness and wild-river designation, conservationists can apply the legislation only to a small proportion of lands and rivers. For most rivers, protection continues to depend on piecemeal application of remedies whenever threats occur.

One such remedy is the 1973 Endangered Species Act. In the notorious case of the snail darter, conservationists temporarily stopped construction of the Tennessee Valley Authority's Tellico Dam (which they had long opposed on the basis of its poor cost-benefit ratio) because the dam's reservoir could have wiped out the endangered fish species. (The reservoir also would have drowned thousands of acres of highly productive farmland and two hundred sites sacred to the Cherokee Indians, but there were no legal remedies to these impacts.) Snail darters belong to a diverse group of droll, popeyed relatives of perch that scoot around stream bottoms, propping themselves on their pectoral fins. As their name implies, snail darters feed on snails that live in free-flowing, relatively shallow streams: neither snails nor darters can survive at the bottom of a reservoir.

The TVA eventually finished the Tellico Dam, but the ever-increasing numbers of fish on the endangered species list has given dam builders pause. Officials added a dozen fish to the list in 1985 alone. Western dam-building interests have advocated amending the Endangered Species Act in an attempt to limit its effects on their projects, even though the act has stopped little, if any, water development to date.

As the snail-darter-controversy illustrates, even the most high-sounding laws may give only token protection to the environment. Wildlife often demonstrates the shortcomings of such laws by dying when its habitat is destroyed. To proclaim the preservation of all species resoundingly is one thing; stopping a multimillion-dollar dam for a tiny fish is another. When wildlife does survive or return, it means that laws are working.

The return of Atlantic salmon to New England rivers is one of the more hopeful developments involving river wildlife, not only because it shows that diligently enforced and well-funded laws have improved the condition of rivers, but also because it suggests that conservationists may be able to maintain those improvements in the face of ever-growing industrial pressures. The very presence of the salmon will be an incentive to protect water quality.

Certainly, salmon would not have returned to the Connecticut, Pawcatuck, Merrimack, Penobscot, and Union rivers if not for the Clean Water Act. Pollution and dams continued to make the rivers uninhabitable for salmon throughout the nineteenth and early twentieth centuries despite many attempts at restocking. Effective restoration began in the 1960s, with passage of an Anadromous Fish and Conservation Act that brought federal funds and agencies into the effort for the first time, and with cooperative agreements between the states involved. In the case of the Connecticut River, for example, no fewer than six state and federal agencies eventually became involved. The U.S. Fish and Wildlife Service established five hatcheries, producing 70 percent of the salmon fry and smolt for restocking, and conducted research on the biology of the restoration process.

With pollution reduced and many dams equipped with fish ladders and other measures that allow fish to swim upstream past them,

SALMON ON THE HIGH SEAS

In the 1950s, already beleaguered Atlantic salmon suffered what seemed likely to be a fatal blow when Danish fishermen accidentally discovered that the salmon congregate off the coast of Greenland to feed during their years in the ocean. Fishing fleets converged on the feeding grounds and began netting salmon in thousand-pound hauls. In 1960, they caught 132,000 pounds off Greenland. By 1971, the catch had increased forty-five times, to six million pounds.

In Iceland, where one of the healthiest Atlantic salmon populations remains, home-water catches dropped 40 percent in thirteen years. The impact on already-fragile populations in Europe and North America was even more severe. In Maine, the only state where Atlantic salmon still spawned at that time, a maximum of 1,500 fish swam through a pitifully shrunken habitat of 464 square miles.

Behind the scenes, though, concern for the salmon's fate had been quietly translating into action. In the aftermath of World War II, the Atlantic Sea Run Salmon Commission was created to restore salmon to Maine rivers. By the 1960s, the Atlantic Salmon

Ocean-fishing vessel in Iceland.

Federation, an organization with increasing reach and power, had joined the commission. When Danish fishing off the coast of Greenland appeared to be dooming salmon, a man named Richard Buck, a longtime conservationist and lover of salmon, organized CASE (Committee on the Atlantic Salmon Emergency). Buck then quickly gave a party in New York City that is still talked about when conservation veterans meet. Celebrities like Bing Crosby and Ted Williams attracted the national media and helped to focus international attention on the Danish fishing problem. A threatened boycott of Danish products swiftly followed, and not long after that, the fishing came to a halt. Countries involved in high-seas fishing formed a commission (ICNAF, or International

Salmon harvest.

Commission on the North Atlantic Fisheries) to study the problem, and signed a treaty to regulate salmon fishing.

the numbers of salmon returning to New England rivers began to climb. In 1970, hatcheries released one hundred thousand salmon smolts (young salmon that have undergone the physiological changes necessary for them to enter salt water for the first time), and 790 adults returned to New England rivers. The first hatchery-bred salmon known to return to the Connecticut was retrieved at the Holyoke Water Power

Company's dam on June 23, 1975, a year during which 2,190 salmon returned to all the rivers under restoration. That number grew to 3,400 in 1984, after a release of over a million smolts. In 1985, 310 salmon returned to the Connecticut: the river and its tributaries now have 275 miles accessible to salmon. By 1990, the Atlantic salmon hatchery program will produce five million fry (recently hatched salmon) and almost a million and a half smolts every year for release in New England rivers. This is expected to double the returning adult salmon population to seven thousand.

Important factors threaten hopes for salmon restoration, however. Commercial ocean fishing is one. After Danish fishermen discovered in the 1950s that salmon congregate off the Greenland coast, the species was under siege during its ocean sojourn as well as its river spawning runs. European fishing boats catch an estimated 50 to 60 percent of salmon that otherwise would return to North America to spawn. Researchers estimate that, for every salmon that returns to New England rivers, one to five are caught off Greenland. International agreements such as the 1983 treaty establishing a North Atlantic Salmon Conservation Organization have set increasingly stringent quotas on the salmon catch. Yet recent catches have actually fallen well below the new quotas, indicating that Atlantic salmon (which were originally distributed from Connecticut to Portugal) are in decline throughout their range.

An even greater threat to New England salmon restoration is a recent surge in construction of small hydroelectric dams under the impetus of federal statutes that provide new incentives for the dam construction. Even small dams stop fish from moving upstream to spawn (the more dams there are, the fewer fish reach native tributaries), and their turbines kill young fish during oceanward migration. The Fish and Wildlife Service has stated that continued licensing of small hydro dams will virtually end the salmon restoration effort. Hydroelectric proponents argue that salmon restoration is not cost-effective because there has been no financial return on the millions spent on the program so far, while restoration advocates point out that such returns can only be expected once a viable population is restored. (Legislation enacted by Congress in 1986 provides for increased protection of fish and wildlife affected by hydropower projects.)

Despite these threats and others (including poaching and destruction of spawning-stream habitat by acid rain), the agencies involved in salmon restoration are optimistic that the program will succeed, as long as hatcheries continue to build up the population and losses from fishing and dams do not increase. So much effort has gone into the program that it is hard to imagine its being destroyed by a commercial fishing industry that will benefit from it in the end, or abandoned in favor of a commodity—electricity—of which there is no present scarcity.

If restoration of such a depleted population seems unlikely, one may look to the recent strong recovery of another river creature whose demise was predicted confidently. Beaver were probably just about as scarce as bison by the 1890s, but instead of remaining only in a few wildlife refuges, they have (with some help from conservation agencies) recolonized most of the continent. They once again are a powerful ecological force on streams, sometimes to the chagrin of road builders and other human stream controllers, but often to considerable human benefit. The multitude of small dams that beavers build on streams draining strip-mined areas, for example, must prevent downstream siltation more efficiently than anything human engineers could do, and at considerably less cost.

Such optimism is somewhat tempered by the plight of river wildlife elsewhere. Beaver have long been extinct in most of Europe. Atlantic salmon no longer spawn in the rivers of Belgium, Czecho-

---

A CONNECTICUT SALMON AT HOLYOKE WATER POWER COMPANY'S DAM

On June 23, 1975, the first hatchery-bred Atlantic salmon to return to the Connecticut River from the ocean was captured at Holyoke Water Power Company's dam in Massachusetts. Environmentalists, fishermen, scientists, and legislators responded jubilantly. The salmon, a male, was taken to the federal fish hatchery in New Marlborough, Massachusetts, where he was to be kept until ready for mating in late October. The treasured fish was placed in a special holding tank for protection, and was visited there, like a royal potentate, by reporters, politicians, and scientists.

On Monday, September 29, however, all celebration came to an abrupt halt when Bill Wallentine,

hatchery project leader, found the salmon dead on the ground beside his pool. Apparently mistaking water running into the pool from a pipe for stream flow, the salmon had leapt out of the pool, slipping under a special net which had been placed over the pool to prevent such a mishap. He had fallen on the grass, dying during the night. Wallentine, a Fish and Wildlife veteran, sat down and cried.

The holding pool at New Marlborough was redesigned, but it wasn't until the spring 1976 spawning run that Wallentine and other regional participants in the salmon-restoration program got their second chance. A big female salmon was caught in the Holyoke dam's fish lift on June 11, 1976. Fish and Wildlife technicians Don Williams and David Curtin rushed out from the New Marlborough hatchery in a truck. With the forty-

inch, twenty-three-pound salmon on board in a special tank, the two men started their ninety-minute trip back to the hatchery. Five minutes later, on the Massachusetts Turnpike, their 1964 pickup truck broke down. The two anxious, furious men took four hours to reach the hatchery at twenty-five miles per hour.

Although she reached the hatchery in apparent health, the salmon became ill two days later. Curtin stayed in her pond with her all night long, helping her stay afloat, but she died on June 16. The trauma of the long ride to the hatchery had lowered her resistance to a pneumonia-like infection. That same year, though, on October 26, another male salmon swam into the Holyoke dam's fish lift. David Curtin raced to the dam in a brand-new truck and rushed the salmon to the hatchery without incident. The slovakia, East and West Germany, Luxembourg, and the Netherlands, and have been severely depleted in those of Spain, Portugal, France, Poland, Finland, Sweden, Norway, and Denmark. Pollution, dams, and dredges threaten river life just as much in the Old World as in the New. If the fate of central European forests is any indication, acid rain may threaten the rivers even more.

River conservation is especially complicated in areas such as Europe because rivers may run through or between two or more countries. In November 1986, a massive toxic chemical spill in the Rhine went unheeded for twenty-four hours because Switzerland, where the spill occurred, did not inform the nations downstream about the accident. An estimated five hundred thousand fish and eels died, and aquatic life will not recover for a decade. On the other hand, rivers in huge nations like the Soviet Union may be threatened by the particularly grandiose development schemes that political homogeneity can foster. The Soviets have long planned to dam the enormous Siberian rivers and divert the water to agricultural projects in central Asia, the equivalent of diverting the Yukon to the Dakotas. The fantastic costs of such

fish's sperm proved to be fertile, and Maine's Craig Brook hatchery shipped four females to New Marlborough. Hatchery personnel stripped their eggs into a basin and expressed the male's milt over them. The thirty thousand eggs were then removed to the Pittsford, Vermont, fish hatchery, site of the Northeast's most sophisticated incubation equipment, to await their return to the river.

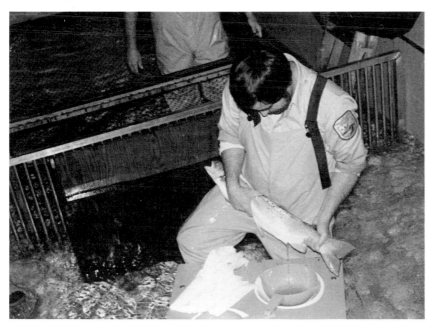

Fish biologist Dan Flint strips eggs from a Connecticut River Atlantic salmon at the National Salmon Station in Sunderland, Massachusetts.

Holyoke fish lift in Massachusetts, where the first hatchery-bred Atlantic salmon to return to the Connecticut River was captured.

projects appear to have led Soviet leadership to shelve at least some of them recently, but river-diverting bureaucracies are tenacious, especially when no private environmental groups sue or lobby against them. (Which is not to say that there *aren't* American bureaucratic plans to divert Yukon or Great Lakes water to the Midwest.) Most other large industrialized or industrializing countries—China, India, Brazil—have ambitious programs for hydroelectric development and water diversion, and considerably less ambitious ones for pollution control and wildlife conservation.

The Amazon River flows from the Peruvian Andes into the Atlantic in northern Brazil.

As in the United States, development worldwide is forcing wildlife to concentrate on the remaining natural parts of rivers. In Europe, the Rhône, Danube, and Guadalquivir deltas form some of the last refuges for otters, pelicans, wading birds, and waterfowl. In India, the Ganges delta is a stronghold of the Bengal tiger, and the river itself harbors a few remaining gharial, a curious, long-snouted crocodile, as well as a species of freshwater dolphin. The lower Yangtze in China may still contain the last Chinese alligators, small relatives of the North American species.

Tropical rivers such as the Amazon and Congo may still seem almost limitless. A number of spectacular and valuable species—giant otters, caimans, manatees, and anacondas, for example—have already been extirpated from many areas, however, and large specimens of fishes such as the arapaima have mostly been fished out. If tropical forest destruction continues at its present rate of 2 percent a year, tropical rivers will rapidly suffer the same downward cycles of siltation and catastrophic flooding as temperate-zone rivers. The potential destruction from such floods is awesome. In the 1970s, a hurricane and flood on the Ganges delta killed one hundred thousand people. In the 1930s, destruction of the Yellow River levees in China caused a flood that killed 3.7 million.

As in the United States, worldwide concentration of river wildlife presents both a danger and an opportunity for conservation. If it continues, the habitat destruction that forced wildlife to concentrate may wipe it out completely. But the more wildlife concentrates, the more spectacular it appears, and the more people are inspired to conserve. As the Atlantic salmon restoration project shows, the more effort conservationists put into wildlife restoration, the more complicated the waste and destruction of wildlife becomes.

T H E
WETLANDS

I T IS JUNE, and southern Florida's rainy season has been underway for a few weeks. Every day, warm, moist air from the Caribbean rises above the hammocks and prairies of the Everglades to form towering thunderheads. When the clouds rise high enough, usually in midafternoon, their moisture precipitates as raindrops, which often fall hard enough to deposit inches of water in the swamp's alligator holes and limestone sinks within hours. As these pools fill, they overflow into the surrounding prairies. Where the sawgrass has grown over cracking black mud during the relatively dry winter months, it now stands in sheets of gently flowing water, making the Everglades live up to its name: a "river of grass."

A wood stork circling in the rising air sees these sheets of water glitter and flash as they reflect the sun through the screen of sawgrass. One might expect the sight to signify abundance to the big, black-and-white bird. With their long beaks and legs, and with the naked, wrinkled heads that prompt local people to call them flintheads, wood storks are eminently adapted to feeding in shallow water. In this way, the only resident stork of the United States is like most of its relatives around the world.

For the stork at this time, however, the Everglades' flooding means not an abundance of food, but a disastrous scarcity of it. This is because of the particular way a wood stork gets food: it moves its partly opened bill around in shallow water until it touches a small fish. The bill then snaps shut on the fish in an instantaneous reflex. It is an efficient way of catching fish: a stork can catch as many as sixty in half an hour.

Wood storks in nest in Corkscrew Swamp, Florida.

Wood storks require a pound of fish a day, minimum, which is a lot for a bird that weighs only a few pounds itself. There is a condition to this efficiency, however. The fish population upon which the stork feeds must be concentrated, or else its bill will not touch, and snap up, enough fish.

The stork soaring in the June thermal is not looking for broad sheets of water in which small catfish and sunfish disperse. He is looking for isolated pools where fish concentrate, and he isn't finding them, even though he has flown over thirty miles from his roost of the night before. In itself, this would not be disastrous for the stork. He can always fly farther, even to Georgia or South Carolina, to find food for himself. But he is also seeking food for a nestling he has left in a mangrove swamp colony to the south. A week before, he sought food for two nestlings, but the weaker one died of starvation three days ago. If the stork does not return to the colony with a full crop of fish today, the surviving nestling is unlikely to last much longer.

Even this situation would not be too disastrous in the natural order of things in the Everglades. Bird nesting is always a chancy affair, and there must have been thousands of bad nesting years during the wood stork's evolution, years when too-early or too-copious rainy seasons cut off the food supply for colonies. Unfortunately, the natural order no longer prevails in the Everglades. The river of grass once flowed uninterrupted from Lake Okeechobee in the north to Florida Bay in the south, its waters contained on east and west only by low, pine-wooded ridges. Now civilization interrupts and impounds it with hundreds of dikes, levees, drainage ditches, canals, and roads, which serve the massive urban conglomerations that have grown up along the coastal ridges in the past century.

Even though much of the Everglades remains wet, seemingly a paradise for fish-eating birds, civilization has changed the patterns of wetness in the great marsh, so that many birds cannot use it as they once did. Wood storks used to nest in November or December, as the marsh dried up, but the creation of water-storage and -transfer systems in the Everglades has caused the marsh to dry up later. Wood storks now start nesting as late as February and March, and this means their young are still in the nest when summer rains cut off the food supply.

This year is the fourth in a row during which the soaring stork's nesting has failed, either because the nestlings died or because none was even produced. In fact, this particular stork has not raised any offspring successfully in his entire life. If he dies without replacing himself, *that* will be a disaster for the species.

A wading, fish-eating bird unable to feed his young in a landscape covered with shallow water demonstrates the complexity of the natural phenomena we call wetlands. Few things are more difficult to measure and define than wetlands because, being both land and water, they are fundamentally ambiguous. Wetlands occur in forests, grasslands, mountains, even in deserts. Wetlands also border every body of water— lake, river, and ocean. They are part of every natural habitat including the skies, since both sky and wetland are integral parts of the hydrologic cycle.

The properties of wetlands continually shift between land and water characteristics. The Everglades shifts between desiccation and inundation, according to seasonal rainfall. Not only rainfall, but also groundwater, sedimentation, earthquakes, glaciation, or growth of vegetation can determine whether this year's wetland becomes next year's dry land or open water. Even when a wetland is clearly a wetland, it can be hard to characterize. A forest wetland is a swamp, unless it is a spruce bog or a cedar fen. A grassland wetland is a marsh, unless it is a sedge meadow (as the Everglades really is, since sawgrass is a sedge instead of a grass) or a vernal pool. Georgia's famous Okefenokee swamp, for example, is a giant sphagnum bog overgrown with sedge prairies, laurel pocosins, and cypress domes—different vegetation types providing different habitats within the same wetland.

The wetland's intermediary role is an ancient and indispensable one in the biosphere. It seems probable that life forms made their first ventures from water to land not by fighting through the surf but by crawling gradually from the shallow margins of primeval rivers and estuaries. Warm, sunlit shallows must have been particularly fertile places long before that, as the oldest wormlike wriggle marks in pre-Cambrian sandstones suggest. Then as now, the interface of land and water at estuaries, deltas, and other wetland sites would have provided an optimal balance of nutrients, moisture, and light for aquatic plant growth and reproduction, and a consequent abundance of animal life. Today's salt marsh plants produce the greatest annual growth of biomass of any ecosystem—four times that of modern cornfields—and about two thirds of the major commercial fishes in the United States depend on coastal wetlands at some point during their life cycles.

We don't really know just how wetland life began, but we probably know as much about how it evolved as we do about any group of organisms. Mud and peat are excellent for making fossils because they often are highly acidic or anaerobic (oxygen-free), which slows organic decomposition. Archaeologists have unearthed the bodies of prehistoric people from Danish bogs whose skin, flesh, and leather garments were almost perfectly preserved by tannic acid. Of course, a few thousand years is very short on the evolutionary scale. There are no such perfect specimens of Paleozoic plants or animals, but their petrified remains are abundant in many places. The giant horsetail and club-moss forests that eventually became Appalachian coal deposits were once swamps growing on estuaries and deltas periodically inundated by shallow seas. The silt that buried the ancient trees served to protect their fossilized remains.

Such vast wetland fossil deposits indicate that there have been long stretches of geological time during which swamps and marshes covered most of the continents. These periods produced some of life's more extravagant manifestations. It seems likely that the largest land animals that ever lived, the sauropod dinosaurs, got much of their food from highly productive Mesozoic wetlands, though they may not have spent their whole lives wallowing in swamps, as researchers assumed originally. Certainly, modern descendants of the sauropod's contemporaries, the turtles and crocodilians, reach some of their largest sizes in wetlands; so do the more recently evolved snakes.

The abundance of ancient wetland fossils leads people to associate swamps with the strangeness of vanished worlds like the dinosaurs'. Many ancient organisms do survive in wetlands, not only crocodiles and turtles, but conifers such as bald cypresses and odd amphibians such as amphiumas and sirens. Yet this "lost-world" impression is something of a romantic illusion. Today's wetlands are no less modern than today's forests, grasslands, or deserts, because they also are dominated by flowering plants, unknown in the sauropod dinosaurs' day. Cattails, sedges, rushes, cordgrasses, pickleweeds, willows, and mangroves do not have conspicuous flowers, but they do have them, all furiously producing pollen and seeds when conditions are right, which is one reason a marsh or swamp can develop quickly on a damp bit of ground.

With their reptiles and flowering plants, wetlands are intermediaries between past and future as well as between water and land. Many plants and animals of tropical and subtropical wetlands such as the Everglades have not changed much since the dinosaurs disap-

Cypress at Duck Lake, Atchafalaya Swamp, Louisiana.

peared, and hardly at all in the past thirty million years. Fossil deposits of about that age in California show evidence of bald cypresses very much like those in Florida today. On the other hand, the glaciated wetlands that stretch across the planet's upper-temperate latitudes are very new in evolutionary terms. Only in the past two million years have continental ice sheets advanced and receded over the flowering plants' world, leaving in their wake a denuded, soggy terrain eminently suited to colonization by wetland organisms. The last North American glaciation receded a mere 14,000 years ago.

Glaciers not only left behind enormous amounts of water as they melted, but they also shaped the land to contain it. They carved out depressions or dammed rivers to form enormous lakes, which then silted in to form marshes and swamp forests. They deposited vast uplands of poorly drained, undulating drift that flooded during wet times to become prairie potholes and sloughs. In some places they left behind buried blocks of ice which, as they melted slowly, formed deep bogs and pools called kettles.

This new terrain was too chilly for many of the more ancient organisms like alligators and bald cypresses, but birds, mammals, and flowering plants adapted to it readily through migration, winter dormancy, or other evolutionary strategies. The glaciated wetlands greatly increased breeding and feeding areas for waterfowl and wading birds. Even today, over ten thousand years after the glaciers melted, North American potholes produce 50 percent of the duck crop in an average year. Glacial potholes are also home to furbearers such as muskrats and minks, although the tendency of potholes to dry up during drought years makes them a more unstable habitat for nonmigratory wildlife than wetlands in more humid areas.

How the earliest humans might have felt about the abundant-but-ambiguous wetlands is hard to imagine. Swamps and marshes around the lakes of the African rift zone were good places for gathering bird eggs, nestlings, and other foods. On the other hand, they were also good places for lurking crocodiles and biting insects. Early hominids were hairier than their descendants, but even the hairiest animals tried to avoid insects that bite and carry ancient primate diseases such as malaria. Our early ancestors probably didn't associate insects directly with disease—modern civilization only made that association in the last century with the discovery of pathogenic microorganisms—but they may have associated wetlands with fevers and untimely deaths. A wetland tree in Kenya is known as the yellow fever tree because it was thought to cause yellow fever if one slept under it. Of course, the fever is actually spread by mosquitoes that breed in treehole pools.

People certainly had made such associations by historical times, when they thought unhealthy air from marshes would cause illness. Yet humans explored and inhabited wetlands anyway, developing cultures like that of the contemporary Marsh Arabs in Iraq's Tigris-Euphrates delta, who live on islands of reeds, travel in reed boats, and eat mainly fish. Some rather sophisticated ways of exploiting wetland life are surprisingly old. Archaeologists have found lifelike canvasback duck decoys in caves inhabited by prehistoric Indians near the marshes of the postglacial American Great Basin, in what is now part of Utah and Nevada. The Indians apparently used the decoys for catching wild ducks with nets. Ancient Egyptian art depicts similar practices.

Clustering in river basins, early civilizations lived on fairly intimate terms with delta marshes and floodplain forests, and doubtless found the reliable food supply a fair exchange for wetland dangers and discomforts. Wetlands were not only a breeding area for fish, shellfish, and waterfowl, but they were also conducive to the development of agriculture. Although most cereal grains came from upland habitats, early civilizations grew them most productively in river valleys, often in irrigated fields, and the earliest irrigation was probably more or less natural, in the manner of the seasonally flooded fields along the Nile. Some crops, especially rice, are natural wetland plants and are grown in artificial marshes to this day.

Wildlife such as storks probably benefited from the proliferation of artificial wetlands by early irrigation. Small fish and crustaceans thrive in paddies and ditches. If people could bring water to the soil to make cropland, however, they could also remove water, and this practice was to have much greater effects on wetland wildlife. As civilization moved north into lands where there was too much water in the soil for crops, wetlands began to disappear. Since the organic mucks that form in wetlands can become extremely fertile soil after drainage, techniques for draining developed rapidly once the idea caught on. Three thousands years ago, Mediterranean city-states used dikes and ditches to drain marshes and lakes for conversion to cropland.

Wetlands often returned after city-states fell, and massive erosion from ancient deforestation created new tidal marshes at the mouths of rivers. On the whole, however, wetlands have shrunk steadily as civilization has grown. Glaciated northern and central Europe apparently was largely swamp and marsh in Roman times, which perhaps is one reason the Romans never conquered much of it. By the end of the medieval period, northern Europeans had so thoroughly drained their land to make new fields that they were forced to begin draining the sea. In Belgium, named for an ancient Gallic tribe which the Romans described as living semiaquatic lives, there are presently two wetlands of significant size. The Netherlands have ten, East and West Germany sixteen, Denmark seven, and Austria three. The numbers are comparable in southern and eastern Europe. Only in the north, in Scandinavia and the Soviet Union, does considerable European wetland remain. The recent rapid decline of the white stork in northern Europe is a result of continuing loss of the pastures and marshes where the species feeds.

European colonists to the New World brought a tradition of hostility toward wetlands with them. This was not without reason. Wetlands in the heavily populated Old World had become reservoirs of disease, and those of the Americas soon did also as colonists imported Old World pathogens in their bloodstreams. Yet the colonies also benefited greatly from America's pristine wetlands. The salt marshes surrounding the earliest, coastal colonies provided food in abundance both for humans, in the form of fish, waterfowl, and shellfish, and for livestock, in the form of enormously productive *Spartina* marsh grasses. Ducks, oysters, and lobsters were such cheap, everyday staples that slaves and indentured servants protested having to eat them all the time. Massachusetts and New Hampshire actually came to armed conflict over salt-marsh pasturage.

Such benefits did not stop colonists from diking and draining coastal marshes to grow rice and indigo, however, and as settlement moved into the interior, settlers drained wetlands for crops as a matter of course. The richest wetlands, those of the tallgrass prairies and lower Great Lakes, disappeared so quickly that relatively little is known about their natural history, except that many creatures now rare or extinct— Carolina parakeets, whooping cranes, trumpeter swans—lived in and around them. Well over 90 percent of the original wetland acreage is gone from Iowa and Illinois.

Other major wetlands have disappeared just about as completely. Of the tule marshes that once filled California's central valley, 90 percent are lost to drainage; fruits and vegetables grow there now. Farmers have converted 80 percent of southeastern bottomland swamps to corn and soybean fields. Only remnants of smaller natural wetlands, like the semitropical "lagunas" of the lower Rio Grande Valley, remain. In all, Americans have drained or filled about 54 percent of the original wetlands in the conterminous United States (according to the U.S. Fish and Wildlife Service's 1984 National Wetlands Inventory), largely for agriculture, but also for urban development, dams, canals, harbors, highways, and other reasons.

Because of traditional prejudice against wetlands, their rapid disappearance from the American landscape did not at first arouse the concern that met forest destruction. While the federal government was establishing the first national parks at Yosemite and Yellowstone, state

DISAPPEARING DUCKS

Ducks in North America are in trouble. The North American waterfowl breeding population is at its lowest level in over thirty years, and many of the most common and economically important species are in dramatic decline. In 1985, mallards were down an estimated 35 percent from their past thirty-year average; pintails were down 50 percent; black ducks showed a 61 percent decline; wigeons were down 37 percent, to their lowest recorded level; gadwalls were down 22 percent, canvasbacks down 28 percent, redheads 17 percent, and scaup 26 percent. The 1986 duck population increased 14 percent from 1985, but was still well below desired levels.

Although none of these species is approaching extinction, some are in danger of "commercial extinction," a term applied most often to fish, and formerly to important game animals. Commercial extinction occurs when a species' population drops to a point at which its pursuit becomes too expensive.

Most of North America's waterfowl breed in the prairie-pothole region of Saskatchewan, Manitoba, and Alberta in Canada. Some of the recent decline in duck populations is the result of a severe

Black duck feeding in salt marsh in Scarborough, Maine.

Male pintail (left) with female on winter migration to Newport Bay in southern California.

drought in this region. Most waterfowl biologists concur, however, that the primary reason for today's record-low waterfowl population is agricultural development of the prairie-pothole region. Canadian farmers have expanded their tilled acreage by 77 percent since the late 1960s, draining thousands of wetland acres the duck need to survive and nest, and destroying the upland cover they need to hide from predators.

legislatures were selling off the Everglades and Okefenokee at a few dozen cents per acre, under authority of the Swamp Lands Acts of the 1850s and '60s, which had simply handed wetlands in the public domain to states. Fortunately for alligators, wood storks, and people, however, these swamps proved more difficult to drain than others. A developer abandoned an attempt to drain the Okefenokee in the 1880s, after taking seven years to dredge twelve of the estimated three hundred miles of canals that finishing the job would have required. Farmers did succeed in draining much of the northern half of the Everglades region, but the southern part, which included extensive marshes and mangrove swamps, remained wild.

When protection finally came to these remnant wetlands, it came less for the sake of the swamps themselves than for that of their most

WINTERING GROUNDS

Although loss of pothole breeding habitat has been the primary cause of recent sharp declines in waterfowl populations, biologists are concerned with problems ducks face in their wintering grounds along four migratory flyways in the United States: the Pacific, Central, Mississippi, and Atlantic.

Each flyway has a unique set of problems, but the Pacific flyway may be in the worst condition. Not only are the ducks there exposed to toxic pollution in the irrigation runoff they often drink, but farmers have converted 90 percent of the wetlands there to agricultural use. Ducks on the remaining habitat are so crowded that they suffer from outbreaks of epidemic diseases. The Interior Department has drained one former waterfowl haven, the Kesterson National Wildlife Refuge in California's San Joaquin Valley, because toxic selenium from irrigation runoff caused birth defects in young birds hatched there.

The Mississippi flyway vies with the Pacific flyway for the largest number of ducks. Four million winter on the coastal marshes of Louisiana alone. Yet habitat is dwindling rapidly, as Arkansas and Mississippi lose bottomland forest to agricultural conversion, and Louisiana coastal marshes erode. Southeast of New Orleans, where construction of the

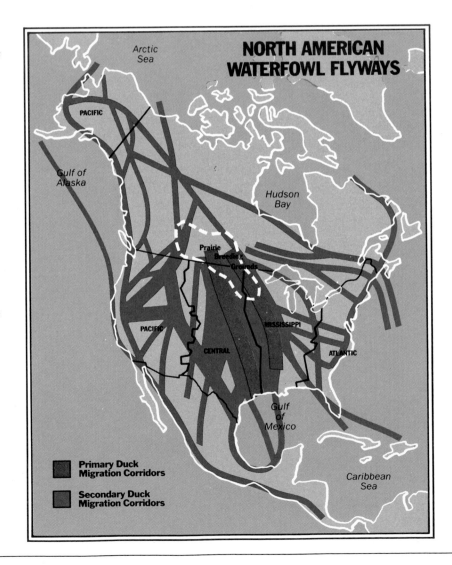

conspicuous inhabitants, waterfowl and wading birds. Most Americans did not yet admire sawgrass prairies and cypress strands as they did mountains and pine forests, but they did admire the flocks of ducks, geese, cranes, and herons that passed overhead in migration, and these had dwindled noticeably by the turn of the century. The greatest species, whooping cranes and trumpeter swans, were almost extinct, and would undoubtedly have followed passenger pigeons and Carolina parakeets into oblivion if parts of their populations had not nested in inaccessible mountains and muskegs (the whooping crane's nesting

Mississippi River Gulf Outlet turned freshwater marsh into open salt water in a matter of years, the mallard population dropped from 250 thousand to 20 thousand. Other water projects and industrial activity ensure that the pattern will repeat itself slowly throughout the rest of the Louisiana coastal marshes. In the past century, Louisiana has lost coastal marsh equal in size to the state of Rhode Island; at fifty thousand acres a year, it is losing wetland faster than any other state, although it still has 45 percent of the nation's remaining marshes. With its potential for waterfowl and fish production, aquifer recharge and purification, and storm and flood buffer, the remaining marshland is valued as high as two hundred thousand dollars per acre.

Primary Goose Migration Corridors

Secondary Goose Migration Corridors

For administrative purposes the North American flyways have been delineated in the United States as shown. Waterfowl do show greater affinity to a particular flyway, and in some cases, where waterfowl migrations are north-south, their flights fit neatly into these patterns. Nearly half the duck and goose populations fly along very distinct corridors.

grounds in Canada's Wood Buffalo National Park were not located until the 1950s). Plume hunters serving the millinery trade pursued the abundant egrets and herons so relentlessly that even they became scarce. Uncontrolled sport and market hunting for ducks and geese also took its toll.

Perhaps because wetlands lacked the popularity of forests and mountains, protection came about in a rather confused and piecemeal fashion at first. Theodore Roosevelt established a national system for forests; in contrast, a complex of legislation and administrative actions concerning wetlands evolved gradually. In 1900, Congress passed the Lacey Act, which authorized the secretary of agriculture to conserve and restore bird species in response to the public outcry against plume hunting. Three years later, Roosevelt established the first national wildlife refuge to protect the Pelican Island colony in Florida. In 1918, Congress passed the Migratory Bird Treaty Act, which placed all migratory birds under protection of federal law, and in 1929 it passed the Migratory Bird Conservation Act, which authorized federal purchase of private lands for bird refuges. It has since passed international bird conservation treaties with Mexico, Japan, and the Soviet Union.

The administration of all this legislation required an agency, and one was put together more or less out of spare parts. A Department of Agriculture Division of Economic Ornithology had concerned itself with birds since 1885. After a name-change to the Bureau of Biological Survey, it took charge of administering the Lacey Act and the new wildlife refuges, as well as other odds and ends such as predator control. In 1940, it became part of the Interior Department and merged with the Bureau of Fisheries to form the Fish and Wildlife Service, which today maintains most of the protected wetland in the United States. A sizable fraction of the over ninety million acres managed by the Fish and Wildlife Service is wetland.

Laws and refuges gradually lessened the decline of wetland birds during the first half of this century, not by stopping or even reducing overall destruction of wetlands, but by protecting the birds themselves and by identifying and protecting the most significant wetlands for breeding and feeding throughout the birds' migration routes. The wildlife-refuge system is perhaps the closest thing we have to the wildlife-habitat corridors that conservationists are concerned with establishing. However, they are not sufficient by themselves to support present wildlife populations.

The whooping crane is a prime example of a vulnerable and wide-ranging species brought back from near extinction by the wildlife-refuge system. Once distributed throughout the prairies and east to Atlantic coastal marshes, the population of five-foot-tall, white cranes had dwindled in 1937, when the establishment of Aransas National Wildlife Refuge on the Texas coast protected their winter feeding habitat. The crane population remains dangerously low now, but it has increased slowly after reaching an all-time low of fifteen birds on the Texas coast in 1941. Protection of the cranes' migration route—refuges exist in Oklahoma, Kansas, Nebraska, and other states—and its nesting grounds in Canada aided the species, along with public education, which reduced hunting. After 1973, the Endangered Species Act gave additional protection to wetlands used by cranes, designating important areas as "critical habitat." This prohibits federal approval of development projects that threaten listed species.

Although habitat protection has not removed the species from danger (the Aransas flock took until 1970 to increase to fifty-two individuals), it has provided leeway for exploring additional ways of restoring whooping cranes. Since cranes usually lay two eggs to a nest but often raise only one chick, biologists were able to establish a captive flock after 1967 by removing second eggs from nests in Canada. In 1974, they began an attempt to create a second wild flock, using what might be called an "ugly duckling" strategy. Biologists placed eggs of captive and wild whooping cranes in the nests of sandhill cranes at Grays Lake National Wildlife Refuge in Idaho. Although they may have been surprised by their unusual offspring, sandhill crane foster parents successfully raised many of the young whoopers. The young whoopers then followed the sandhill flock to wintering grounds along the Rio Grande in New Mexico, and returned to their northern Rocky Mountain homes in summer. About thirty-five whooping cranes now live in the Rockies. None has successfully reproduced yet, but some have shown pairing behavior (with other whoopers), and biologists expect them to start laying eggs in a few years.

By late 1985, the wild and captive whooping crane population stood at 170 birds, an eleven-fold increase in forty-four years. This is by no means a large population for an entire species, of course, and disease or disaster could threaten the cranes' survival again. Yet biologists are hopeful that they can meet the goal of "delisting" the whooping crane from endangered to threatened status by increasing the populations of the two present wild flocks and by creating another on the eastern seaboard, until the number of wild cranes stands at about ninety nesting pairs. This is nowhere near as many whooping cranes as once lived in North America, and biologists hope that the population eventually will become larger.

A problem with such projections is that civilization continues to grow as whooping crane populations do, adding new threats to whooping crane survival. This problem has plagued the refuge system since its inception. Within a few years of the Lacey Act, Congress also passed the Rivers and Harbours Act and the Reclamation Act, which brought the Army Corps of Engineers and the Bureau of Reclamation into the business of draining, filling, dredging, and drowning wetlands. These agencies have devoted as much effort (and a lot more money) to destroying wetlands as the Fish and Wildlife Service has to protecting them.

In the 1940s, agricultural exploitation of wetlands acquired a new twist with the widespread application of new, persistent pesticides. Because ditches and streams often drain into marshes and swamps, and because wetlands often receive direct spraying for mosquito control, these pesticides accumulated rapidly and in great magnitude. After twenty years of applications, Long Island coastal marshes contained thirteen pounds of DDT per acre. Wetlands also became the repositories of many other toxic substances—oil refinery wastes, radioactive materials, and PCBs.

Such problems have gradually led to a broader conservation approach than the setting aside of prime habitat for choice species while other wetlands are left to their fate. So have other factors. As modern health technology has reduced insect-borne diseases, wetlands have joined mountains and forests in the general public's concept of natural beauty. Establishment of Everglades National Park in 1947 confirmed this shift in values, and wetlands are quite popular with recreationists today. One must make reservations well in advance to canoe through Okefenokee National Wildlife Refuge.

Even more important, scientific research of the past few decades has shown how much civilization itself depends on the existence of healthy wetlands. Various studies have indicated not only that salt marshes produce most of our seafood, but that swamps store water with much less evaporation than reservoirs, that marshes and swamps purify sewage effluent more cheaply than treatment plants, and that floodplain forests regulate stream flow more cheaply than flood-control reservoirs. Wetlands are not simply living museums for the preservation of alligators and storks, but a vital part of the hydrologic system that produces clean and reliable water supplies.

As the scope of wetland conservation has broadened, it has become even more complicated. Early on, wetland-protection organizations were few, like the Fish and Wildlife Service and the National Audubon Society (which created the first private wading-bird sanctuaries in southern Florida around the turn of the century). Now, dozens of federal, state, local, and private organizations wholly or partly devoted to wetlands have joined them. The Clean Water Act amendments of 1972 brought in the Environmental Protection Agency, making wetlands protection part of its responsibility to control and prevent water pollution. Ironically, the amendments also took the Army Corps of Engineers partially away from its traditional concern with dams and dredging, by making it responsible, under Section 404, for enforcing the EPA-established regulations against industrial and urban wetland destruction.

Under Section 404, anybody who wants to fill or dredge a swamp—to grow crops, to build a parking lot or shopping mall, or to undertake any other commercial or industrial construction—has to get a permit to do so from the Corps of Engineers. The corps has been less than enthusiastic about its new role as mother hen to spring peepers and snapping turtles, and has tried to abdicate it by defining wetlands so narrowly as to leave most of them outside its jurisdiction, or simply by failing to pay attention to offenders. So far, however, Congress and the courts have continued to reaffirm the corps' responsibility.

Increased public and governmental concern has brought improvements for wetlands and their wildlife. In the 1950s and '60s, hide poachers nearly exterminated alligators in much of the Southeast. The species enjoyed various legal protections, but potential profits from selling the skins for handbags and shoes negated the protection effort. Listing of the alligators under the Endangered Species Act finally brought an end to the hide trade. Since then, alligators have been one of the few species to recover from endangered status. In 1985, the Florida population joined those of Texas and Louisiana in being removed from the endangered list, although populations in the rest of the Southeast are still endangered.

In the early 1970s, concern for the integrity of Everglades National Park led to the defeat of plans for a huge airport on its northern border, which would have altered much of the Big Cypress Swamp and degraded the wilderness quality of the park itself. Another massive project, a cross-state barge canal in northern Florida that would have destroyed a considerable amount of wetlands, also met defeat, and the Big Cypress Swamp was designated a 570,000-acre national preserve. Designation under the Wilderness and Wild River acts put thousands of acres of wetlands off limits to development. This is particularly significant for wildlife refuges, which, like national forests, may otherwise be subject to oil exploration, logging, and other developments.

Proliferation of wetland organizations also has brought progress in protecting some of the highly threatened southern bottomland hardwood swamps and midwestern prairie potholes. Despite their enormous importance to waterfowl—and, in the case of bottomland forest, to black bear and other dwindling southeastern species—these two wetland types have the greatest cropland potential of all remaining undeveloped wetlands. Consequently, they have disappeared fastest, and they are hard to protect, being scattered over wide areas and largely in private hands. Section 404 of the Clean Water Act applies in most cases to dredge or fill activities in these areas (although ongoing farm

BOTTOMLAND HARDWOODS

The seasonally flooded forests of gum, bald cypress, oak, hickory, elm, and pecan along the Mississippi and its tributaries in upper Louisiana, Arkansas, and Mississippi remained true wilderness far into the twentieth century. The forests harbored ivory-billed woodpeckers and red wolves, as well as more than fifty mammal species, including black bears, and seventy non-game bird species. They also served as wintering habitat for migrating waterfowl, especially mallards and wood ducks.

Agricultural conversion has claimed most of these bottomland forests: of an original twenty-five million acres, only three to four million remain, with the rest cleared during the 1950s, '60s, and '70s. Only one-fourth of the remainder is under state or federal ownership, so even more forest could easily be lost, although Section 404 of the Clean Water Act should slow the rate of loss.

Ivory-billed woodpecker.

Sweetgum and red maple reflected in swamp in the Tidewater area of Virginia.

activities are exempt), and the Environmental Protection Agency has shown increased interest in protecting bottomland hardwoods and potholes in recent years. In 1985, Congress passed the Food Security Act, with provisions denying federal aid such as price-support payments, crop insurance, and loans to farmers who convert wetlands or highly erodible lands to cropland. The 1986 Tax Reform Act withdrew some tax benefits from farmers who convert wetlands to commodity production. Such regulation and legislation should slow the rate of destruction.

So far, the most effective way to save particular potholes and bottomland has been for public or private conservation organizations to purchase or lease them. The federal Migratory Bird Conservation Fund began acquiring wetlands in 1934 with money from the Duck Stamp Program, which requires waterfowl hunters to buy federal duck stamps every season. Congressional appropriations under the Wetlands Loan Act of 1961 augmented the fund, which has acquired 3.6 million acres of wetlands for the National Wildlife Refuge System. Acquisition, however, has not kept up with federally declared goals. The Fish and Wildlife Service, National Park Service, and various state and local agencies have also acquired substantial wetland acreage with Land and Water Conservation Fund appropriations.

As federal conservation budgets declined in recent years, some of the most aggressive and effective wetland acquisition has been carried out by private conservation organizations. Funded by public-spirited individuals and foundations, The Nature Conservancy has implemented programs to acquire at least fifty million dollars' worth of wetlands, with a special emphasis on southern bottomlands. By 1985, it had acquired 250 thousand acres along rivers of the Southeast. The Nature Conservancy manages some of these acquisitions itself and conveys others to public agencies as funds become available. Ducks Unlimited is another private organization, specializing (as its name implies) in leasing and rehabilitating waterfowl habitat, mostly in Canadian prairie provinces. Various private industrial firms also have donated thousands of acres of southern swamplands either to the Nature Conservancy or public agencies, combining public service with tax write-offs. The entire 120 thousand-acre Alligator River Wildlife Refuge in North Carolina was one such donation.

Despite progress, most of the estimated remaining ninety-five million wetland acres in the conterminous United States are inadequately protected today, and they are continuing to disappear at a rate somewhere between 300 and 450 thousand acres a year, according to the Fish and Wildlife Service. The rate may be slower than it was during the grain and soybean boom of the 1970s, but it is still fast enough to destroy all unprotected wetland by the mid to late-twenty-first century. As unprotected wetlands dwindle, pressures on protected ones will increase. Consumptive activities—hunting, grazing, and trapping—have already caused crisis in some wildlife refuges. At the Malheur Refuge in Oregon, trampling, irrigation, and fencing asso-

RESTORING A PRAIRIE POTHOLE

In an attempt to restore some of the waterfowl habitat lost to agriculture, the Midcontinental Waterfowl Project funded by the United States Fish and Wildlife Service offered sixty-four dollars per acre per year to farmers in three Minnesota counties who would lease part of their land for wetlands and upland cover. The FWS accepted only farmers willing to sign up for ten years. Despite initial resistance from skeptical farmers, the program is now fully subscribed.

"It took me one and a half months to sign up," said one participant in the program, Charlie Piekarski, of Fergus Falls, Minnesota. "A ten-year hitch is hard on a farmer. You're geared to production." He says the perils of farming today increased his interest in the program. "Farming is like Las Vegas. Every year you gamble with the weather, world markets, you try to anticipate what the consumer wants." But the attraction was that for ten years he wouldn't have to worry about a portion of the farm.

Today, the restored pothole on Piekarski's farm is a migration resting station for redheads, blue-winged teal, grebes, and a variety of other birds. In a few years, when marsh vegetation grows thickly enough, it will become a good breeding spot. Piekarski actively enjoys the addition to his farm. "I come down to listen to the ducks. I bring a chair in spring. They're jumping and swimming. When it's freshly flooded, in early spring, the bugs rise up and it's a dinner plate for the ducks. I get a new lease on life. I come down here, don't worry about my problems . . . get lost here in times of frustration."

Farmland at the edge of prairie pothole in North Dakota.

ciated with grazing increases between 1940 and 1970 resulted in a drop of more than 40 percent in waterfowl nesting success.

Wetlands are so complex that increased human pressures will affect wildlife in far-reaching and often unexpected ways. The wood stork's fate is an excellent example. A few decades ago, nobody dreamed the species might become endangered. As egrets and whooping cranes disappeared at the turn of the century, wood storks thrived, being lucky enough to possess neither showy plumes nor palatable flesh. Nobody knows how many wood storks lived in the United States originally, but estimates of nesting colony populations in the 1930s cited fifteen to twenty thousand breeding pairs at that time. Most of these nested in southern Florida, and since much of the area was protected in the Everglades or the National Audubon Society's Corkscrew Swamp Refuge, the species seemed fairly secure.

The year after Everglades National Park was established, hurricane floods south of Lake Okeechobee caused considerable loss of life and property in drained areas. In response, the Army Corps of Engineers created a flood-control system to protect the farmlands and cities that had grown up on former sawgrass and pinelands. The corps built or improved fourteen hundred miles of canals and levees for moving water from where agribusinesses and developers didn't want it to where they did. It also turned the Kissimmee River north of Lake Okeechobee —the headwaters of the Everglades system—from a meandering, one-hundred-mile river to a fifty-mile drainage ditch, which increased the pasture and farmland along the former river, but also greatly increased rate of eutrophication and siltation in shallow Lake Okeechobee.

Agribusinesses and developers did not particularly care how water moved southward from their lands into the national park, and evidently the corps didn't either. Its projects effectively ended the natural movement of water into the park. After the construction, water which used to flow into the park's prairies and sloughs ran instead in canals and through water storage impoundments. In times of drought, canal control structures stayed shut, starving the park of water; in flood times, they stayed open, drowning the park. In 1970, Congress required the corps to provide a minimum amount of water to the park every year, but the corps delivered the water in monthly spurts, not in the natural manner—a seasonal surge that begins with the summer rainy season and tapers into the fall. Since Congress stipulated no maximum, moreover, the corps continued to drown the park when its storage areas contained more water than it wanted.

When the corps projects began, no one monitored wood stork populations because they seemed so safe. By the late 1950s, however, nesting populations in the Corkscrew Swamp and Everglades seemed abnormally low. The National Audubon Society conducted aerial surveys, which indicated that Florida's stork population had declined to eleven thousand breeding pairs. Populations continued to decline by about one thousand pairs every four years, and in 1974 the society began a study to find out why.

Surveyors studied nesting colonies throughout Florida during the breeding season, weighing and measuring young storks to determine their growth and survival rates, a risky enterprise considering the expectant attitudes of alligators underneath nest trees. More than five years of studies indicated that storks were declining because their food supply was no longer sufficient to support the nesting colonies. Between 1961, when the Corps of Engineers had largely completed construction of its projects, and 1975, Everglades National Park storks had only five good reproductive years. Their population dropped from 2,500 pairs in 1960 to 1,300 pairs in 1975. After that year, Everglades Park storks had only one good breeding year, 1976. Population declines coincided with the completion of water-control structures on the northern and eastern borders of the park, suggesting that man-made changes in southern Florida water supply threatened the storks.

By 1984, the total number of breeding stork pairs in all of Florida and Georgia had declined to about five thousand, and the species appeared on the federal endangered list (Florida had considered it endangered since 1972). A large proportion of these birds was no longer in southern Florida, where the species had been most abundant originally, but scattered in small colonies farther north, wherever they could find adequate feeding habitat. Evidence even showed that southern Florida storks were emigrating northward, to areas where food supplies were more reliable. It is sadly ironic that wildlife was forced to abandon one of the world's most famous national parks because they were unable to feed their young in it.

The wood stork's endangered status is only the most dramatic symptom of a general degradation in the Everglades ecosystem. Wading birds overall have declined by about 90 percent in the region since the 1930s. Fewer than forty thousand of all kinds live there now; the area may have supported as many as two and a half million in the nineteenth century. Sport and commercial fisheries in Florida Bay have declined disastrously as the fresh water supply to estuaries and sloughs, where fish and shrimp breed, has fallen off. Alligators have suffered along with wood storks from the alternate drowning and parching of the Everglades, because an unreliable water supply affects their nesting success, too. Rare species such as manatees and American crocodiles, both of which have been on the federal endangered list for many years, also suffer from civilization's expansion. Collision with power-boat propellers kills and injures the slow-moving manatees, while coastal development destroys the mangrove and salt-marsh habitats of North America's only native crocodile.

AMERICA'S STORK

The wood stork is one of three species of New World storks, but it is the only one that nests or occurs regularly in the United States. It ranges in wetlands across the southern United States, from southern California to South Carolina, southward through the tropical and subtropical regions of Mexico, Central America, and South America to central Argentina.

Storks have historically nested in coastal states from eastern Texas to South Carolina, although the largest and most consistently used nesting sites in the United States are in Florida. In recent decades, storks in the United States have nested in peninsular Florida, in a few small colonies in southeastern Georgia, and, rarely, in southeastern South Carolina. This shrinkage of stork nesting range has resulted from loss of habitat, and stork populations have declined so much in recent years that the species has been declared endangered. Wood storks are highly social birds that nest in colonies and forage in flocks.

Stork colonies, often called rookeries in Florida, traditionally have been located in cypress or mangrove swamps. Less often, they occur in thickets on islands or in marshes or in stands of swamp hardwoods. Colonies range in size from only a few nests to as many as several thousand. Storks may nest in "pure" colonies containing no other species or in mixed colonies containing many herons, egrets, ibis, cormorants, or pelicans.

Male and female storks participate about equally in the construction of nests, incubation of eggs, and feeding of chicks. Nests are large, bulky platforms of sticks. In a crowded colony, they may be located within two or three feet of each other. A stork lays between two and four large white eggs; incubation takes about thirty days. Parent birds feed chicks by regurgitating whole fish onto the bottom of the nest, where nestlings quickly consume it. One adult remains at or near the nest to shade and protect the young while the nestlings are downy. When chicks are four to five weeks old and beginning to develop feathers, both parents spend most of each day gathering food. Young birds make their first flights at about fifty-five to sixty days, but continue to return to the nest to be fed until they are seventy-five days or older.

Adapted from "The Wood Stork," by John C. Ogden, *Audubon Wildlife Report*, 1985.

Wood stork feeding at Mrazek Pond in the Florida Everglades.

RESTORING THE EVERGLADES

There is no other place on Earth quite like the Everglades, no other subtropical wetland of such magnitude and diversity. Early American settlers in southern Florida found a river of grass, fifty miles wide and 250 miles long, flowing gently toward the sea, a seemingly endless golden-green wet prairie interrupted here and there by dark green hardwood hammocks and silvery patches of open water, inhabited by seemingly countless birds, alligators, and other wildlife.

Today, half the Everglades is gone: nearly 4.5 million people live around the shrinking wilderness, and their numbers increase daily. In addition to the cities of the east and west coasts, vast sugar-cane fields, cattle ranches, and vegetable farms have taken the place of wetland. Developers have drained and filled the land and, with the help of the federal government and the Army Corps of Engineers, have built an elaborate system of canals, dikes, locks, and levees to manipulate water flows and provide for municipal and agricultural water supplies.

This has proved disastrous for wildlife in the region. Unnatural containment has dried out great sections of the swamp and sent enormous fires sweeping across places once lush and green. On the other hand, releasing huge quantities of water for flood-control purposes at various locks and levees has wiped out countless alligator nests. Diversion of water has changed the normal saline balance in coastal estuaries, with disastrous consequences to fish-breeding waters. Along with the wood stork, numerous bird species have had their nesting patterns disrupted. Everglades' natural hydrology is also threatening human water supplies. Canals and drainage have sharply reduced freshwater flow into the Biscayne Aquifer upon which millions of Florida city dwellers depend for drinking water.

Twenty years ago it may have seemed wise for the Army Corps of Engineers to reroute the scenic Kissimmee River and turn it from a shallow, meandering stream one hundred miles long to a straight fifty-mile-canal. Now, however, in the words of Florida Senator Bob Graham, such changes have "reduced a natural work of art into a thing pedestrian and mundane." Channeling the Kissimmee has also backfired. Runoff from the channelled stream is choking Lake Okeechobee with chemicals and manure, a problem not only for wildlife but for people around the lake. The river's original meandering course filtered the water.

Over twenty-one environmental and conservation groups have joined to remake the Everglades in its former image by returning the Kissimmee to its original course, reducing pollution of Lake Okeechobee, and restoring natural seasonal sheet flow to the still wild part of the Everglades. The proposed changes are controversial and will be difficult to implement, but they are necessary for the salvation of a wilderness of global significance.

ABOVE: *Roseate spoonbills.*

ABOVE, RIGHT: *The great blue heron's rare white phase occurs only in southern Florida.*

OPPOSITE PAGE, LEFT: *American alligator.*

OPPOSITE PAGE, RIGHT: *American anhinga.*

RIGHT: *Whooping crane with sandhill cranes.*

The wetland vegetation upon which swamp fauna ultimately depend is in decline as well. The freshwater marshes are flooded for shorter periods each year, and this has allowed an alien weed tree, melaleuca, to take over areas suffering frost or hurricane damage. Casuarina, or Australian pine, another alien weed tree is invading beaches and coastal marshes, while yet another, Brazilian pepper, is spreading in disturbed pine and hardwood forests. By reducing evaporation and humidity, drainage of much of southern Florida may even be changing the climate, making it cooler in winter and warmer in summer.

Developments similar to those affecting the Everglades are destroying other protected wetlands completely. Kesterson National Wildlife Refuge in California's San Joaquin Valley is one of the last remnants of the native bunch-grass prairies, wildflower-rich vernal pools, and tule-rush marshes that once filled the valley. It was an important wintering and breeding area for dozens of waterfowl, shorebird, and wading-bird species. Nevertheless, the Interior Department has had to close the refuge, shutting off its water supply so that birds will not nest or feed there.

That water supply came from farmland irrigated and drained by a vast Bureau of Reclamation canal system, and it was poisoning the refuge. Soils in the San Joaquin Valley contain high levels of selenium, a naturally occurring element which is toxic to living organisms in more-than-minute doses. Irrigation water dissolved the selenium in the soil, then carried it into drainage ditches. When the water drained out of the fields and flowed down the Bureau of Reclamation canal system into the refuge's 1,200-acre pond complex, it contained four hundred times the amount of selenium considered safe for human consumption.

Not surprisingly, the selenium-laced water had highly unpleasant effects on wildlife. In 1983, refuge personnel noticed that a large proportion of waterfowl and wading-bird chicks were being hatched with horrible deformities: misshapen beaks, exposed brains, clubfeet, useless wings. Many eggs were infertile, and adult birds were dying, too. In 1985, the California Water Resources Board, determining that the poisoned water threatened human health as well, ordered the Bureau of Reclamation either to find a way of ending the poisoning or to close the Kesterson pond system.

Since closing the ponds means that many San Joaquin farmers will have nowhere to dispose of their waste irrigation water, the situation has been quite controversial. The Bureau of Reclamation's original idea had been to dispose of the waste water not at Kesterson, but farther downstream, in San Francisco Bay. San Francisco Bay residents

were unenthusiastic about the plan, however, and the scheme died
for lack of funding in 1975. Finding yet another way to dispose of the
water will be costly, as will digging out and disposing of the poisoned
pond sediments at Kesterson.

In Louisiana, yet another wetland refuge is disappearing. Delta
National Wildlife Refuge is one of the nation's oldest, established as
a haven for waterfowl at the mouth of the Mississippi. The government
purchased most of its almost fifty thousand acres of marshland at a
cost of over two hundred thousand dollars. Since 1956, however, fifty-
one percent of the refuge has disappeared into the Gulf of Mexico,
which is eroding the Mississippi Delta's southern tip at a current rate
of about thirty-nine square miles a year. In a hundred years, the Delta
Refuge may very well not exist.

The various causes include hurricanes, rising sea levels, changing
river channels, and other natural phenomena. But the many changes
humans—and in particular, the Army Corps of Engineers—have made
on the Mississippi River and its tributaries have also contributed to
disintegration of the refuge. Deltas form as free-flowing rivers carry
large amounts of sediment down to their mouths. The Mississippi and
most of its tributaries are no longer free-flowing rivers, so sediment
stays upstream, behind dams or on the bottoms of reservoirs. Unless
more sediment continually replenishes them, deltas stop growing; once
they stop, they erode.

On top of this, human alterations to the Mississippi Delta itself
have accelerated erosion. People have channeled the river's course
through the delta and have built canals for transportation and oil
development. Canals allow Gulf water to intrude deep into marshes
and hasten their disintegration. If the entire delta washes away, as now
appears likely, the effects not only on waterfowl but on Louisiana's
important fishing industry will be incalculable.

The problems facing the delta and Everglades are similar to those
of Yellowstone Park: both mountains and wetlands are wildland pockets
surrounded by expanding development. The difference, of course, is
that civilization generally finds draining or filling wetlands easier than
leveling mountains (although strip-mining for coal endangers much
mountain wilderness). Farming and ranching on the plains and valleys
east and west of Yellowstone won't directly threaten grizzlies as long
as they have enough habitat in the mountains. Even a wetland like
the Okefenokee can coexist with adjacent farmland and commercial
forest because it is a headwater wetland. Its main drainages, the Suwannee and St. Mary's rivers, begin in the swamp.

The Everglades and the Delta and Kesterson refuges are all downstream from major agricultural and/or urban conglomerations, so their

water quality is much more vulnerable to disturbance than headwater wildlands. If they are to survive, we shall have to modify the artificial systems that are choking and poisoning them. This will be a taller order even than keeping logging and mining out of the Yellowstone ecosystem.

In the case of the Everglades, at least, conservationists are making an ambitious attempt to repair some of the damage. Pointing to evidence that the destruction of southern Florida's natural hydrology is threatening human water supplies as well as wildlife (salt water is infiltrating the Biscayne Aquifer that provides drinking water for greater Miami because not enough fresh water reaches it anymore), a coalition of citizen's groups and the state of Florida has proposed to "turn the clock back" on the Everglades: to return the Kissimmee River to its natural, one-hundred-mile river channel, and to modify the Corps of Engineers' canal system so that water once again will flow into the Everglades as a wide, seasonally rising and falling river of grass. Other proposals call for acquiring more wetland for preservation, restoring drained areas to wetland, plugging canals that now drain water from the Everglades' eastern edge, cleaning up badly polluted Lake Okeechobee, and redesigning Alligator Alley, the trans-Everglades highway, so that it is less of a barrier to water and wildlife movement. The ultimate purpose of the proposals, as expressed by Senator (then Governor) Bob Graham of Florida, will be "to provide that by the year 2000 the Everglades will look and function more as it did in 1900 than it does today."

Some of these proposals—land purchases, highway redesign, plugging of a few canals—are being implemented. The Corps of Engineers has balked, however, at the two most important ones—restoration of natural flows to the Kissimmee and the "river of grass." Although some berms and culverts newly installed in the present Kissimmee ditch allow water back into natural river meanders and oxbows, the corps' district officer has recommended that it not participate in restoring the river on the grounds that "economic benefits" would be insufficient.

Restoring natural flow to the "river of grass" will be even more difficult than restoring the Kissimmee, which after all is *above* the Corps of Engineers' canal system. Everglades National Park must share water with the corporate sugar farms and other developments that lie upstream of it. Since Congress establishes the park's annual water allocation, conservationists will have to look to Congress to change it. Given the lobbying power of agribusiness and other development interests, this will be an arduous process. If it drags on too long, however, there may not be any wood storks left in the Everglades to protect.

Squeezed on three sides by an exploding population, the Everglades' precarious situation typifies that of wetlands globally. Most temperate-zone wetlands are already drained, and tropical wetlands are going the same way as tropical forests, for much the same reasons (although wetland drainage requires more capital investment than forest clearing and thus tends to proceed more slowly). In their natural state, wetlands can provide abundant supplies of high-quality protein foods, but they may provide even larger supplies of lower-quality carbohydrates once converted to cropland. Nations desperate to feed fast-growing populations may choose quantity over quality.

Insect-borne diseases continue to be a major problem in tropical countries, contributing to pressure to drain wetlands or to pump large amounts of pesticide into them, although rice paddies can breed malaria mosquitoes just as natural marshes can. Wetlands also get drowned or dredged during dam, harbor, and barge-canal construction. Even in places where wetlands benefit from official protection—Rumania's Danube Delta, for instance—well-meant developments like fish-farming can put added pressure on wildlife. International banking organizations with capital to invest have been less than sensitive to the ecological consequences of wetland exploitation (or to the destruction of other natural habitats).

Though wetlands are subject to similar threats worldwide, the beauty of wading birds seems to have a universal appeal for humans. Cranes, storks, and herons figure largely in the folklore and art of most cultures. Many of the earliest wildlife refuges in places like Japan, the Soviet Union, and India were set aside for wading birds. For example, China has an active wading-bird conservation program. The sizeable Zhalong Reserve in northwest China offers feeding and breeding habitat to six crane species—the red-crowned, common, white-naped, demoiselle, hooded, and Siberian—perpetuating a Chinese tradition that goes back to the fifth century B.C. when the legendary Duke Yi of Wei welcomed cranes to his lands as honored guests.

Certainly, the role of wading birds in the American conservation movement has been pivotal. There was no conservation movement at all until the plume-trade threat banded scientists and private citizens together in the first effective political coalitions. Determination to save the birds became determination to save the habitat on which they depend.

T H E
OCEANS

PRECEDING PHOTO: *Crinoid and gorgonian coral typical of reefs in Southeast Asia and the Philippines.*

I

T IS SUCH A STILL SUMMER EVENING on the Bay of Fundy that
the sound of waves on the granite shores of Campobello Island
has sunk to murmur. Bay and sky seem empty: no planes or
boats are in sight. Yet occasionally there is a sharp, explosive sound,
almost like a shot, although muffled from echoing across the water.
It evidently comes from some distance, and in the quiet, the explosive
report seems unearthly.

The sound is not really made by extraterrestrials, but if summer
vacationers knew its origin, they might be as surprised as if little green
men had produced it. A baby right whale lies in the water several
miles offshore, slapping its flippers and flukes against the surface, and
the resultant sound waves are strong enough to echo off the shore
cliffs. This may seem an excessive distance for baby sounds to reach,
but sound carries far over water, and six-month-old right whales are
over twenty feet long. Babies tend to make surprising amounts of noise
when signaling their mothers anyway, and that may be what this baby
is doing, although we don't know enough about right whales to be
sure.

The mother left her calf at the surface while she dove to feed on
a swarm of copepods. He amused himself for a while by playing with
a patch of floating kelp, but whales can stay underwater for many
minutes, and perhaps he has grown impatient. Or perhaps the tail-
slapping is just another form of play. In any case, his mother surfaces
a few minutes later, making the right whale's characteristic J-shaped
double spout that once brought excited cries from the crow's nests of

whaling ships. The calf hurries over and slides on her back, and she rolls and bats him away with a flipper, perhaps playfully, perhaps in annoyance at this disturbance while she is getting her breath.

Someone who could have watched her feeding underwater, or who had watched right whales surface-feeding as they do in Cape Cod Bay in the summer, might have been a little surprised at this frisky behavior. Right whales are the slowest, stoutest whales. Compared to the other group of baleen-feeding whales, the rorquals (which includes blue, humpback, fin, sei, and minke whales), right whales are what sailing ships would be to steamships. Whereas blue whales sometimes pursue their krill prey at speeds of over ten miles an hour, engulfing entire swarms with a single gulp of their expandable gullets, right whales plod along at two to six miles an hour. They simply hold their huge underslung jaws open as they swim through copepod swarms and let the screens of baleen hanging from their upper jaws filter the small crustaceans out of the water. When enough accumulates, they scrape the baleen with their tongues and throw the food down gullets about as wide as stovepipes.

Pokey as this method of feeding may seem, it suffices to nourish right whales to an average weight of seventy tons and a length of fifty feet. It also gives them the energy for other apparently playful behavior. Like their more streamlined relatives, right whales occasionally breach, leaping out of the water, sometimes almost completely, and twisting to fall on their backs or sides with thunderous splashes. Breaching may have a practical function in that it gets rid of external parasites such as whale lice, but some right-whale behavior seems purely for fun. They like to go "sailing." A whale extends its flukes in the air and lets the wind drive it across the surface as though it were a sloop. Whales have been seen sailing a certain distance thus, then swimming back to the starting point and doing it again. Off the Argentina coast, right-whale calves have been observed wrapping themselves in kelp strands, rather as human youngsters do with crepe streamers at a birthday party.

The calf quiets down after his mother's slap, perhaps feeling rebuked, perhaps simply because he is tired. They have just arrived in the bay after a very long trip for an infant, even a twenty-foot-long one. Western Atlantic right whales winter off the Georgia-Florida coast, so the calf probably was born there, then followed his mother on a six-month migration up the coast to the New Brunswick shore. Nobody can be entirely sure about this, however, because nobody really knows that much about the right whales, even though they live alongshore the most populous part of the United States. They are so rare now that they are very difficult to study. Their wintering and calving grounds off Georgia and Florida went undiscovered until 1984.

Sperm whale sounding.

(Even common whales are little-known because they spend most of their lives underwater.)

What we do know about right whales suggests that they are less specialized, perhaps less intelligent than other whale species. Their brains are not as large in proportion to their bodies as those of sperm whales or some dolphin species. They don't vocalize as much as dolphins or make the eerie, majestic "songs" of humpback whales. They don't dive deeper than three thousand feet and stay submerged for more than ninety minutes, as sperm whales do.

Because we know so little about them, of course, right whales may prove to have undreamed-of talents. Yet for the present, they seem like standard models of whaledom: basic, medium-sized (for a whale), warty, black tubs ambling through the plankton. Rights certainly have been the standard whales for whaling fleets during the roughly eight hundred years of commercial whale-catching. Their slowness made them the easiest whales to catch, and their stoutness made them float after they were killed, whereas rorquals sink. That is why they are called right whales. Before modern whaling technology became fast and efficient enough to exploit more streamlined species, they were the "right" whales to hunt. Sperm or gray whales might smash a boat, and rorquals might drag it for hours and then get away. Right whales generally were neither aggressive nor fast enough to make such difficulties.

That a fifty-foot-long, seventy-ton, oceanic descendant of smaller land mammals (related to cows) should be considered in any way ordinary says a great deal about the extraordinary nature of that creature's habitat. Compared to the oceans, the land and sky habitats are really rather insignificant, important as they seem to the creatures that inhabit them. Indeed, land and skies would not be inhabited if not for the oceans; the water and oxygen upon which sky and land life depend come from the oceans.

Most things in the biosphere begin, end, and begin again in the oceans. They cover seventy-one percent of the globe and contain over eighty percent of its living matter, or biomass. Most of the sedimentary and metamorphic rocks that form today's continents lay under salt water once, as the seashells Charles Darwin found high in the Andes demonstrated. Most of them will lie under salt water again, once rain, wind, and glaciers have scraped them away into river deltas and estuaries. Then those deltas and estuaries will rise to mountaintops again, scraped up by drifting continents.

Almost certainly, life itself began in the oceans. Life is still mostly water, and salt water at that: blood and other organic fluids have chemistries similar to sea water. Fossils of sea life long predate those of land and skies. The question of how life might have begun in the oceans is much less certain, of course. The general belief used to be that life began at the ocean surface, where energy from ultraviolet radiation or lightning caused formation of giant, self-replicating organic molecules from a "primordial soup" of methane, ammonia, and other organic chemicals dissolved into the water from the preoxygen atmosphere. More recently, scientists have come to doubt that the early atmosphere could have contained significant amounts of such unstable compounds. They suspect life evolved in the ocean bottom, in the mud, or perhaps around volcanic vents. We know such vents to be sources of methane and other organic chemicals, and in fact primitive organisms live around such vents today, hydrogen sulfide powering their metabolisms.

There is no fossil evidence to show how life began in the oceans, but there is evidence that it has been there a very long time. Concentrated masses of thick-walled cells resembling today's bacteria have been found in South African chert (a silica-based rock similar to flint) estimated to be 3.5 billion years old. Since the planet itself is roughly five billion years old, the living ocean's antiquity is impressive. Of course, the forms that ocean life took during the first two billion years were not impressive by today's standards: they were all single-celled organisms resembling bacteria and blue-green algae. But things eventually got more complicated, although, again, we have no fossil evidence of how single-celled organisms evolved into many-celled ones.

There is ample evidence that they did evolve. Remains of creatures resembling (but only distantly related to) worms and jellyfish lie in billion-year-old rocks, and by the beginning of the Cambrian period most of the animal phyla that now exist (mollusks, arthropods, chordates, and others) had appeared. There also were some phyla that *don't* exist now, which we can determine from rare deposits like the Burgess Shale of British Columbia, formed by sudden mud avalanches that buried and preserved an unusual array of 530-million-year-old soft-bodied creatures. As many as a dozen of these creatures cannot readily be placed within any living animal group: one is so weird that scientists named it *Hallucigenia*.

Since then, the oceans have repeatedly demonstrated an ability to produce the most extraordinary creatures, from the jawless fishes, scorpion-like eurypterids, and cone-shelled nautiloids of the Paleozoic era, to the sharks and lobe-finned fishes, giant marine reptiles, and giant ammonoids of the Mesozoic, to the cod and tuna, whales, and octopi of the Cenozoic. Ocean life has nearly been wiped out a number of times, including a great extinction at the end of the Permian period when trilobites died out, and another at the end of the Cretaceous period when giant reptiles and ammonoids (shell-dwelling relatives of octopi) did. Yet evolution has refilled emptied oceans gradually with forms that exceeded extinct predecessors in biological specialization. For example, ocean-going reptiles appear never to have evolved the ability to strain plankton from the water with seive-like jaw structures such as whale baleen. The nutritional advantage that this adaptation

Fossils of trilobites, early marine arthropods.

Plankton.

gives whales apparently has allowed them to become the biggest animals that ever lived.

For all their novelty, the oceans retain an even more impressive environmental stability. The most ancient creatures continue to inhabit them along with the most modern because the conditions that allowed life to prosper in pre-Cambrian waters still prevail. Although rain has been washing dissolved minerals into the oceans throughout life's tenure, ocean waters remain within tolerable limits of salinity. Science probably will continue to find living examples of ocean life forms once thought extinct, like the lobe-finned coelocanth discovered in deep waters off Madagascar in the 1930s.

The oceans' combination of stability and novelty produces an abundance that seems limitless from the perspective of dry-land life. Yet ocean life is limited by the same fundamental factor as land life—the availability of food—and most ocean food comes from the same basic process—photosynthesis by green plants. Considerably more photosynthesis occurs in the oceans than on land. The one-celled algae that make up 99 percent of ocean plankton are the main source of atmospheric oxygen. It doesn't occur everywhere in the oceans with equal abundance, however. In fact, rich swarms of plankton, consisting of small crustaceans and fish as well as algae, are the exception rather than the rule, because the mineral nutrients that algae need to photosynthesize are available only in certain parts of the oceans.

The oceans are not simply global fishponds. They are as moody and changeable as the skies. Like the skies, they flow and eddy constantly across the Earth's surface, driven by solar energy. Water warmed by the equatorial sun rises and flows north and south in great currents such as the Gulf Stream of the western Atlantic. Such warm tropical waters are not rich in mineral nutrients, because they flow far above the fertile ooze of the sea floor. Underneath them, however, flow other currents of cold water moving south or north from the poles. Where these currents rise to the surface, forced upward by collision with a continent or underwater plateau such as the Grand Banks off Newfoundland, they raise huge amounts of nutrients from the ocean floor to where algae can use it (there is light enough for photosynthesis only at the upper layer). Ocean life concentrates in such places, or along continental shallows, where rivers and offshore currents sweep nutrients into the water. Of the world's fish catch, 90 percent comes from 30 percent of the oceans.

Of course, there are a great many food-rich places scattered about the oceans. Since so many are located at the edges of continents, it is easy to see how a land creature would get a deceptive impression of limitless abundance. Indeed, such a creature would have to expend quite a lot of effort to discover that the abundance does have limits. The ancestors of whales must have made that discovery as they gradually wandered out of the food-rich rivers and estuaries, in which they originally swam, into the largely barren open oceans. The worldwide migrations which their descendants presently make to polar or continental shelf feeding grounds are a response to the discovery of limits.

We don't know exactly when or why humans first ventured onto salt water, but they seem likely to have done so along the routes that whales used—rivers, estuaries, and coastlines. They are also likely to have sought the same thing whales did—food. Of course, humans had not been swimming in rivers for millions of years before they entered the seas, so they had to invent boats. Most of the known Neolithic cultures that lived near water had boats of some kind: dugouts and bark canoes in North America, balsa rafts and reed canoes in South America, outriggers in Polynesia, bamboo rafts in east Asia, papyrus boats in the Near East, skin curraghs in Europe, kayaks and umiaks in Greenland. As recent experiments by Norwegian explorer Thor Heyerdahl and others have demonstrated, some of these early boats were surprisingly seaworthy: enough to get aborigines to Australia and Polynesians to Tahiti and Hawaii.

OCEAN DIVERSITY—OCEAN PROTEIN

Although tropical forest may have more species of organisms (largely insects and flowering plants), no habitat on earth has more phyla of organisms than the marine environment. Oceans contain not only vertebrates, mollusks, and arthropods, but also sponges, coelenterates (jellyfish), and echinoderms (seastars), as well as brachiopods (which resemble clams but aren't mollusks) and many other obscure groups.

The diversity of ocean animal life has made the seas a cornucopia of protein for human consumers. Various cultures have gained sustenance not only from marine mammals, birds, reptiles, and fish, but from shrimp, crabs, clams, oysters, mussels, squid, sea urchins, abalones, snails, and sea cucumbers. Cultural use of marine foods remains diverse, from the American tuna sandwich to the Japanese and southern European enthusiasm for squid. More than a hundred species of finfish, crustaceans, and shellfish are caught commercially, and twenty-two of these commonly yield one hundred thousand tons of seafood or more annually. Five fish species and associated relatives—herrings, cods, jacks, redfishes, and mackerels—make up more than half of the yearly catch. Per capita fish consumption is lower in Third World nations than in industrialized nations, but fish is still a key protein source in the diet of coastal peoples, often making the difference between protein deficiency and a nutritionally adequate diet.

This Fiji chalice coral provides shelter for many species of fish.

Despite their wanderings, early humans didn't really test ocean abundance. They lived in relatively small communities and caught only enough food for their own needs. If they fished out village waters, they could always move. Larger prey such as whales were sufficiently hard to catch that they were virtually invulnerable to depletion by human hunters. Although Inuit and northwest Indian whalers were highly skilled, their expeditions had relatively low success rates. It remains possible that prehistoric humans may have exterminated some ocean creatures as they seem to have exterminated some land ones, but we have no evidence of it.

Only with the rise of civilization did humans discover ocean limits, and the knowledge came late, even though saltwater trade routes and fisheries quickly became indispensable to growing city states. Sailing fleets plied the Mediterranean as early as ten thousand years ago, and dried fish was a staple food throughout Greek and Roman times. Yet classical civilization did not send its fishing fleets beyond the relatively limited areas of the Mediterranean and Black seas. Past the coastal waters of Gaul and Spain, the Atlantic remained unknown territory. Not until commerce and industry had spread throughout Europe in the late Middle Ages did demand for commercial supplies of whale and seal oil, baleen (used to make items such as brushes, springs, chair seats, and knife handles), salt fish, and other ocean goods expand enough to send fleets across the Atlantic.

The Portuguese fishermen and Basque whalers had already depleted the right whales and herring of the Bay of Biscay, but the herds and schools they found off the coast of Newfoundland after 1535 must have made the scarcity in the Bay of Biscay seem unimportant. Nobody knows how many right whales lived in the Atlantic at that time; probably hundreds of thousands. Other fleets quickly joined the Portuguese and Basques.

The Dutch, seeking a northern passage to the Indies, chanced upon huge herds of bowhead whales (close, polar relatives of the right whale) in the waters east of Greenland; they established a town called Smeerenberg (which translates roughly as Fat City) on the Island of Spitsbergen north of Norway to process blubber and baleen. English, French, German, and Danish whalers also arrived and quickly fell into various squabbles with the Dutch and one another over the whale supply. There was big money to be made. According to estimates, every whale killed by the Dutch in that period brought in the equivalent of 33,500 dollars, and the overall income of the seventeenth-century Dutch industry more or less matched that of twentieth-century whaling in Antarctica, even though the former was carried out with sailing ships and hand-thrown harpoons, the latter with factory ships and harpoon cannons.

Yet the busy fleets discovered within decades that the new whale supply wasn't as endless as it seemed. Annual catches averaging in the thousands of whales in the seventeenth century began to drop into the hundreds in the eighteenth. Despite their initial abundance, right whales proved to have a low reproductive potential. Like females of other whale species, right and bowhead females almost always bear single young and breed only every other year or so. Young whales take many years to reach maturity. Having few natural predators, whale populations are not adapted to fast growth. Although whalers haven't hunted rights significantly in over a century, and agreements have protected them completely since 1938, right numbers have never recovered from early whaling. About three thousand survive in the southern hemisphere, where hunting began later, but only five hundred are thought to live in the North Atlantic, and fewer than 200 in the North Pacific. These populations may have become so scattered that males and females simply have difficulty finding each other.

The disappearance of right and bowhead whales discouraged Basque and Dutch whalers, but not others. New England colonists had caught small numbers of right and gray whales off their coast since the mid-seventeenth century. In the beginning of the eighteenth, they ventured farther offshore to hunt a species that had not been exploited much before, the sperm whale. Sperm whales are toothed whales (like dolphins and killer whales), rather than baleen whales. They get their food by diving deep to catch squid, a much more active prey than plantonic crustaceans. Sperm whales are sleeker, faster, and more aggressive than right whales, prompting Basque and Dutch whalers to leave them alone when rights were abundant. They also spend most of their time on the open ocean instead of coastal waters like the rights, which misled some early whalers into thinking they were rare.

On the contrary, sperm whales actually were much more abundant than rights and bowheads. They were the most numerous of the great whales, and remain so even today, with a global population of several hundred thousand. Their blubber might not have been as thick as baleen whales', but it and the fatty material in sperm whales' huge, bulbous foreheads produced an oil of much higher quality than right-whale oil. Although sperm whales had no baleen, their stomachs sometimes contained ambergris, an extremely valuable substance from which one could make fixatives for perfumes and volatile essences.

New England whalers discovered all this as they extended their voyages past George's Bank to the Gulf Stream and Baffin Bay. By the Revolutionary War, they had over four hundred ships, produced hundreds of thousands of dollars worth of oil annually, and had crossed the equator to African and South American coasts and down to the Falkland Islands. In the ninteenth century, ships went on two-year, worldwide voyages, killing any and all whales they could catch, the only ones they couldn't being the fast-swimming rorquals. Whaling was the third-largest industry in Massachusetts, producing about seventy million dollars of income a year at a time when the gross national product was less than ten billion. Yankee whaling eventually killed an estimated half-million whales, enough so that traditional whaling methods be-

MELVILLE'S LEVIATHAN

The sperm whale, reaching a maximum length of sixty feet, is the only one of the great whales that belongs to the toothed-whale family, which also includes dolphins and killer whales. Sperm whales hunt large, deep-ocean squid and cuttlefish aggressively, and prey occasionally on fish, including sharks. They have been known also to counterattack whalers. In one well-documented case, a large male sperm whale twice rammed and eventually sank the 238-ton Nantucket whaler *Essex* off South America on November 20, 1820. The sinking of the *Essex* is believed to have provided much of the inspiration for *Moby Dick*.

Sperm whales have the largest and most complex brains on earth, and a highly developed social structure. Females and young live in pods. Males live in groups or singly, and compete to mate with females.

Cetologist Hal Whitehead has described a group of sperm whales feeding: "They often seemed to be coordinating by forming a rank several kilometers long, with the whales swimming abreast of one another. These ranks swept through the deep ocean at a steady three knots for twenty-four hours or more. Individuals would come to the surface every forty minutes or so to breathe, but the whole phalanx bore on. But once every day the whales ceased their feeding to congregate at the surface in groups of five to forty animals for an hour or more. Snorkeling, we saw them gracefully turn to watch us with deep blinking eyes, gently stroke one another with their small flippers, or nuzzle a smooth bulbous brow against a vast wrinkled flank."

They make a variety of sounds, including "clicks" that show individual variations, the significance of which is not yet understood. It has been suggested that sperm whales may use their "click" sounds not only to locate their prey (as dolphins are believed to locate fish schools by listening to the echo of their own "clicks" off the fish), but to capture it. In 1982, Kenneth Norris of the University of Santa Cruz in California suggested that toothed whales can emit and focus "sonic booms" accurately enough to stun or even kill the fish and squid they eat. The sperm whale's great head might serve as a resonating chamber for amplifying and focusing such sounds.

Male and female sperm whales.

came unprofitable by the end of the century. Replacement of whale oil by petroleum and of baleen by spring steel contributed to the decline, but the main cause of American whaling's demise was a scarcity of whales that could be caught with available technology.

As the American whaling business collapsed, new technologies brought a revival to the industry elsewhere. A Norwegian invented a cannon that shot a grenade-tipped harpoon into whales from the prow of a small, fast ship. With this deadly weapon, whalers could finally kill rorquals (and then keep them afloat by injecting them with compressed air). Technological innovations also extended the industrial uses of whale products: as the twentieth century dawned, whale oil became an ingredient in margarine, lipstick, and machine lubricants. Like the Americans before them, the Norwegian fleet spread throughout the world, and in the 1890s, they came upon whale populations which, again, must have made depletion elsewhere seem unimportant.

An estimated eight hundred thousand rorquals then lived in the waters of Antarctica, feeding on the vast swarms of krill that thrive during short Antarctic summers. By 1912, Norwegian and British whalers were catching over twenty thousand whales a year in southern waters, twice the annual catch of the American industry's heyday. With the introduction of the factory ship, which allowed whalers simply to haul their gigantic catch aboard and process it with the latest industrial facilities, the killing increased even more. By the 1930-to-1931 season, the kill had doubled to 40,201.

Rorquals don't breed any faster than other whales, so one species after another dwindled; first the relatively slow humpbacks, then the huge blues, which factory-ship whalers especially coveted because one kill produced so many tons of meat and oil. After a certain point, oil production declined even though more and more whales were being caught, because the oldest and biggest whales were gone. This size reduction was an ominous sign for whale populations, because the oldest and biggest whales were also the breeders.

Yet depletion of these last whales didn't stop whalers from trying even harder to catch them. As whaling became more technologically sophisticated, it also became more capital-intensive. Whaling countries, of which there were increasing numbers, invested too much money in their fleets to let them lie idle simply because they were threatening to exterminate the whales. They would get the best return on their investment if they killed whales as long and hard as possible, then simply junked or converted the fleets.

With only a short break during World War II, the whaling countries continued in this way. Technology improved even more after the war, and demand for animal protein and fat in war-torn countries raised the price of whale oil and meat. As kills of depleted blue whales declined from 7,781 in 1948 and 1949 to fewer than 1,500 ten years later, kills of smaller fin whales increased to 25 thousand. As fins declined, the even smaller sei and minke whales became the prey. Although the annual kill reached an all time high of 66,097 in 1960, Antarctic whaling declined steadily thereafter. In 1962, a jump in the price of sperm-whale oil used in industrial lubricants sent Russian and Japanese factory ships after the Pacific sperm whales, the last population that could have been called abundant. In all, the whaling industry has killed some 2,234,000 whales in this century, and has rendered most species rare or endangered to some degree.

Given the intensity of exploitation, most whale species undoubtedly would have gone the way of the mastodon if they hadn't lived in the oceans. Certainly, conservation measures taken throughout all but the last few years of whaling history had virtually no success in stopping their decimation. Whalers do not seem to have even begun thinking about conservation until the 1920s, when the British established regulations to protect breeding whales and reduce waste at their Antarctic shore stations. Other whalers simply evaded these regulations by switching their processing to floating factories, however, and this response to regulation set the tone for the next five decades.

Various agencies, first national governments and the League of Nations, then the International Whaling Commission after its founding in 1946, would set quotas, seasons, size limits, and other regulations. Established with the express purpose of conserving whale numbers, the regulations proved ineffective for reasons that became increasingly plain over the years. The whalers themselves, or the scientists and bureaucrats whose careers they could influence, established and enforced the regulations, and they did not allow those regulations to interfere with the profitable killing of whales. Thus quotas tended to be higher than the numbers of whales actually being killed. Size limits tended to reflect the convenience of factory ships more than the needs of whale reproduction. Regulators declared whale species or whaling areas protected only after whalers had depleted them.

Conservationists and the general public did not pay much attention to Antarctic whale slaughter in its heyday. It took place far from civilization at a time when communication was much slower than it is today. Moreover, people knew much less about the whales' fascinating qualities; science had yet to discover many of them. According to popular perception, cetaceans were either rather dull, or rather dangerous creatures (except the small-toothed whales—the dolphins and porpoises).

This perception has changed radically in the past three decades,

as restricting commercial taking, the Endangered Species Act requires federal agencies to ensure that their activities don't threaten listed species, and also provides for designation and acquisition of critical habitat, which may be important to survival of coastal species such as rights and grays as offshore oil drilling increases.

In 1976, Congress passed the Fisheries Conservation Management Act which, along with other measures to conserve saltwater fisheries, extended the United States Conservation Zone (over which it claims exclusive fishing rights) from twelve to two hundred miles into the oceans. Congress approved the measure mainly to halt depletion of offshore fisheries by foreign factory trawlers, but the law also had direct and indirect applications to whale conservation. It established instant de facto whale sanctuaries within the two-hundred mile zone, which is the largest offshore area owned by any nation. Soviet factory ships that had been catching sperm whales in Hawaiian waters had to stop.

The Fisheries Conservation Management Act also gave the United States increased leverage over whaling nations under the Packwood-Magnuson amendments passed in 1979. These require the secretary of commerce to reduce allocations of fish made to a foreign nation using American waters (the United States still allows foreign fleets to fish within the two-hundred-mile limit under a permit system) if that nation jeopardizes the effectiveness of the International Whaling Commission. The amendments came into play when Soviet whalers exceeded its quota of Southern Hemisphere minke whales in 1985. Another legislative provision, the Pelly amendment to the Fisherman's Protective Act of 1967, calls for the government to prohibit the importation of fish products from countries known to be violating an international fisheries conservation program. Merely the threat of the Pelly amendment has encouraged Japanese and Soviet delegations to the IWC to cooperate with reforms.

In the late 1970s, the IWC became a much more effective conservation body than previously. As well as reforming its regulatory procedures, it declared the entire Indian Ocean north of fifty-five degrees latitude a whale sanctuary, and it banned factory-ship whaling except for the taking of minke whales in Antarctica. These changes were not entirely the result of a change of heart in favor of conservation among whaling nations. More and more were dropping out of the industry as whales and profits dwindled, so die-hards like the Soviet Union and Japan increasingly found themselves outvoted. Even the Soviet Union and Japan had to idle or convert most of their fleets. When the 1982 moratorium (scheduled to take effect in 1986) passed, it was partly a victory for conservationists, partly a repetition of the historical pattern whereby whales had been killed as long as it paid.

The IWC moratorium is unlikely to stop the killing of whales entirely. Japan defied an earlier ban on sperm whaling in the North Pacific and has opposed the moratorium on the grounds that whale meat is an important food for its people (whale meat presently makes up about 6 percent of Japan's annual meat consumption; tariffs keep out foreign beef that could serve as a substitute). The Soviet Union, Norway, Iceland, and South Korea also may continue whaling to some extent. Whaling will even continue in United States waters, since special provisions of the Marine Mammal Protection Act and the Endangered Species Act permit Alaska natives to engage in a subsistence hunt of bowhead whales.

This Alaska bowhead hunt has complicated the United States' role in whale conservation in recent years, having brought the federal government into conflict with the newly conservation-oriented IWC: the commission has tried to lower bowhead quotas, and the United States has tried to raise them. The United States has tarnished its whale-conservation record further: the government has failed to invoke the Pelly and Packwood-Magnuson amendments to force Japan to observe the moratorium, a failure related to balance-of-trade concerns and increasingly close ties between Japanese and American fishing companies. There is hope that Japan will eventually stop whaling, however. In June 1986, the United States Supreme Court upheld an American-Japanese agreement that would allow continued Japanese fishing in United States waters if Japan is out of whaling by 1988.

Even if all IWC countries abide by the moratorium, illegal whaling might continue to kill many whales. Pirate whalers like the *Sierra* (a ship that sank when anti-whalers mined it in Lisbon harbor) may kill whales much more cruelly and wastefully than legal whalers. The *Sierra* took only meat, killing forty- to fifty-ton animals for two or three tons of prime cuts, and it killed whales without explosive harpoons. This saved meat, but whales sometimes took hours to die. Since the ownership and nationality of such ships is usually obscured and complicated, the enforcement of laws against them is difficult. Some nations have also continued to kill whales for "scientific purposes," while selling the meat to the Japanese. In November 1986, an anti-whaling group sank two whaling ships and destroyed a rendering plant belonging to Iceland, which planned to continue "scientific" whaling.

Although threats to whale survival probably will continue, whales still have a major advantage: they inhabit the most remote, wild ecosystem on Earth. Spending their lives on the open sea, mating and calving there, they remain less vulnerable to disturbance than land animals and other less pelagic sea creatures. A group of ocean animals that is just as fascinating as whales has a much more troubled outlook because it doesn't reproduce at sea: the sea turtles.

Sea turtles have inhabited the oceans much longer than whales. Fossils of turtles even larger than the seven-foot leatherbacks that are today's largest species are common in Mesozoic marine deposits, indicating that turtles shared the oceans with the seagoing giant reptiles of that era. Contemporary sea turtles are supremely adapted to life in the oceans, the various species feeding on a variety of organisms, from jellyfish to underwater grasses and sponges. Like whales, they make trans-oceanic migrations as a matter of course.

Sea turtles' ability to find their way around the oceans is one of the most intriguing scientific mysteries. For example, green turtles that spend most of their lives grazing on turtle grass in the warm, shallow waters of Brazil's east coast somehow make their way across half the Atlantic to tiny, volcanic Ascension Island to breed, a feat which humans could not accomplish without sophisticated navigation gear. Scientists speculate that the turtles may follow star patterns, scent trails, or other natural pathways to the island, but have little experimental evidence upon which to base such ideas. They are also unsure how baby turtles hatched on Ascension return from there to Brazil. The prevailing current runs in that direction, which suggests that the turtle hatchlings simply drift, but since hatchlings not only of green turtles but of all the five living sea-turtle genera virtually disappear from human sight and knowledge during the first year after they enter the ocean (another major scientific mystery), nobody can be sure.

Unfortunately, the sea turtle's uncanny ability to find a mid-ocean nesting island suggests its fatal vulnerability to the modern world. Unlike whales, turtles cannot reproduce in water. Although some reptiles, for instance snakes and lizards, have evolved the ability to incubate eggs in their bodies, turtles haven't. Despite their long ocean evolution, all sea turtles must come out onto beaches to lay their eggs.

Beach nesting evidently was not a major threat to turtle survival for most of their hundreds of millions of years in the oceans. A wide variety of land predators—raccoons, coyotes, gulls, wild pigs, snakes, crabs—will eat turtle eggs and hatchlings, and some of them are quite adept at doing so. At the Mexican nesting grounds of the Kemp's ridley turtle, for example, coyotes seem to know beforehand when turtles will nest. Yet turtles have a number of defenses against natural predation. The exact locations of nestings are unpredictable, and most species scatter their nests over wide stretches of coastline. Moreover, predators have a very difficult time locating nests once wind has obliterated traces of the female's egg-laying activities from the sand. Hatchlings are highly vulnerable when they first emerge from the sand, but they move into the water fairly quickly, and there often are so many (a single female can lay a hundred eggs) that even very busy and numerous predators don't get them all. Kemp's ridley turtles dealt with prescient Mexican coyote's by nesting in massive aggregations (called *arribadas*, Spanish for arrivals) of tens of thousands of females, thus overloading even the coyote's appetite for turtle eggs.

These natural defenses have proved inadequate to human predation, however. Turtle eggs and meat are quite edible (and in the case of the grass-eating green turtle, highly delicious) to humans, who probably ate them long before they began to catch whales. Even technologically primitive *Homo habilis* would have had little difficulty taking nesting females and their eggs along the African coast. Turtles evidently were abundant enough so that subsistence hunting didn't deplete their populations. They were still numerous over most of their mainly tropical range when European explorers and fishing ships penetrated it in the fifteenth century.

This ancient situation changed in a few centuries as commercial civilization spread throughout the tropics. If the people on a coastline couldn't eat all the turtle eggs they found, they could take the rest to market, often along with the nesting females. Also, hunters caught huge numbers of adult turtles on the high seas. They were greatly in demand to provision ships, because they would live for long periods turned upside-down in holds, thus providing fresh meat. The outlook grew worse as sea turtles became the target of luxury markets. The cartilage around the bottom shells of green turtles is the basis for green turtle soup, a gourmet food on a par with caviar. The shell of another species, the hawksbill, is the main source of tortoiseshell, long in demand for many craft items. Sea-turtle skin has also been made into expensive leathers, and the eggs are thought to be aphrodisiac in some areas.

Sea-turtle exploitation has not been as systematical as whales', so the turtles' decline is less well-documented. There is no doubt that it has been steep, despite protective laws such as the one passed by Bermuda as early as 1620. In Florida, the commercial catch fell from 643,616 pounds in 1897 to 10,000 pounds in 1936. Nesting has declined with the numbers of breeding adults, and many former turtle beaches are now empty. The Kemp's ridley now nests on a single stretch of Mexican beach, although it apparently nested further north and south once.

The highly coveted green turtle has been reduced to two major nesting areas in the entire Caribbean—one on a Costa Rican beach and one on a rapidly eroding little island in the eastern Caribbean. Loggerhead turtles may once have nested on the East Coast of the

United States as far north as Virginia, but now do so only up to the Carolinas, and much more sparsely than before. All these species have other populations or closely related species that nest along African, Asian, and South American coasts, but given the rising human population pressures in those areas, they are no safer than turtles near the United States. In 1979 alone, Ecuadorean fishermen killed as many as 148,000 Olive ridley turtles; in western Mexico, mass-production

CONSERVING SEA TURTLES

Conservationists have devised a number of ways to try to protect the seven species of sea turtle, all of which are threatened to some degree by human exploitation. Perhaps the most important is protecting the beaches where turtles lay their eggs from predation and overexploitation. The Caribbean Conservation Corporation has been working to protect and restore the population of green turtles that nests at the beach called Tortuguero in Costa Rica for over thirty years. For two decades, the Mexican Departmento de Pesca has been guarding the northeast Mexican nesting beach of the most endangered turtle species, the Kemp's ridley, with armed marines during its breeding season. There may be as few as 520 adult female Kemp's ridley turtles remaining in the world. In the 1940s, forty thousand nested at one time.

Conservationists also try to protect turtles on the open ocean, where hunters pursue green turtles for their meat and calipee (a cartilaginous material which is the basis for the delicacy green turtle soup) and hawksbill turtles for their beautifully patterned shells. The Convention on International Trade in Endangered Species prohibits trade in sea turtles among the eighty-nine nations that have signed it.

TOP: *Green turtle*.

BOTTOM: *Hawksbill turtle*.

factory processing has been a factor in the heavy exploitation of the species. The greatest turtle, the leatherback, has only four major nesting sites throughout the world, although individuals are scattered and nest in other places.

The problems of sea-turtle conservation are different from whale-conservation problems. For the most part, developed nations have carried out modern whaling, having invested a great deal of capital in it. Except to the Inuit and a few other indigenous peoples, whales are not an important subsistence-food item. Most turtle hunters, on the other hand, are individual fishermen with small boats who hunt offshore from poor tropical nations. Although some turtle products are international luxury items, turtle eggs and meat are also subsistence foods for many coastal populations in the tropics.

Given the local, small-scale nature of most turtle exploitation, a worldwide moratorium like the one on whaling would probably be impossible even to propose, much less enforce. No international agency exists to regulate sea-turtle fishing or to declare a moratorium, and no mechanism exists to inform hundreds of thousands of affected people that a moratorium would be in force. Even if such a moratorium could apply only to commercial exploitation, the legal and social complications of differentiating between commerce and subsistence might be insurmountable.

Given the grave ecological dilemmas facing virtually all tropical nations today, the prospects for controlling such an anarchic phenomenon as turtle killing may not seem bright. Determined scientists and conservationists have tried to control aspects of it for over forty years, however, and with some success. The major green-turtle nesting beach at Tortuguero in Costa Rica would not likely have turtles today if herpetologist Archie Carr and his associates had not begun to study and protect it in the 1950s. At that time, wild dogs and poachers took most turtle eggs, and poachers also turned nesting females upside down until catcher boats could come and take them away. Carr came first to study turtle migration, but since it was obvious that there soon would be little left to study if the situation continued unchanged, he became involved in conservation.

Carr's activities led to the founding of the Caribbean Conservation Corporation, a nonprofit organization that established a turtle hatchery at Tortuguero with the idea of releasing hatchlings on re-established nesting beaches in other parts of the Caribbean. Carr and his coworkers hoped the hatchlings would return to the beaches after they matured, rather as hatchery salmon return to the streams in which they are released. Turtle conservation efforts in the area also led the Costa Rican Department of Agriculture to set aside some miles of the beach as a turtle nesting sanctuary, and eventually to prohibit turtle-turning and egg poaching on the country's entire Caribbean coast.

Tortuguero has been a major center of sea-turtle research and conservation since. In the 1970s, the Costa Rican government established a nineteen-thousand-hectare Tortuguero National Park, which includes fifteen miles of nesting beach, most of the turtle colony. The park may be a mixed blessing to nesting turtles and conservationists, since it provides increased public access to the beach that may increase disturbance by poachers and tourists. Like the Marine Mammal Protection Act, however, the park constitutes an overt acknowledgment that wildlife once valued only for its economic potential also has great ecological and aesthetic significance.

Techniques developed at Tortuguero have been applied in a last-ditch attempt to save the Kemp's ridley, the most endangered species. One of the smallest sea turtles, with an average weight of seventy to ninety pounds, the Kemp's ridley also was one of the most mysterious for many years because scientists had never observed it nesting. Some people even thought it might not nest at all, but bear live young on the open sea. Then in 1961, Professor Henry Hildebrand of the University of Corpus Christi in Texas located a 1947 amateur film that showed an estimated forty thousand Kemp's ridleys nesting on a stretch of beach in the northern Mexican state of Tamaulipas. Scientists evidently had not been able to find the species nesting because all the females nested together within a few hours on a single isolated beach.

Unfortunately, scientists have never been able to see a big Kemp's ridley *arribada* like the one the film showed, because the species had declined to fewer than a thousand individuals by the time Hildebrand found the film. No more than a few hundred females have been seen nesting since. These low numbers, combined with the possibility of major contamination of the breeding grounds by oil spills like the massive Intox I blowout in the Bay of Campeche in 1979, have raised the definite possibility of extermination for the species, which lives nowhere else. In response to the ridley's decline the Mexican government's Departmento de Pesca has for two decades pursued a program to protect the nesting beach and offshore waters.

Biologists, technicians, armed Mexican marines, and other conservation personnel set up camp on the nesting beach from April to mid-August each year. They patrol fifteen miles of beach twice a day, seven days a week, looking for tracks and turtles. When turtles do come ashore to nest, marines guard the nesting area; biologists gather the eggs and relocate them in corrals safe from poachers and coyotes. When the eggs hatch, biologists release the hatchlings.

Since 1977, the U.S. Fish and Wildlife Service has furnished workers, vehicles, and other assistance to the Mexican program in exchange for about two percent of the annual egg production. These eggs incubate not in the Mexican beach, but in sand from Texas's Padre Island National Seashore. By the time the small turtles hatch, they have been flown 250 miles north to Padre Island. Workers release them there and allow them to crawl down to the water, in the hope that they "imprint" on the Padre Island beach and will return to breed there when they mature. Instead of letting them swim away, however, biologists gather them up again and keep them in a laboratory for a year so that they will grow large enough to escape ocean predators. Then the biologists return them to Padre Island and release them into the Gulf of Mexico.

Mexico, a country with one of the longest turtle-nesting coastlines in the world, also has a beach-protection program on its west coast. The Pacific's black turtle, a close relative of the Atlantic's green, has long been an important resource for the Nahuatl inhabitants of the Michoacan coast. But growing human population and commercial exploitation were decimating Michoacan black-turtle nesting beaches. In the 1980s, the World Wildlife Fund has supported a program whereby local people patrol the beaches against poaching, while a student team led by biologist Javier Alvarado tags nesting turtles and protects eggs. In a single year, the program watched over five hundred thousand eggs, from which three hundred thousand hatchlings were eventually released into the ocean.

The trouble with turtle-restoration programs such as the ones at Tortuguero and Tamaulipas, however, is that nobody knows if they will work. Nobody has tried transplanting turtle hatchlings before, so nobody knows if they will "imprint" to new beaches and return to breed on them. Hatchlings released so far have yet to do so. Sea turtles take many years to reach breeding age, so transplanted hatchlings may return eventually, but until they start doing so, hatchery programs can't be counted on to aid sea-turtle conservation. The only sure thing is simply to stop people from killing turtles whenever and wherever possible.

Although they may have no nesting beaches, northern industrial countries can assist turtle conservation by helping to limit the luxury trade, most importantly by participating in the 1973 Convention on International Trade in Endangered Species of Flora and Fauna (CITES). Signed by some eighty-nine countries including the United States, CITES regulates international trade in species listed as threatened or endangered during biennial meetings of member countries. CITES has prohibited international trade in sea turtles, a considerable conservation advance over the situation in the early 1970s, when traders exported as many as ten thousand green turtles a year from Nicaragua's Miskito Banks (a major turtle grass area), mostly to United States markets.

But compliance with CITES is even harder to enforce than compliance with the whaling moratorium. Unwilling to forego traditional ornamental uses of tortoiseshell, Japan has continued to import thousands of hawksbill turtles. It reportedly refused to stop supporting the netting of turtles off the Ecuadorian coast despite repeated protests by that country. When Ecuador closed its turtle processing plants, Japanese turtle buyers simply moved processing operations to Colombia. Although a CITES signatory, France appears to be a major importer of banned sea-turtle products, while Panama and Cuba are trafficking centers. Despite its turtle-conservation programs, Mexico has not signed CITES and allows the sale of turtle products.

Not all threats result from the turtles' commercial value. Shrimp trawlers catch sea turtles accidentally in their nets; although unintentional, this has drowned thousands of turtles, since the nets prevent their rising to the surface to breathe. The National Marine Fisheries Service estimates that more than forty-five thousand sea turtles a year are caught in trawler nets in the Gulf of Mexico alone (along with two billion pounds of fish and other nontarget organisms). Of these, over twelve thousand turtles drown, many of them washing onto beaches.

Since the Endangered Species Act protects sea turtles, the Fisheries Service began research in 1978 to develop new fishing-gear designs that would keep turtles, fish, and other unwanted creatures out of shrimp nets. In 1981, it came up with the Trawling Efficiency Device, which consists of a grid set in the neck of the net. The grid lets shrimp into the net, but shunts turtles, sponges, fish and other large objects to the top, where trapdoors guide them into open water. The TED reduces turtle capture by 97 percent and actually increases the shrimp catch, since nets don't get weighed down with turtles and fish. Installation costs about four hundred dollars, less than one percent of the yearly outlay for rigging a shrimp boat.

Unfortunately, the response of American shrimp fishermen to the device was less than enthusiastic, despite the encouraging name and a government, conservation community, and industry campaign to spur voluntary use. Fewer than two hundred of the more than six thousand American vessels used the device at any time during the 1985 season. Assuming that the TED works as well as its supporters say, this lack of enthusiasm probably arose more from conservatism and lack of time than from fondness for drowning turtles, so the device may come into wider use with time. Perhaps not soon enough for remaining Kemp's ridleys that live in prime Gulf of Mexicao shrimping grounds, however, and the United States Fish and Wildlife Service Turtle Recovery Team and other interested groups have called for mandatory TED use. Predictable resistance to such a measure by the shrimp industry may bring the matter into the courts.

Of course, sea turtles and whales don't define the oceans' limits. If both became extinct, the oceans would continue to function. Yet civilization also has begun to deplete organisms much more basic to ocean functions, and to its own. We can function without whales or turtles, but without fish we would face real difficulties. The annual global catch of fish substantially exceeds yearly beef production and provides twenty-three percent of all animal protein consumed by humans. As world population has doubled since 1950, the annual fish catch has more than tripled. A global fish depletion would cause massive malnutrition.

Until quite recently, people did not believe ocean fish could be depleted. Before 1970, fisheries experts confidently predicted that global annual catches eventually would reach two to four hundred million tons a year, an enormous increase over the roughly twenty-five million tons caught in 1950. Many nations thus invested heavily in sophisticated fishing fleets and other ocean-taming schemes. Futurologists envisioned an age of ocean settlement, when underwater or floating cities would serve domesticated fisheries, deep-sea mining, and other industries of unprecedented bounty.

Instead, fishing nations discovered limits with surprising swiftness. The fishing industry expanded rapidly for two decades, but then growth of annual catches slowed to less than one percent after 1970. Since human population is growing much faster, this has meant a per-capita decline in availability of fish as food. Even more ominously, some local fish populations began to disappear entirely, the Peruvian anchoveta being a case in point. Its disappearance has destroyed profitable guano industry, as seabirds that had fed on the fish declined. (Guano, the nitrogen-rich droppings covering seabird colonies, makes excellent fertilizer.) By the 1980s, six Atlantic fisheries and five Pacific ones were depleted to the point of collapse, and the annual global catch had declined by about eleven million tons from its peak in the early 1970s.

Like whales and turtles, fish declined because they were being caught faster than they could reproduce; human exploitation will have to be controlled if their populations are to be restored. The establishment by many nations of two-hundred-mile coastal zones is one step in this direction; it has led many of the factory ships that once emptied vast coastlines of fish to cease operating. Leveling off to ocean catches (at about seventy million tons a year) has also encouraged considerable

FISH AND SEABIRDS

Humans are not the only ones faced with malnutrition if overfishing depletes stocks of ocean fishes. The many species of seabirds that enliven coastlines also may suffer as efficient modern fishing fleets exploit the small-fish species upon which the birds depend. Usually, humans do not eat these fish directly, but convert them into fishmeal as a protein supplement for livestock feeds. (Ironically, these small fish are often major food sources for larger fish that humans do eat, such as salmon, halibut, cod, and haddock. Overfishing of them may reduce the numbers of fish for human consumption.)

A recent example of such overfishing and its side effects is that of the capelin, a small, silvery, smelt-like fish of immense importance in Western North Atlantic food chains. Soviet and Norwegian trawlers began taking hundreds of thousands of tons of capelin off the Canadian coast in the 1970s. By the end of the decade, commercial fishermen had begun to notice declines in reproduction of salmon and cod that seemed to be tied to the scarcity of their capelin prey.

In the early 1980s, capelin depletion began to affect the colonies of puffins that nest along the coast of Newfoundland. The comical-looking puffins depend particularly on capelin for a number of reasons. They cannot fly far or dive deeply like murres and gannets; capelin swim near the surface, fairly close offshore. Puffins must swallow their food whole; capelin are small enough for both adult and nestling puffins to ingest.

Whereas surveys in earlier years had shown that puffins at one colony in Newfoundland fledged 60 percent of their young, they fledged only 45 percent in 1981. Fledglings in 1981 also weighed significantly less than in previous years, so that a larger percentage than usual probably did not survive their first year in harsh northern seas. The commercial offshore capelin fishery had collapsed by 1978, undoubtedly because of overfishing. Possible food substitutes for the puffins such as young herring and mackerel were unavailable because these fish species tend to remain beyond the limited foraging range of puffin colonies.

Atlantic puffins.

Adapted from "The Fish Factor" by Frank Graham, Jr., *Audubon*, July, 1985.

growth in fish farming of freshwater species such as carp, tilapia, prawns, and catfish.

Fish farming is not necessarily a boon to wildlife, since it can preempt wetland, riparian, and estuarine habitat and, in the case of turtle and crocodilian farms, lead to illegal trafficking in wild animals passed off as farmed ones. Renowned sea-turtle expert Archie Carr has expressed opposition to sea-turtle farming for this reason. Fish farming or aquaculture *is* a highly efficient way of producing animal protein, considerably more efficient than the growing of warm-blooded livestock. While it takes seven pounds of grain to produce a pound of beef, it takes only 1.7 pounds to produce a pound of fish. Farming now produces about a sixth of the fish and other "underwater livestock" consumed worldwide, and with a growth rate of over seven percent a year, it probably will produce much more eventually.

It is unlikely, however, that futurologists will ever realize dreams of turning the oceans into giant fish farms. It would be hard to raise

FERTILIZERS AND FISHERIES IN CHESAPEAKE BAY

Chesapeake Bay has long been one of the most abundant sources of seafood on the Atlantic coast of the United States. In recent years, however, its yields of oysters, crabs, striped bass, and other high-quality foods have fallen because of pollution, not only with toxic chemicals from oil spills and industrial discharges, but with fertilizers from agricultural lands adjacent to tributaries of the bay—the Susquehanna River, for instance. Nourished by the fertilizers, a thick growth of algae flourishes along the bay, using up the vital dissolved oxygen in the water. A 1983 Environmental Protection Agency report cited pollution from farmlands as the largest nonpoint source of pollution in the bay.

The Susquehanna River Valley above the bay supports more livestock per square mile than any other place in the country, and one of the byproducts of all this livestock is manure, a rich source of nitrogen and an ideal fertilizer. Yet area farmers spend an average of 2,200 dollars a year on commercial fertilizers such as anhydrous ammonia. A program called the Chesapeake Bay Water Quality Project has been studying the relationship of farm fertilizers and water pollution in the area. Project researchers have concluded that valley dairymen who grow their own feed crops apply twice as much fertilizer to their soil as they need, and that millions of dollars worth of commercial nitrogen runs off the soil into the underground reservoirs that connect with the Susquehanna River.

Paul Clugston is a dairy farmer with 110 holsteins in the Susquehanna Valley. Until Clugston got involved in the Chesapeake Bay Water Quality Project in 1985, he'd spent thousands of dollars a year on fertilizer he didn't really need. At the suggestion of project workers, he built a pit to compost and store the manure from his own cows for use on his three hundred acres of grain and hay. Manure now provides half the fertilizer he uses, and Clugston saves four thousand dollars a year.

Chesapeake Bay waterman fleet dredges oysters near Smith Island, Maryland.

their productive capacity beyond what it was in the natural state. Instead, civilization is lowering that capacity by overfishing the oceans, and, even more ominously, by polluting them. The limits of the oceans' ability to absorb sewage, toxic chemicals, radioactive wastes, and oil spills are the most crucial limits of all. If we exceed them, recovery will be much more problematic than restoration of whale, sea turtle, or fish populations.

Like water, pollutants eventually find their way into the oceans. Unlike water, pollutants are not distributed evenly throughout the ocean basins. They accumulate near their sources, the coastlines, which are also the most important areas for ocean life. Such areas may therefore reach their pollution-absorbing capacities long before entire oceans reach their limits. For example, in New York Bight, a portion of the Atlantic off New York City, a lifeless blanket of "black mayonnaise" comprising sewage sludge and other pollutants spreads for miles out to sea, and when wind and tides are right, occasionally covers beaches. Oil spills may also blanket miles of sea floor with toxic ooze that takes years to dissipate, but at least the pollution of an individual oil spill eventually does dissipate. The pollution at the mouths of the rivers into which cities, factories and farms dump their wastes is never-ending.

BELOW: *Oil on the beach after a Gulf-coast spill in Texas.*

BELOW, RIGHT: *Collecting dead birds after an oil spill on the Pacific coast south of San Francisco.*

Ocean pollution is a vast, complicated problem. Yet civilization's responses to depletion of whales, sea turtles, and fish suggest what can be done to confront this more fundamental limit of the oceans. Civilization can reform its institutions, as the International Whaling Commission has been reformed. It can change its customs, as Mexico and Costa Rica have changed their traditional subsistence uses of green, black, and Kemp's ridley turtles. And it can redistribute its investments, as international banking organizations have redistributed their loans from trawler fleets to fish farms.

Sonoma County, California.

T H E
ISLANDS

I N THE MORNING MIST, the green plain resembles a midwestern pasture. The grass is cropped smooth as a lawn, and the stout, rounded shapes resting or moving slowly among scattered small trees might be black angus steers. As the sun ascends and the mist thins, the illusion of familiarity fades. The largest of the stout, rounded shapes might weigh as much as a black angus, but there the similarity ends. Instead of hair and hooves, these animals have high-domed shells, elephantine clawed feet, and long, snaky necks. They are tortoises.

The giant turtles become more active as the air warms. Larger ones climb out of puddles in which they have been lying and begin to crop the grass with their toothless jaws, swallowing the fodder unchewed. Smaller tortoises emerge from thickets and also begin to graze. Occasionally one of the large tortoises will approach one of the small ones and nose at its hind end, but the smaller one moves away and the larger, still a little stiff in the morning air, does not pursue it far. The smooth, polished shells of the smaller individuals, which are the female of the species, indicate that larger ones, the males, have mated them in the past. Despite their ponderousness, male tortoises are very interested in romance during their rainy-season mating time, evidenced even this morning by the hoarse moans of one successful suitor farther off on the plain.

There are other encounters in this strange landscape, even odder than that between male and female giant tortoises. A blackish hawk, about the size and shape of an American red-tail, lands on a tortoise's

Giant tortoise and Galápagos hawk.

back and rides along for several minutes as the reptile ambles from one grass clump to another. Hawk and tortoise seem to take this hitchhiking entirely for granted, the tortoise apparently oblivious to its passenger, the hawk only blinking sleepily as its conveyance lurches. Another tortoise responds more alertly to another bird, however. When a small, brown, sparrow-like finch lands in front of it and begins fluttering about, the giant turtle raises itself on extended legs and rears back its head as though coming to attention. Ludicrous as the idea of a four-hundred pound reptile presenting itself for the inspection of a few ounces of songbird may seem, that is more or less what is happening: the finch flutters onto the leathery skin exposed around the tortoise's neck and picks a tick off it. The tick is a nuisance to the tortoise, but a nutritious mouthful to the finch.

Land tortoises, hawks, and finches are common creatures in many parts of the world (tortoises live in many warm, dry areas of Eurasia, Africa, and the Americas), but tortoises do not commonly approach steer size, and hawks and finches do not normally behave so familiarly with them. Clearly, there is something highly unusual about this place. As the morning mist dissipates toward noon, the extent of that peculiarity is revealed further. What seems to be simply a plain is actually the floor of a collapsed volcanic crater, or caldera, surrounded on all sides by steep walls of lava rock. Shreds of white vapor clinging to these walls show where the volcano's heat still escapes to the surface as hot springs and muddy fumaroles.

A walk to the top of one of the walls reveals an even more unusual circumstance: the Pacific Ocean stretches away on all sides. The volcano is not part of any continent, but one of three volcanoes (its name is Alcedo) that form a small island some six hundred miles west of South America, and a few dozen miles south of the Equator. Named Isabella Island, it is part of a group of small islands that a gradual but massive upwelling of lava from the ocean floor has formed over the past two million years. Although inhabited by tortoises, finches, hawks, grasses, and trees, none of these islands has ever been less than hundreds of miles from other land.

The Spanish mariners who chanced on the islands in the early sixteenth century called them the Encantadas, or enchanted islands. The name seems appropriate; however, it applied not to the odd antics of the islands' animals but to the strong ocean currents that flow among them and make navigation difficult for sailing ships. The islands seemed to appear and disappear magically as the currents carried the ships toward or away from them. Later, the islands' name changed to Galápagos, Spanish for tortoises.

Since their discovery, these islands have become famous for a peculiarity that goes even deeper than their isolation and the bizarre behavior of their fauna and ocean currents. There is nothing quite like them in the entire world. The giant tortoises, hawks, and finches of Isabella Island's Alcedo Caldera belong to species that live nowhere else on earth except the Galápagos. Isabella Island tortoises are different even from those that live on other islands in the group, although classed in the same species. Birds similar to Galápagos hawks and finches live on the American mainland, but the only other giant tortoises surviving in the world live on small islands of the Indian Ocean, thousands of miles from the Galápagos.

Most native Galápagos organisms are unique to some degree. The only seagoing lizard in the world, the marine iguana, lives there. It dives in the surf for its kelp diet. One of the few habitually tool-using bird species, the woodpecker finch, lives there. It uses cactus thorns to pry grubs out of trees. It is closely related to the tick-eating finch in Alcedo Caldera, and eleven other species of these small finches live only on the Galápagos. The various species have differing feeding habits, on the ground or in vegetation, and the shapes and sizes of their bills reflect these differences. Species of rail, mockingbird, heron, flightless cormorant, snake, land iguana, lava lizard, rice rat, and bat also live there, but nowhere else. Despite their equatorial location, the Galápagos even have an endemic species of penguin, which thrives (along with sea lions and fur seals) because currents and deep-ocean upwellings make the waters around the islands quite cold, as well as rich in plankton and fish. About 40 percent of Galápagos plant species grow nowhere else.

The isolated strangeness of the Galápagos Islands might make them seem truly *encantadas*, outside the natural order of things. Yet, although there are no places *quite* like them, there are places of similar peculiarity scattered about the world, not a great many, but enough to establish a natural pattern. Some of the places are like the Galápagos geologically, chains of volcanic islands formed where oceanic plates of the Earth's crust passed over "hot spots" in the deeper planetary mantle, causing massive upwellings of lava. The mid-ocean islands of Hawaii or the Azores are examples. Some came into being as movements of the crustal plates broke pieces from continents and rafted them out into the oceans. The granitic islands of the Madagascar and the Seychelles in the Indian Ocean are examples. Some are mountains and highlands surrounded by shallow continental seas. Crete, Sicily, and other Mediterranean Islands are examples. Some arose as sandbars or coral reefs or mangrove flats accumulated in the shallow waters of continental shelves or eroded volcanoes.

A GALÁPAGOS NATURALIST

Tui De Roy has lived on the Galápagos Islands since the age of two, when her parents rejected modern urban living and sought a life close to nature in those remote islands. The islands have been her education, and she knows them with a lifelong intimacy expressed in her photographs and writings, and in the lectures she gives advocating conservation of the unique flora and fauna of the Galápagos.

"When I was about eleven or twelve, I started to see more of the islands. That's when my parents acquired another boat and we started to travel a little bit more. I started to see some of the sea-bird colonies and a lot of the bird-nesting activities, and that got me really interested. I even remember one time when I said, 'Oh, I want to become an ornithologist,' and then I began to realize what that meant . . . gathering data or plucking feathers or putting bands, and I realized that wasn't at all what I was talking about. I was just interested in seeing what these birds do and how they go about doing it.

". . . I decided right then that I was going to record all of the behavior, nesting behavior, of all the birds in the Galápagos, which seemed like a very simple goal then, and here I am twenty years later and I still haven't finished.

"I think the world could become a better place if enough people were a little bit more attuned to what's around them. It doesn't really matter where you live or where you go. If you are going to feel that the natural world and natural balances really mean something to you . . . it's everywhere."

Naturalist Tui De Roy with sea lion.

Despite different origins, such places have something in common. Wide stretches of salt water isolate them from other land, yet they are covered with land life, and the more isolated they are, the more their life differs from that of other land. This pattern transcends the individual oddity of islands, because it demonstrates something very important about life as a whole: that it is never finished. When island isolation cuts animals or plants off from their mainland relatives (perhaps because the sea has risen over a former land bridge, perhaps because a storm, or vegetation spewed from a flooding river's mouth swept organisms out to sea), they begin, generation by generation, to differ from those relatives. They evolve, demonstrating that the ancient process that began in the pre-Cambrian oceans and gradually filled empty skies and lands is ever ready to fill any new patch of emptiness that rises above water.

Our present scientific ideas of evolution arose to some extent from a visit to the Galápagos. When the young naturalist Charles Darwin spent three weeks visiting four of the islands in 1835, the oddness of the fauna unsettled his conventional ideas of unchanging species. After returning to England, he submitted the specimens he had collected there to specialists and discovered that they were new species, related to organisms of the American mainland, but distinct. As he noted in his published journal of the worldwide cruise of the *Beagle*, the isolated, unique Galápagos fauna made Darwin feel "brought somewhat close to that great fact—that mystery of mysteries—the first appearance of new beings on Earth."

Today, the thirteen species of Galápagos finches (now called Darwin's finches) are viewed as classic examples of how species originate through the evolutionary process of adaptive radiation. The finches are believed to have originated from a single ancestral species that arrived accidentally on the islands from South America and, finding little competition from other land birds, gradually adapted to a variety of new habitats. During this process, populations became so isolated by their varying physiques and habits that they stopped interbreeding with others, with the result that the thirteen finch species eventually came to exist, playing the ecological roles of woodpeckers and other kinds of birds that never reached the Galápagos. Similarly, the other unique creatures—tortoises, iguanas, hawks, mockingbirds, plants— are descended from ancestors carried accidentally to the islands by wind or water (tortoises float and can survive long periods without food or water).

The evolutionary concept of the species has had a profound effect on human attitudes toward wildlife as a whole. Once seen as an unchanging, passive background to the dramas of human history, wild plants and animals became more significant once people realized that each species has its own history, its own drama of survival and development. This knowledge has brought a new sense of responsibility: we are aware that not only natural events, but also human interference can end a species' history forever.

The potential for such interference has been demonstrated with particular frequency, and tragedy, on islands, where millenia of peaceful isolation have ill-prepared giant tortoises, hawks, and finches for human aggression. People encountered islands as soon as man began using boats, and they seemed to have begun devastating them just about as quickly. Neolithic people exterminated endemic species of elephants, hippos, and deer from Mediterranean islands about 8000 B.C. Even earlier, aborigines introduced dogs to the island continent

AT HOME WITH
DARWIN'S FINCHES

The Galápagos' most scientifically renowned birds, the drab-colored but fascinatingly adapted Darwin's finches, are regular visitors at Tui De Roy's house overlooking Academy Bay on Santa Cruz Island.

"We've got three species here, four species, a pair of cactus finches, a couple of medium ground finches, a large ground finch and a small ground finch sitting in a tree. Of course, ground finches sit in trees and tree finches sit on the ground. You have to remember that there's never something so simple as a well pigeonholed role.

"There's been a lot of work done to show that finches feed on different things and their feeding habits keep them from getting to be in competition, but as you can see here, they don't mind sharing whenever the opportunity arrives.

"It's a neat relationship because the finches aren't really dependent on us. And yet when they're not nesting they'll come here and sit by the hundreds. They're very much a part of my life here. I can remember when I was quite small they came around the house, but we didn't actually have any tame ones. I started to really try to get them to come to my hand. The first ones were very hesitant, and then it caught on. And I guess they just got bolder and bolder when they saw that it was worth it and we've had tame finches ever since.

"You feel that there's really a basic understanding between all these living creatures, including ourselves. We're not apart as man, we're not man as a different entity from the rest of the wild world, but we're part of the natural world. They accept us, and of course, this gives incredible opportunities for photography. But I think it's even more moving just to watch them, just to see how they relate to us and how they try to understand, just like we try to understand them."

Tui De Roy

Galápagos finches.

of Australia, and the dogs exterminated native, marsupial predators, and probably other species as well.

The greatest early ocean wanderers of all, the Polynesians, decimated a number of island ecosystems as they spread across the South Pacific, wiping out the forests of Easter Island, the giant, flightless moas of New Zealand, and much of the native lowland flora and fauna of the Hawaiian Islands. Even though early Polynesians did not commercially exploit island ecosystems to any great extent, native plants and animals simply were not able to resist the spread of agriculture and the introduction of domestic or pest animals such as pigs, dogs, poultry, and rats. Despite their popular reputation as a primeval, unspoiled paradise, the Hawaiian Islands were something of an ecological disaster long before Captain Cook set foot on them. Recent archaeological investigations indicate that at least forty native bird species became extinct there after the first Polynesian settlers arrived around 400 A.D., and that the settlers cut or burned off the most diverse forest types below three-thousand-foot elevation, with consequent extinction of endemic mollusk, insect, and reptile species.

Some of the island extinctions caused by non-Western peoples were quite recent. The moas of New Zealand, for example, may have survived into the nineteenth century; well-preserved carcasses have been found in bogs. Another flightless giant, the eight-foot elephant bird of Madagascar, lasted until the mid-eighteenth century and probably was the origin of the giant roc in the Sinbad-the-Sailor legends of the Arabian Nights. Long isolated from the continents, Madagascar has a highly unusual ecosystem that includes many species of lemurs, very ancient primates driven to extinction elsewhere by competition, possibly with the more recent monkeys and apes. Fossils indicate there were lemurs as big as humans and some as big as small horses on Madagascar fairly recently, and local legends suggest the human-sized species was still alive when people reached the island.

Yet if early humans used islands destructively, their destruction was limited. Many islands simply were too small, isolated, or inhospitable for early cultures to exploit. This situation changed quickly after 1500, however, as European mercantile fleets combed the oceans in search of wealth. Early ships could carry only limited supplies of water and fresh food, so sailors depended heavily on mid-voyage sources for such necessities and kept a sharp eye out for islands that might provide them. Even the most remote and rugged islands, if they offered food or water became stopping-off places for increasing numbers of vessels.

The history of the Galápagos was typical. Despite relative proximity to South America, early cultures never inhabited them, although

Mongoose lemur, Madagascar.

Inca legends suggest pre-Columbian Indians may have visited them. Their volcanic terrain, limited rainfall, and somewhat sparse vegetation would have discouraged any wanderers that happened on them, and the strong currents among them would have made such visits difficult. Even after the Spanish discovered them, the Galápagos remained isolated from major trade routes.

The larger Galápagos do get enough rainfall to produce permanent springs, however, and mariners discovered that they could locate the springs by following giant-tortoise paths. They also found a very convenient source of fresh meat in the tortoises, which not only were too slow to escape human predation, but were too naive even to try. Like all other Galápagos species, the tortoises had no fear of humans because they had never encountered them. They simply watched curiously as sailors arrived with barrows to cart them to beaches. There, the sailors either butchered them or rowed them out to the ships where they would be kept alive in holds until their meat was required.

Ships did not arrive very often at first. Pirates were the main visitors during the seventeenth and eighteenth centuries. The spread of whaling and sealing brought greatly increased exploitation in the nineteenth century, however. Charles Darwin found harbors full of whalers and beaches littered with the barrows used to transport the tortoises. Whalers making two-year voyages would take hundreds of tortoises at a single stop on the islands. This eventually reduced a tortoise population that originally had numbered in the hundreds of thousands—so dense that a man could walk some distance over their backs without touching ground—to fewer than ten thousand. The Alcedo Caldera tortoises on Isabella—located a half-day's hot, uphill walk from the beach—are the last population on the islands to escape substantial depletion. The tortoises on Pinta Island, the northernmost island, became extinct except for a solitary male, appropriately called Lonesome George, that was discovered in recent years. Another lonesome male, the last tortoise of Fernandina Island, died in 1906.

Exploitation of tortoises was only the most direct human impact on the islands; others were equally damaging. To create another source of fresh meat, ships left goats on the islands. These hardy animals multiplied rapidly, competed with tortoises for forage, and destroyed much of the native vegetation and wildlife habitat. Ships also accidentally introduced black rats onto many islands, which displaced the innocuous native rice rats and preyed on the nests and young of native birds and reptiles. The innocence of Galápagos wildlife also made it subject to simple vandalism. Darwin wrote of knocking hawks off branches with his gun barrel and killing numbers of finches with his hat. He was doing this to obtain scientific specimens, but other visitors did such things simply for amusement.

In 1832, Ecuador annexed the Galápagos and set up a colony. Although this settlement never grew very large, colonists added to pressures on tortoises and other vulnerable species. They also introduced more alien animals, including horses, cattle, burros, sheep, pigs, cats, and dogs. Pigs and dogs proved particularly destructive, not only of tortoises and native land birds and mammals, but of land iguanas and of dark-rumped petrels, sea birds that nest in tunnels in the ground, which the pigs and dogs learned to dig up. On the island of Floreana alone, six native species were extirpated in recent historical times.

A GALÁPAGOS SEABIRD COLONY

Punta Vicente Roca has to be one of my favorite places in Galápagos because it's so very wild, it's almost never visited. And the blue-footed boobies come here in vast numbers. The boobies are the most prominent right now because they're just starting to nest and beginning their courtship. . . . The females are honking and the males are whistling.

The whole courtship of the boobies seems to revolve around those incredible blue feet. They really show them when they dance around in slow motion and when they come in with that landing stunt where they throw their feet up and expose the undersoles. It really must be quite spectacular from the mate's point of view on the ground.

It's really incredible to look into the way they feed. You'll see them flying along maybe fifty to one hundred feet over the sea and all of a sudden they just drop out of the sky, and not only do they drop, but they actually fly downwards to add speed, and then at the very last moment before they hit the surface, they extend their wings behind their body and just enter the water like an arrowhead.

Their whole life cycle when they're nesting depends on making many short trips to feed and coming back to feed their young. Once or twice I've seen a colony where all of a sudden the fish will move away for some reason, and the boobies can no longer come in to feed their young. And so rather than try and feed their young and perhaps starve in the process, which would mean starvation for the young anyway, they just desert the nesting area. This can happen almost overnight.

That way the adults can survive, and a few months later they come back and start again when conditions are better. So it's a harsh, but very effective way of being able to raise just as many chicks as possible under varying conditions.

A lot of these seabirds are totally oblivious to people. That's one of the greatest experiences, just to sit here and be disregarded. They carry on as if we weren't here. But then again the young ones are often curious. They have time to spend, they have a lot of things to learn about life, and part of this learning process is to get to know what the other creatures around them are, and I guess we fit the bill as being other creatures.

Tui De Roy

Still, human impacts on the Galápagos were relatively light; foraging sailing ships had much more deadly effects on other places. On Mauritius and Rodrigues in the Indian Ocean, for example, isolation from predators allowed birds called dodos and solitaires to become flightless and gigantic. Although probably descended from small ancestors such as rails or pigeons, they had become as large as turkeys, with

Blue-footed booby. This dance is part of his courting behavior.

heavy bones and fat deposits. The crews of Dutch vessels plying the East Indies spice trade found them a welcome variation of monotonous shipboard diets, and the dodos and solitaires apparently lacked instincts for self-defense. Sailors clubbed them easily or drove them into ship holds like sheep. As humans logged their native forest and brushland habitats and converted them to plantations, the last remnants dwindled.

Both species were extinct in the nineteenth century. Giant tortoises native to Mauritius also became extinct.

Habitat destruction generally has been a more important cause of island extinctions than direct killing for meat. Such killing becomes inconvenient as the exploited population gets scarce, so a few survivors may remain. Even these will die if they have no habitat, however. The Hawaiian Islands did not have any tortoises or dodos that sailors could cart casually into their holds, but this did not stop aliens from devastating native wildlife more thoroughly than in the Galápagos.

Despite extinctions caused by the Polynesians, at least seventy kinds of endemic bird still lived on the Hawaiian Islands when Cook arrived in 1778. Great expanses of native vegetation persisted in the mountains, and a group of birds lived in these forests that support Darwin's theories of species origin even more dramatically than the Galápagos finches. These Hawaiian songbirds, called honeycreepers or Hawaiian finches, are believed to have descended from a pair or flock of small birds (possibly related to American goldfinches) blown to the islands. They eventually evolved into over forty species and subspecies that differ from one another even more than the Galápagos finches do. The bills of the various species (which have Hawaiian names such as 'i'iwi, 'apapane, mamo, and 'akialoa) have taken on just about every shape imaginable for a small forest bird, from massive seedcrackers worthy of a parrot to slender, decurved nectar siphons worthy of a hummingbird. In a few species, the upper and lower halves of the bill have evolved to different lengths, and a bird uses the long upper half to drink nectar and the short lower half to flip over twigs or probe bark in search of insects. Hawaiian finch plumage is also more showy and diverse than that of Galápagos finches. Males of some species are brilliant red, while most have yellowish or greenish feathers. One species, the crested honeycreeper, has an orange-red nape and a startling tuft of white feathers on its forehead.

Hawaii's forest finches are only the most striking example of the unique diversity that the first European visitors found on the islands. There also were endemic thrushes, geese (called nene and descended from Canada geese), rails, herons, ducks, gallinules, coots, stilts, and owls. There was even a species of crow that lived nowhere else. Invertebrate diversity was, as usual, even greater: eight hundred species of fruit flies, many of which had evolved characteristics unknown elsewhere; forty species of colorful agate-shell land snails on the island of Oahu alone.

Hawaii's native plants displayed the highest level of endemism in the world: more than 95 percent of them were species unique to the

islands. As birds and fruit flies did, the plants included many spectacular forms derived from more mundane mainland ancestors. The majestic, yucca-like silversword plants that grow on the slopes of the islands' volcanoes, for example, may have descended from tarweeds—inconspicuous, sticky forbs of dry California grasslands. Lobelias, common flowering herbs of the mainland, grew to tree size in Hawaii. So did ferns.

Unfortunately, the advent of Western civilization continued a decimation of Hawaii's native wildlife that probably could not have been more effective if it had been deliberate. As in the Galápagos, ships and settlers released goats, cows, sheep, rats, dogs, and cats that destroyed native animals and the vegetation upon which they depended. Many Hawaiian plants—native raspberries, mints, and nettles, for instance—had lost the thorns and bitter or stinging chemicals that protected their mainland ancestors from grazing animals. They succumbed, and alien plants eventually replaced them.

In Hawaii, the list of highly destructive introductions didn't stop with goats and cats. Around 1826, mosquitoes were introduced to the

A hardy succulent is the first plant to grow on the cooled lava near the ocean, Island of Hawaii, Hawaii.

islands, and in turn introduced avian malaria and avian pox. The diseases have since devastated the native bird populations. Native birds also suffered from competition with introduced exotic species such as cardinals. Over fifty exotic bird species became established. Other animals that have gone wild and destroyed native wildlife or habitat include European boars, axis deer, mule deer, mouflon (a wild sheep from the Mediterranean region) and mongooses.

While introduced organisms competed with natives, agriculture and urbanization devoured natural areas at a fast rate: farmers converted mountain forest to pasture, valley grassland and wetland to pineapple and sugar cane fields. The result of some two hundred years of this has been that native vegetation survives mainly on cliffs, mountaintops, steep slopes, and high plateaus, and that many species have become extinct or endangered. In the past century, 40 percent of native perching birds have become extinct, and 40 percent have become endangered, leaving only a small percentage of common native species. Almost half of the Hawaiian finch species are extinct. In all, only 37 percent of Hawaii's historically endemic land and water bird species are *not* either extinct or endangered.

Hawaii's preponderance of endangered native species is typical of islands worldwide. Over 80 percent of the species that became extinct over the past few centuries were island ones, and they continue to dominate international endangered lists. Rampant deforestation endangers most of Madagascar's surviving lemur species; habitat loss and introduced predators endanger most of New Zealand's remaining ground-dwelling birds. The solendons (shrew-like relatives of primates) of Cuba and Hispaniola; the fruit pigeons of New Caledonia and the Marquesas; the amazona parrots of Puerto Rico and Dominica: all are endangered.

For all their dismal history, however, islands present numerous opportunities for wildlife conservation. The very isolation that made them so vulnerable in combination with human destructiveness may become an asset if people become serious about protecting island species. An island park or preserve is not surrounded by an ocean of development, as most continental ones are, but by an actual ocean. Although the ubiquity of air and sea travel has made the oceans much smaller than they once were, they remain formidable barriers to many kinds of pollution and habitat encroachment.

In spite of past problems, the Galápagos have become an encouraging example of island wildlife conservation, and of the benefits it can provide. Concerned about the future of what it recognized as an internationally significant natural area, the Ecuadorian government in 1959 declared all uninhabited parts of the islands (about 97 percent) a national park. It set strict regulations for public access to the areas

THE GALÁPAGOS OFFSHORE

In the last few decades the Galápagos ecosystem has drawn a lot of attention around the world because it's so unique and so special on land. But I think very few people realize just how unique it is underwater. . . . All the vast amount of life that borders the shoreline is dependent on the sea, and if anything were to happen to the marine environment, this life on land would disappear as well. It's only recently that there's more and more interest in trying to preserve the marine environment as well and actually extend the status of National Park to the marine environment.

The Galápagos penguin is the only penguin that is actually found at the equator. Of course, the water is quite cold around Fernandina Island, which is where they normally live. They nest in these deep caves, and they're mostly active in the evening.

The marine iguana is actually the only lizard in the world that's become marine. And there's a lot of speculation as to why this happened in Galápagos and nowhere else. There really isn't a good answer to that. You can find thousands and thousands of them in great masses, sunning themselves along the shore. When the tide goes down all these iguanas move down towards the water's edge and start to feed on the algae in the intertidal zone; a lot of them also go into the water and swim some distance offshore. They don't actually use their legs for swimming, but they use their tails. They undulate their tails, which are

Male marine iguana, Point Espinosa, Galápagos.

flattened, and dive down and just graze the algae off the rocky bottom. That's like cows in a pasture but underwater. It's just an incredible sight to see, these iguanas, they look very pale grayish underwater, and they just cling to the rocks and graze away.

Tui De Roy

and declared them off-limits to private development. A few years later, the government established a park administration, which has grown over the years to include a sizable staff of conservation administrators and wardens responsible for tourist control, eradication of introduced species, captive breeding of endangered native species, and education of Galápagos residents in conservation and natural history. The Charles Darwin Foundation has assisted park development; established with the support of UNESCO and other international organizations, the foundation fosters concern for Galápagos conservation and raises funds for it. Its Charles Darwin Research Station has been the focus of research and conservation programs.

As a result of these national and international efforts, the historical deterioration of the Galápagos ecosystem has been arrested, perhaps reversed. Populations of goats and other destructive exotics have been reduced. The park staff and Darwin station have cooperated to collect hundreds of tortoise and iguana eggs, raise the hatchlings until they are large enough to be safe from introduced predators, and return them to their native islands.

The islands' human population has benefited economically as a tourist trade developed. Beginning in 1970, tourism has increased rapidly as visitors have been attracted by the reputation for exotic beauty and fascination that the work of popular naturalists such as the Galápagos resident photographer Tui De Roy has fostered. Although many tourists are not particularly conservation-minded, most probably go away with some sense of the value of protecting giant tortoises and Darwin's finches. This may change if proposals for construction of a large hotel complex on one island are realized, but for the present, tourism has had a positive effect on Galápagos conservation.

Despite successes, conservation in the Galápagos is similar to evolution—it is an on-going process. If programs to eradicate destructive exotics, control visitor use, and restore native species were discontinued, the islands would start slipping back toward a state of biotic impoverishment. Recently, a drastic shortage of funds threatened the Darwin Station's ability to continue important programs. The Nature Conservancy and Smithsonian Institution have been trying to remedy this by raising an endowment fund, but the possibility that even such a well-known place as the Galápagos should be threatened by faltering support is disturbing.

The problems of the Galápagos seem minor compared with those facing the endemic remnants of "earthly paradise" Hawaii—ironic considering that the Galápagos belong to a small, developing country while Hawaii is one of the richest states in the richest country on earth.

Yet it also is encouraging, in a way, because it shows that economic prosperity is not a necessary condition of environmental sensibility. Indeed, the exploitation of Hawaii's great natural wealth—copious watersheds, rich volcanic soils, and highly marketable climate—has been the main cause of its ecological degredation.

Because most of the Hawaiian Islands are heavily developed, the parks and refuges there are in a state closer to that of Yellowstone or the Everglades than the Galápagos. Although Hawaii is much farther out in the Pacific, the ocean provides it much less protective isolation than it does the Galápagos. Surrounded by introduced species, Hawaiian wildlife does not even have the advantage of genetic resistance to a variety of natural enemies and diseases. Given its situation, some people have expressed surprise that any endemic species have survived at all.

Yet native wildlife does survive in a few places remote from the highrises and freeways of Honolulu. On the big island of Hawaii, a few nene geese (the state bird) still fly around the slopes of the great volcanoes, Mauna Kea and Mauna Loa. Nene geese have become less aquatic than their ancestors during adaptation to island life: their feet are no longer fully webbed. Mauna Kea is also the home of the endangercd palila, a yellow-headed Hawaiian finch with a stout bill reminiscent of a grosbeak's. There once were another sixteen closely related species: thirteen are extinct, and the other three are endangered as well. Palilas depend on the seeds of a small, leguminous tree called the mamane that presently grows between 6,000 and 9,500 feet on Mauna Kea. The last native crow species, the alala, still lives on the drier parts of Hawaii, although its numbers have declined to fewer than twenty in the wild. Clearing of forest understory for agriculture and housing has destroyed its feeding and breeding habitat, while disease and wanton shooting have reduced its numbers.

On the island of Maui, Haleakala Volcano and the adjacent, heavily-forested Kipahulu Valley support some 370 native plant species and dozens of native forest bird species. Five endangered Hawaiian finches live in the area. One of these, the Maui nukupu'u, was thought to be extinct until a 1967 expedition rediscovered it. Another, the poo-uli, wasn't even discovered until 1973.

On Kauai, parts of which get some of the heaviest rainfall in the world, a high-elevation swamp forest called the Alakai is a refuge for an estimated quarter-million birds, three-fourths of which are native. All of the thirteen forest bird species historically native to the island are thought still to live in the Alakai, although the numbers of some have become so low that they may not last much longer. One species,

HAWAII'S SPECTACULAR EVOLUTION

Like other volcanic islands, the Hawaiian Islands formed as an oceanic crustal plate passed over a hot spot in the Earth's mantle, causing massive upwellings of magma. The Pacific Plate, which underlies the Hawaiian Islands, has been moving northward; therefore the southern islands, such as Hawaii, contain active volcanoes and are more recent. More northern islands are much older, do not have active volcanoes, and are more eroded.

The Hawaiian Islands are the most remote islands in the world, never having been connected to any continent or other islands. Their tropical climate is very hospitable, with abundant rainfall in most places and no frost below six thousand feet, so the relatively few species of organisms that have managed to get to them have evolved great diversity. A single ancestral species of Hawaiian finch, or honeycreeper—small forest birds resembling American goldfinches—evolved into many species and subspecies after its arrival on the islands millions of years ago. Forty kinds of Hawaiian finches are known to have existed after 1778, and the list would be longer if one includes fossil kinds. This is one of the most striking examples of adaptive radiation known to science. Many of the finches have spectacularly beautiful plumage and strikingly elongated bills for feeding on flowers.

Scientists believe that the entire native bird fauna of the Hawaiian Islands, which perhaps included over a hundred species before human-caused extinctions began, may have evolved from as few as fifteen colonizing species. Yet this pales beside the amazing diversity of Hawaiian insects. The seven thousand native Hawaiian insect species are thought to have evolved from fewer than three hundred colonizing species. Since these three hundred colonizing species represent only 15 percent of the families of insects in the world, Hawaii's native insects have evolved to fill many strange ecological niches. Winged insects such as moths and leafhoppers usually evolved wingless forms that fill burrowing and ground-dwelling niches; on the continents, insects such as silverfish, ants, and cockroaches occupy those niches.

Adapted from "Hawaiian Birds," by J. Michael Scott and John L. Sincock, *Audubon Wildlife Report,* 1985.

Laysian finch.

Male Nihoa finch (left) and female.

the o'o, appeared to have declined to a single male in the early 1980s. A dark, medium-sized, long-billed bird that feeds on flower nectar and insects, the o'o is the last Hawaiian member of a South Pacific bird family, the Australian honey eaters. Several other honey-eater species once lived on the islands, but Hawaiians coveted their bright scarlet and yellow leg feathers for the feather cloaks and helmets worn by Hawaiian royalty, which may have contributed to their extinction.

On Molokai, the lush, rugged Kamakou plateau between two ancient volcanoes may still contain two species feared extinct on the island: the Molokai thrush and Molokai creeper, a Hawaiian finch not seen on the island since 1963. One of the most beautiful Hawaiian finches, the bright red, long-billed 'i'iwi, remains fairly common on some other islands, but the Kamakou is its last refuge on Molokai.

None of these areas would have remained in their present states without the efforts of conservationists. Congress set aside Mauna Loa and Mauna Kea on Hawaii, and Haleakala on Maui, as national parks in 1916. The Alakai Swamp on Kauai has long been a state forest reserve. The Nature Conservancy and the University of Hawaii acquired the Kipahulu Valley and turned its crucial upper portion over to Kaleakala National Park in 1969. The Kamakou area on Molokai has also become a Nature Conservancy preserve, part of an extensive project that protects forest-bird habitat throughout the islands.

Even establishing parks and preserves isn't enough to assure survival of nature organisms in the Hawaiian Islands. Invading exotic species do not recognize conservation boundaries. Feral pigs and goats continued to eat up national park vegetation after 1916. In the 1920s, siltation and flooding from devegetated watersheds became so bad that communities and landowners created forest preserves and tried to extirpate the feral ungulates in them. This relieved pressure on native organisms somewhat. Feral pigs, goats, and sheep breed so quickly that they are very hard to get rid of, however, and since they were the only game available to sport hunters, state wildlife agencies sometimes showed more interest in managing them than the native species.

This political conflict between natives and exotics came to a head in 1979, when the National Audubon Society and Sierra Club sued the Hawaii Department of Land and Natural Resources on behalf of the endangered palila, maintaining that the department was destroying the bird's critical habitat of mamane forest on state lands and Mauna Kea by allowing feral sheep, pigs, and goats to run loose. The court ruled in favor of the palila, and required the state to extirpate the animals, although a herd of mouflon sheep remained. Now conservationists are suing to get the mouflon removed.

Feral ungulates have continued to pose problems in many areas, moving onto parks and preserves from adjacent lands. Given the likely impossibility of removing them from entire islands, the only alternative is to fence them out of protected areas. This is what managers are beginning to do, despite the herculean proportions of the task. Haleakala National Park is conducting a four-year boundary fence project which, if funding permits its completion, should make goat control possible. Volunteers are doing much of the work on the fence.

Fences won't stop mongooses, exotic birds, avian malaria, avian pox or invasive alien weeds such as blackberry and ginger, however.

GOATS AND ISLANDS

Overgrazing by domestic goats has contributed to the deforestation of large parts of the continents, but on islands, their effects are even more devastating. Between 1927 and 1970, park rangers removed more than seventy thousand goats from Hawaii Volcanoes National Park to protect native vegetation and wildlife. Even so, a 1970 aerial census revealed a goat population of fifteen thousand within the park boundaries, about as many as when goat control began.

This led to the completion of a long-term anti-goat plan. The heart of the plan called for fencing goats out of the park, but before undertaking this costly project, the staff needed to know what excluding goats would accomplish. They built a goat-proof fence around a three-hundred- by thirty-foot test area, and within a year the vegetation inside and that outside the fence contrasted sharply. Even inside the fence, there was a barren strip as wide as a goat's neck would stretch, but the block of new green plants beyond that line was visible a mile away.

In the shade of this new vegetation, an unfamiliar vine appeared and spread widely. Botanists examining the vine realized they had found a new species. During all the years of goat depredation, at least one seed of the native vine had remained hidden in the ground. When the area was relieved of goats, it sprouted. Botanists wonder how many other native plant species might reappear if grazing by goats, sheep, and other ungulates ends soon enough.

Adapted from "A Scourge of Goats," by George Laycock, *Audubon*, January 1984.

Long-haired island goat.

Silversword on Haleakala Crater, Maui, Hawaii. These bloom once every nine to fourteen years.

They also can't stop potentially harmful developments such as a hydroelectric dam that has been proposed for one of the streams that originate in Kaui's Alakai Swamp. The reservoir behind the dam would provide increased breeding habitat for mosquitoes, and construction activities would disturb native plants and animals. Natural areas need more protection from such incursions.

Even this won't be enough for some species. The nene goose would be extinct in the wild now if its population weren't continually replenished with captive-bred birds. For reasons that are unclear, 95 percent of wild nene goslings fail to survive. It may be that the food they get in the mountains isn't nutritious enough: they originally spent much of their time in the lowlands. It may be because of mongoose predation. Many land birds such as the Hawaiian crow are on a similarly unexplained downward spiral, perhaps because of avian malaria, habitat loss, inbreeding, or predation.

Recovery plans prepared by biologists in accordance with the Endangered Species Act outline what will be required to restore such species: immediate implementation of increased research, habitat protection and improvement, control of exotics, and programs for treatment of disease-affected populations and captive propagation to develop immunization. Unfortunately, funding even for existing measures such as land acquisition and fencing is hard to come by, so it seems quite possible that a number of species will slip away.

Considering the popularity of the Galápagos with tourists, it seems strange that a state as dependent on tourism as Hawaii hasn't emphasized the attractions of its unique, globally significant native fauna and flora more. Even Hawaiian citizens, 80 percent of whom live in heavily urbanized Oahu, may not be particularly aware of their natural heritage, perhaps partly because schools don't teach native natural history, and neither national parks nor state conservation agencies have significant interpretive programs. Increased public awareness by both visitors and residents would probably help to save what's left of Hawaii.

Of course, Hawaiian crows, geese, finches, koa trees and land snails are not as eye-catching and bizarre as Galápagos tortoises and iguanas, but they are just as significant, and many are quite beautiful. Tourists who never even hear of them under present circumstances might get just as much enjoyment from seeing 'i'iwis and papanes as

West Maui Mountains, Maui, Hawaii.

they do from the luaus, leis, and beaches they could just as easily enjoy in Miami or Malibu. Increased tourist access to remaining natural areas might not be a good idea, but perhaps new natural areas could be created. Considering the concern that Americans have expressed about the global disappearance of tropical forest, protecting and restoring some of our own wildlife would seem appropriate.

TOMORROW'S WILDLIFE

WILDERNESS EARTH REMAINS a realm of enormous, largely unrealized potential. During most of humanity's existence, our relationship to that potential has been more one of exploration than of exploitation. In exploration, we have learned much. Our knowledge of Earth's habitats—skies, forests, grasslands, mountains, deserts, poles, rivers, wetlands, oceans, islands—is one of our greatest evolutionary achievements. Having evolved with wildlife, the human mind is deeply connected to it. One can trace many human ideas of ethics, aesthetics, and metaphysics back to life in the wild, and an appreciation for wildlife is a part of every culture. We may be separated by thousands of years from our prehistoric experiences, but we still readily respond to the sight of a leaping antelope or a prowling tiger.

Given the ancient relationship between wildlife and humans, the sensible human response to the impending extinction of any species is not whether it should be saved, but *how* it is to be saved. In the long term, no more important challenge faces humanity than wildlife conservation. We may survive the threat of nuclear annihilation, but to survive on a planet emptied of its vast biotic potential would be a Pyrrhic victory indeed.

Growing numbers of people face the challenge of wildlife conservation today. Although government and institutional funding for it has been a tiny fraction of the sums spent on industry, past decades have seen considerable refinement of techniques for studying and conserving wildlife. One great advantage is that wildlife conservation is not a field restricted to specialists, but a wide spectrum of activities—songbird censusing or prairie restoration, legislative lobbying or electoral politics—in which all kinds of people can participate. The restoration of vanished wilderness is not a utopian daydream but a practical project already underway in many parts of the world. The Arabian oryx, European and American bison, and many others have already been returned to the wild.

A world in which we can nurture the beauty of the wild and the economic ambitions of humanity side by side is possible to imagine. A world in which wildlife corridors bring native forest, grassland, and wetland within walking distance of urban populations is possible to imagine. A world in which few species are threatened with extinction, and in which species once extinct are restored to the wild is possible to imagine.

Of course, there are formidable obstacles to the realization of these goals. Human demands on the biosphere have grown even faster than wildlife conservation. The world population has doubled since wildlife scientists developed technology to supplement traditional forms of research. That number doubles every thirty-five years at present growth rates, and the rapidly expanding economies of the industrialized nations consume more and more resources. In nonindustrialized nations, poverty is increasing as rapidly as population. People who can't get adequate food and shelter can't be expected to care about wildlife.

Yet wildlife and wilderness are not the cause of poverty. Humans would hardly be better off were the last forest logged, grassland plowed, mountain mined, desert irrigated, tundra drilled, river dammed, wetland drained, ocean depleted, and island stripped of native flora and fauna.

Scientific evidence and simple logic both suggest that civilization cannot deface the planet with impunity. Massive environmental contamination and major climactic changes could result. Thermonuclear war might throw so thick a blanket of dust and smoke over the northern hemisphere that most living organisms would deep-freeze in a prolonged, sunless nuclear winter. And, if we continue to burn the planet's supply of fossil fuels wantonly, we may well raise overall temperatures enough to melt polar ice caps and bring the oceans into our most populated areas.

It would be reasonable to predict such follies if humans came from outer space, since we could wash our hands and go home. It also would be reasonable to predict them if we were an essentially suicidal species. Yet scientific evidence does little more to support such an assumption than it does an extraterrestrial origin for *Homo sapiens*. Several million years of survival among glaciers and deserts have demonstrated *Homo* to be one of the more durable genera. Of course, human life has changed immeasurably in the past ten thousand years, and some of these changes have led people to dissociate their lives from that of the natural world. The life of apartments and automobiles does seem alien to that of caves and footpaths. Yet we may overestimate the differences between ourselves and our ancestors.

The more we learn about our ancestors, the more familiar their lives seem. Like us, they appear to have developed technologies that allowed them to overexploit their resources, as when late Paleolithic tribes became so expert at hunting that they exterminated the mammoth. But they did not proceed from exterminating mammoths to exterminating every other species of big game. They may have lacked the ability to do so, of course. Tracking and killing a small group of shaggy elephants is not the same as wiping out large populations of bison or antelope. Projecting modern problems on prehistoric people is dubious at best, yet it is possible that our ancestors learned something from this early conservation crisis, something about restraint and about the need to be flexible and diversified—something about limits.

It is on learning—on knowledge—that our own fate ultimately depends. We need to learn about interconnections, and we need to understand balance. An education in survival might well begin with this simple and powerful truth: in abandoning our environment we begin to abandon ourselves. The logic, however grim, is elementary enough. But if we are logical beings, we are reasonable, too. And reason tells us there is another, happier perspective on that truth. It is equally powerful: in conserving our environment we insure our future.

ACKNOWLEDGMENTS

Christopher N. Palmer
Vice President, National Audubon Society

As Executive Producer of the Audubon television specials, it was my privilege to initiate and oversee the production of this companion book. It is being published at the same time that the television programs are becoming available on cassettes in shops and rental stores, our hope being that the programs and this book will complement and enrich each other. The National Audubon Society offers both to the public with the conviction that they say something important about the world's future.

The goals of both the book and the Audubon television specials are:

- To show that the sustainable and efficient use of the world's natural resources and the protection of our wildlife are important worldwide goals.
- To show that microorganisms, plants, animals, habitat, and above all people are not isolated entities but are dependent on one another.
- To reach those who do not ordinarily see themselves as conservationists by celebrating the natural beauty all around us.

The Audubon television specials have covered the California condor, the black-footed ferret, the Galápagos Islands, biological diversity, alternative agriculture, waterfowl and wetlands, the Florida Everglades, whales, grizzly bears, birds as environmental messengers, sea turtles, illegal trafficking in wildlife, sharks, and the sandhill cranes of the Platte River. More are in preparation. Some of the programs are about a particular species, habitat, or ecosystem. Others deal with resources like groundwater, wild rivers, energy, and soil. Still others are on biotechnology as it is applied to the conservation of species and ecosystems. And all are about individuals who are making a difference.

The essence of each film is that we must live in harmony with our natural ecosystems. If we damage them, we cannot meet basic human needs and have economic growth. There can be no civilization without a healthy environment. We need to build for future generations rather than steal from them.

The Audubon television specials (called "World of Audubon Specials" on cable SuperStation WTBS and "National Audubon Society Specials" on public television) are the brainchild of the National Audubon Society and Ted Turner. Soon after the Turner Broadcasting System and Audubon started working together, we persuaded Ward Chamberlin, President of public television station WETA in Washington, D.C., to join the partnership. This triumvirate of Audubon, TBS and WETA is responsible for the Audubon television specials and for this companion book. None of it would be possible without a major underwriting grant from the Stroh Brewery Company.

It was not hard to select the author for this book. David Rains Wallace has published seven other books and dozens of articles about wildlife, conservation, and natural history. His work ranges from essays on gardening to articles on conservation politics to a mystery thriller about an endangered species. His third book, *The Klamath Knot*, about evolution in a West Coast wilderness region, won the coveted John Burroughs Medal for Nature Writing in 1984. On presenting the award, Paul Brooks remarked, "David Wallace seems to me a sort of Lewis Thomas with the wilderness as his laboratory."

Marie Arana-Ward, senior editor of Harcourt Brace Jovanovich, has been an invaluable partner on this project. Other people whose help I gratefully acknowledge include:

Durward Allen	Bob Cahn
Pam Amster	Marshal Case
Frosty Anderson	David Clark
Dede Armentrout	Dave Cline
Hope Babcock	Inez Connor
Pat Baldi	Leslie Dach
Ben Beach	Alan Dater
Chris Beldin	Lisa DiMona
Peter Berle	Amos Eno
Jan Beyea	Brock Evans
Carlyle Blakeney	Roger DiSilvestro
Dave Blankinship	Charlene Dougherty
John Borneman	Sam Dovie
Mary Joy Breton	Susan Drennan
Bill Butler	Mike Duever

Ron Goldfarb
Steve Hillebrand
Maureen Hinkle
Pam Hogan
Jack Holowell
Hardy Jones
Jeff Jouett
Jane Kinne
Ron Klataske
Gene Knoder
Larry Kruckenberg
Mercedes Lee
Dick Martyr
Bill Myer
Bob Nelson
John Ogden
Don Pfitzer
Walt Pomeroy
George Powell
Bart Rea
Ron Rinaldo

Tammy Robinson
Gail Ross
Jim Ross
Claire Rusowicz
Carl Safina
Rob SanGeorge
Mike Scott
Chris Servheen
Gail Shearer
Delores Simmons
Tom Smylie
Gary Soucie
Sandy Sprunt
Lawrence Stolte
Larry Thompson
Whit Tilt
Bob Turner
Tom Watkins
Fran Weber
Mike Weber
Chris Wille

PHOTO CREDITS

All photographs researched by Pamela Amster.
Photographs from the National Audubon Collection of Photo Researchers,
except where noted.

Front cover: Phyllis Greenberg
Frontispiece: Alex Kerstitch

WILDERNESS EARTH
Page X: John Mitchell. 6: Gordon Gahan.

THE SKIES
Page 8: George W. Calef. 13: John Borneman. 14: Tom McHugh. 15: Phyllis Greenberg. 24: Anne La Bastille. 29: Zoological Society of San Diego. 30: Tom McHugh. 31: Zoological Society of San Diego.

THE FORESTS
Page 34: Keith Gunnar/Bruce Coleman, Inc. 38: Pat Caulfield. 51: Joe Van Wormer. 52: Larry Engel/Cineworks, Inc. 53: William A. Greer/Florida Game and Fish. 55: Jeff Foott/Bruce Coleman, Inc. 57 Left: Jeanne White; right: Wolfgang Bayer/Bruce Coleman, Inc. 60: Tom McHugh. 61: G. Ronald Austing.

THE GRASSLANDS
Page 64: Tom McHugh. 68: Ray Paunovich/The Natural Image. 75: G. C. Kelley. 78: Earl Gustkey. 80 Top: Harry Engels; bottom: LuRay Parker/Wyoming Game and Fish. 83: A. W. Ambler. 84: Margot Granitsas. 86: Mitch Mandel/Rodale Press. 89: Noble Proctor.

THE MOUNTAINS
Page 92: John V.A.F. Neal. 97: Tom McHugh. 98: Tom McHugh. 102: Tom McHugh. 107: G. C. Kelley. 110: Stephen J. Krasemann. 112: Michael Giannechini. 115 Left: Leonard Lee Rue, III; right: Len Rue, Jr.

THE DESERTS
Page 120: Bill Curtsinger. 124: Leonard Lee Rue, III. 129: C. Max Dunham. 130: Jeff Apoian. 131: M. P. Kahl. 133: Jerry L. Ferrara. 137: Phil Degginger/Bruce Coleman, Inc. 138: Peggy Olwell/U.S. Fish and Wildlife Service. 140: R. Rowan.

THE POLAR REGIONS
Page 142: Dan Guravich. 147 Top and bottom: Phyllis Greenberg. 151: Leonard Lee Rue, III. 157: Tom McHugh. 158: Robert W. Hernandez. 160: Michael Male. 161: Steve Krasemann. 163 Top: Jen and Des Bartlett; bottom: Karl H. Maslowski. 164: Dan Guravich. 166: Dotte Larsen/Bruce Coleman, Inc.

THE RIVERS
Page 170: Charlie Ott. 178: Leonard Lee Rue, III. 180 Top: Karl H. and Stephen Maslowski; bottom: Earl Roberge. 182: Dan Guravich. 188: Pat and Tom Leeson. 190: Dan Guravich. 194 Top: Pavlovsky; bottom: Joe Munroe. 197 Left and right: Dan Flint. 198: George Love.

THE WETLANDS
Page 200: Dr. Georg Gerster. 204: Phyllis Greenberg. 207: Eastcott/Momatiuk. 211 Top: Townsend P. Dickinson; bottom: Lawrence E. Naylor. 218 Left: A. A. Allen; right: Pamela Harper/Harper Horticultural Library. 220: Jim Brandenburg/Bruce Coleman, Inc. 223: Michael Giannechini. 224 Left: Russ Kinne; right: Townsend P. Dickinson. 225 Top, left: Peter B. Kaplan; right: Townsend P. Dickinson; bottom: G. C. Kelley.

THE OCEANS
Page 230: Mike Neumann. 235: Robert W. Hernandez. 237: Townsend P. Dickinson. 238: George C. Lower. 240: David Hall. 243: painting by Richard Ellis. 252 Top and bottom: Tom McHugh. 258: Alvin E. Staffan. 259: Lowell Georgia. 260 Left: Sam C. Pierson, Jr.; right: Townsend P. Dickinson. 261: Al Lowry.

THE ISLANDS
Page 262: Jack Fields. 266: Tui De Roy. 268: David Clark. 270: Roger Tory Peterson. 272: A. W. Ambler. 275: Tui De Roy. 277: Ray Fairbanks. 279: Frans Lanting. 282 Left and right: Karl W. Kenyon. 284: Stan Goldblatt. 285: Fred McConnaughey. 286: Mindy E. Klarman.

TOMORROW'S WILDLIFE
Page 288: Leonard Lee Rue, III.

INDEX